AA

BRITAIN

FOR

FREE

HUNDREDS OF PLACES TO VISIT

No admission fees charged

2

Produced by the Publishing Division of the Automobile Association

Maps: produced by the Cartographic Department of the Automobile Association

Printed by: Grosvenor Press (Portsmouth) Ltd.

Every effort is made to ensure accuracy, but the publishers do not hold themselves responsible for any consequences that may arise from errors or omissions. Whilst the contents are believed correct at the time of going to press; changes may have occurred since that time or will occur during the currency of this book. The up-to-date position may be checked through AA regional offices.

Please note that, in line with Government policy, some museums and places of interest now operate a system of voluntary contributions.

ISBN 0 86145 732 3   **AA Ref: 55961**

Published by the Automobile Association, Fanum House, Basingstoke, Hampshire RG21 2EA.

CONTENTS

Ancient Monuments, National Trust Properties and The National Gardens Scheme

Ancient Monuments

AM Ancient Monuments in England are in the care of the Historic Buildings and Monuments Commission for England, popularly known as English Heritage, PO Box 43, Ruislip, Middlesex HA4 0XW, with the exception of seven properties in and around London which are administered by the Department of the Environment. Ancient Monuments in Scotland (with the exception of Holyrood House) are the responsibility of the Scottish Development Department, 3-11 Melville St, Edinburgh EH3 7QD.

Ancient Monuments in Wales are the responsibility of CADW, Brunel House, Fitzalan Rd, Cardiff CF2 1UY.

Except where otherwise stated, the standard times of opening for all Ancient Monuments, except Scotland, are as follows:

16 Oct-14 Mar:
      weekdays 9.30-4
      Sunday 2-4
15 Mar-15 Oct:
      weekdays 9.30-6.30
      Sunday 2-6.30

Standard times of opening for all Ancient Monuments in Scotland are as follows:

Apr-Sep:
      weekdays 9.30-7
      Sundays 2-7
Oct-Mar:
      weekdays 9.30-4
      Sundays 2-4

All monuments in England and Wales are closed on 1 January and 24-26 December. Those in Scotland are closed on 25 and 26 December, also 1 and 2 January. Some of the smaller monuments may close for the lunch hour and may be closed for one or two days a week. It is advisable to check before visiting.

The National Trusts

NT Indicates the properties in England and Wales administered by the National Trust for Places of Historic Interest or Natural Beauty, 42 Queen Anne's Gate, London SW1H 9AS.

NTS National Trust for Scotland, 5 Charlotte Square, Edinburgh EH2 4DU.

The National Gardens Scheme

NGS National Gardens Scheme, 57 Lower Belgrave St, London SW1W 0LR.

Over 2,300 gardens (some entries are in this book) open to the public, mostly for one or two days a year.

Proceeds for charity. Booklet £2.25 including postage.

Symbols and abbreviations

Other symbols and abbreviations used throughout this publication will be found inside the front cover, whilst an explanation of how to use the gazetteer section appears on the page opposite under the heading 'About this Book'.

About this Book

In this book we list hundreds of places to visit and try to provide as much information as possible for the intending visitor.

Gazetteer

The gazetteer is listed in strict alphabetical order throughout. As far as possible, the places of interest situated within one or two miles of a town or village are placed under the nearest town or village heading. However, some establishments are too remote for this to be done and such places are listed under their own name. Should you be in any doubt about a particular place, the comprehensive index at the back of the book will indicate where it can be found.

Atlas

If you are planning a day out or a holiday in a particular area, you might find it useful to refer in the first instance to the atlas at the back of the book where all of the towns and individual establishments that we list are located. A useful key at the front of the atlas section will help you find the area you require. Each gazetteer entry also gives a map reference which includes the atlas page number and grid code.

Open dates

The dates quoted in the gazetteer are inclusive, so that Apr-Oct indicates that the establishment is open from the beginning of April to the end of October. (For Ancient Monuments see page 4.)

Telephone

Unless otherwise stated the telephone exchange given in the gazetteer is that of the town under which the establishment is listed. Where the exchange for a particular establishment is not that of the town under which it appears the name of the exchange is given after the telephone symbol and before the dialling code and number.

In some areas telephone numbers are likely to be changed by the telephone authorities during the currency of this publication. It you have any difficulty it is advisable to check with the operator.

Donation and Charity Boxes

Some of the places of interest listed in the gazetteer are administered by Charities, Trusts and Associations. They are responsible for carrying out much of the restoration work in order to promote Britain's heritage and rely on public generosity to continue their work. They do not charge for admission, but donations are appreciated.

Care of the Countryside

The gazetteer contains a selection of countryside sites and nature reserves. Many have public footpaths or waymarked trails leading through them, and these should always be followed, since the object of such reserves is that these areas should remain undisturbed. Irreparable damage can be done to reserves by those who, perhaps quite innocently, wander over them at will. Access to some reserves, or parts of reserves, is often limited and these details should always be checked before making a visit.

Please always follow the Country Code:

Enjoy the countryside and respect its life and work
Guard against all risk of fire
Fasten all gates
Keep dogs under close control
Keep to public paths across farmland
Use gates and stiles to cross fences, hedges and walls
Leave livestock, crops and machinery alone
Take your litter home
Help to keep all water clean
Protect wildlife, plants and trees
Take special care on country roads
Make no unnecessary noise

Please note that, in line with Government policy, some museums and other places of interest now operate a system of voluntary contributions.

ORDNANCE SURVEY
LEISURE GUIDES

LAKE DISTRICT

Voted the best new publication about the area in 1984, this superb guide describes the topography and traditions of the area and offers scenic drives, walks, and masses of information about what to see and where to stay, linked to large-scale Ordnance Survey maps, and illustrated throughout in colour.

NEW FOREST

Walks, drives, places to see, things to do, where to stay, all linked to large-scale Ordnance Survey mapping, with useful background information to the area. Illustrated throughout with superb colour photography.

YORKSHIRE DALES

Descriptions of scenery, history, customs and 'a day in the life of a dalesman' evoke the atmosphere of this remote and beautiful region and introduce the walks, drives and directory of places of interest. Large-scale Ordnance Survey maps and a wealth of colour photography make this guide a must for tourist and walker alike.

COTSWOLDS

Pretty villages of native limestone, impressive churches built on the wealth of the wool trade, ancient hillforts and Roman roads, rolling upland and gentle river valleys – these and much more are described and colourfully illustrated in this guide. Walks, drives and Ordnance Survey maps complete this ideal companion to the area.

SCOTTISH HIGHLANDS

Scottish Highlands – a treasure house of nature, packed with breathtaking scenery and fascinating traditions. The book captures the flavour, the scents and the grandeur of Europe's foremost 'wilderness' area. Walks, drives, things to do, places to stay are listed, with maps to show the way.

All available in hardback or paperback

GAZETTEER

The gazetteer gives locations and details of AA-listed establishments in England, Wales, Scotland, the Channel Isles and Isle of Man.
Locations for islands are shown under the appropriate island headings.
A useful first point of reference is to consult the location maps which show where establishments are situated.
(There is no map for the Isles of Scilly.)

ABERDEEN

Grampian (Aberdeenshire)
                              Map 15 NJ90.

Aberdeen Art Gallery and Museums
Schoolhill
Scottish art from 16th century to present day, with outstanding collection of 20th-century paintings. Water colours, print-room, and art library; contemporary sculpture and decorative arts; special exhibitions and events throughout the year.

∅ (0224) 646333.
Open: Mon-Sat 10-5 (8pm Thu) Sun 2-5. (Closed: Xmas and 1 & 2 Jan.)
⌨ ☒ Shop ⌘
(ex guide dogs).

Cruickshank Botanic Garden
University of Aberdeen
Developed at the end of the 19th century, the 10 acres include rock and water gardens, a heather garden, collections of spring bulbs, gentians and Alpine plants. There is also an extensive collection of trees and shrubs.

∅ (0224) 480241 ext 2696 or 2704.

Open: all year Mon-Fri 9-4.30; also Sat & Sun May-Sep 2-5.
☒

Duthie Park Winter Gardens
Polmuir Road/Riverside Drive
This fine park, with beautifully laid-out gardens occupies an area in the south of the city and on the north bank of the River Dee. It has many exotic plants, flowers, turtles, birds and fish. Of particular interest is a cactus house and a famous 'hill of roses'.

∅ Leisure and Recreation Dept of Aberdeen City Council (0224) 642121.
Open: Dawn-dusk.
☒ ⌨ (⌘ in Winter Gardens).

James Dun's House
61 Schoolhill
18th-century house used as a museum with changing exhibitions.

∅ (0224) 646333.
Open: Mon-Sat 10-5
(Closed: Xmas and 1 & 2 Jan.)
Shop ⌘ (ex guide dogs).

Kings College
High Street
The college was founded in 1494, but its crown tower is 17th century. The chapel with its richly carved woodwork, dates from the 16th century.

∅ (0224) 272000.
Open: Mon-Fri 9-5, Sat 9-12.30 (ex weddings).
☒ ⌘

Marischal College
Broad Street
The college was founded in 1593 but the present building dates from 1844. Forming part of Aberdeen University, it is said to be one of the finest granite buildings in the world with its Mitchell Tower

233 ft high. The College houses the University Anthropological Museum, the Henderson Collection of classical vases, the Grant-Bey Egyptian Collection, a collection of Chinese art (with bronzes of the Shang Yin period). Tang Dynasty horses, and carved jade of the Ming Dynasty.

∅ (0224) 272000 ext 3133.
Open: Mon-Thu 9am-10pm; Fri 9-5, Sat 9-5; Sun 2-5.
⌘

Maritime Museum
Provost Ross's House, Shiprow.
This new museum, housed in Aberdeen's 3rd oldest surviving building built in 1593 and a National Trust of Scotland property, highlights Aberdeen's maritime history in dramatic and graphic fashion. Trust visitor centre shop.

∅ (0224) 572215. For group bookings (0224) 646333.
Open: Mon-Sat 10-5 (Closed: Xmas and 1 & 2 Jan). Visitor Centre May, Sep & 1-19 Dec, Mon-Sat 10-4 (5pm, Jun, Jul & Aug)
☒ (ground floor only) Shop ⌘ (ex guide dogs).

Provost Skene's House
Guestrow
A 17th-century house restored as a museum of local history and social life. Furnishings, panelling and plaster ceilings of 17th and 18th century.

∅ (0224) 641086.
Open: Mon-Sat 10-5,
(Closed: Xmas and 1 & 2 Jan)
⌨ ☒ (ground floor only)
Shop ⌘ (ex guide dogs).

St Machar's Cathedral
Chanonry (Old Aberdeen)
Located in Old Aberdeen the partly castellated Cathedral

is a magnificent granite building dating from the 14th century. The ceiling is of oak and is painted with emblems of spiritual and temporal monarchs and dates from the 16th century. There are two squat west towers surmounted by spires.

℘ (0224) 485988.
Open: daily 9-5
 ⅃ ⚹

ABERDOUR
Fife (Fife)   *Map 11 NT18*
Moray Workshop
High Street
The workshop is housed in a former 18th-century village hospital. Visitors can see the various stages involved in the manufacture of silver and gold jewellery.

℘ (0383) 860248.
Open: Mar-Oct
Mon-Sat 9-5.30.
Shop.

ABERYSTWYTH
Dyfed   *Map 6 SN58.*
National Library of Wales
Penglais Hill
One of Britain's six copyright libraries, housed in imposing building of 1911-16, with later additions. Large number of books in all languages, musical publications, prints, drawings and old deeds; specialises in Welsh and Celtic literature. Exhibitions of pictures.

℘ (0970) 3816.
Open: all year Mon-Fri 9.30-6, Sat until 5pm. (Closed BHs & 1st wk Oct.) Exhibition Gallery only, open Whitsun & Aug BH.
⌨ ⅃ Shop ⚹

Yr Hen Gapel
Tre'r-ddôl
This museum of 19th-century religious life in Wales reflects those activities which

had such far-reaching effects on the social life of both rural and industrial Wales. The collection consists of a permanent exhibition and a few temporary displays.

℘ (0970) 86407
Open Apr-Sep Mon-Sat 10-5
Shop ⚹

ACCRINGTON
Lancashire   *Map 7 SD72.*
Haworth Art Gallery
Haworth Park
Standing in a 13½-acre park, the art gallery houses what is considered to be one of the finest collections of Tiffany Favrille glass in the world. Also on display are fine collections of 19th-century watercolours and 18th- and 19th-century oil paintings, the most notable being 'The Tempest' by Claude Vernet.

℘ (0254) 33782.
Open: daily 2-5 (closed Fri).
⚹

ACHILTIBUIE
Highland (Ross and Cromarty)
                    Map 14 NC00.
The Smokehouse
(3m NW)
Although not allowed into the premises for hygiene reasons, visitors can look through the viewing-gallery windows and see the traditional craft of curing and smoking of local meat, fish and game being carried out.

℘ (085482) 353.
Open: Mon-Sat 9.30-6.
Shop

ACTON BURNELL
Shropshire   *Map 7 SJ50.*
Acton Burnell Castle
Ruined 13th-century fortified manor house where the first English Parliament is said to have met in 1283.

Open: at all reasonable times.
⅃
(AM)

ALDERSHOT
Hampshire   *Map 4 SU85.*
Royal Corps of Transport Museum
Buller Barracks
Uniforms and badges of Royal Corps of Transport and predecessors. In addition models and photographs of vehicles used from 1795 to present day.

℘ (0252) 24431 (ext 3837 or 3834).
Open: Mon-Fri 9-12.30, 2-4.30. 'At Home Day' 16 Jul. (Closed BH.)
⅃ Shop ⚹

ALLEN BANKS
Northumberland   *Map 12 NY76.*
(3m W of Haydon Bridge ½m S of A69)
Covering 185 acres, Allen Banks is located in the deep valley of the River Allen shortly before it flows into the River South Tyne. The valley is noted for its deciduous woodland of mature beech and oak inhabited by roe deer and the rare red squirrel. There are attractive riverside trails and in Morralee Wood on the eastern side of the river, a steep climb gives rewarding views.

Open: accessible at all reasonable times.
⊫ NT.

ALTON
Hampshire   *Map 4 SU73.*
Curtis Museum & Allen Gallery
High St
Contains local collections of geology, botany, zoology, archaeology and history, also craft tools, dolls, toys and games. The Allen Gallery

houses a changing programme of temporary exhibitions and the Bignell collection of English ceramics.

℗ (0420) 82802.
Open: Tue-Sat 10-5
🚻 ♿ (ground floor only)
Shop ♫

AMBLESIDE
Cumbria   Map 11 NY30.
Hayes Garden World
(½m S on A591)
The knowledge of six generations of the Hayes family has gone into developing this, one of the most outstanding nurseries in Europe. Beautiful landscaped gardens display an abundance of plants, shrubs and trees, while fascinating tropical plants thrive in the Plant House.

℗ (0966) 33434.
Open: Mon-Fri 9-5.30 (or dusk) Sun & BH 10-5 (or dusk). (Closed 25-26 Dec, 1 Jan.) ♿ ▭ 🚻 Shop. No disabled toilets available, wheel chairs available.

AMPTHILL
Bedfordshire   Map 4 TL03.
Houghton House
(N off A418)
Ruined 17th-century mansion with associations with the Countess of Pembroke, sister of Sir Philip Sidney.

Open: at all reasonable times.
(AM) ♿ (ground floor & gardens only)

ANDERTON
Cheshire   Map 7 SJ67.
Anderton Canal Lift
Designed by Sir E Leader Williams, this unique electric canal lift hoists vessels from the River Weaver Navigation to the Trent and Mersey Canal. The lift, formerly worked hydraulically, lifts barges 50 ft in just two and a half minutes.

Open: accessible at all reasonable times along canal towpath.

ANDOVER
Hampshire   Map 4 SU34.
Andover Museum
Church Close
The museum is housed in a fine Georgian building; among its displays are locally manufactured agricultural machinery and an aquarium designed to display local fish found in the Test Valley. There is a new natural history gallery. Temporary exhibitions.

℗ (0264) 66283.
Open: Tue-Sat 10-5
♿ (ground floor only) Shop ♫.

ARBORFIELD
Berkshire   Map 4 SU76.
Royal Electrical and Mechanical Engineers' Museum
Isaac Newton Road
The museum tells the story of the REME, whose function is to repair and maintain army vehicles and equipment. Photographs, models and a variety of other related items cover the military and technical aspects of the corps' history.

℗ Arborfield Cross (0734) 760421 Ext 2567.
Open: Mon-Fri 9-12.30 & 2-4.30 (4 on Fri) (Closed BH and week-ends).
♿ (ground floor only) ♫ Shop.

ARBOR LOW
Derbyshire   Map 7 SK16.
Arbor Low Henge
(off unclass road ¾m E of A515 at Parsley Hay)
A particularly fine example of a henge monument with two entrances in the containing bank which is 6 ft high and has a diameter of 250 ft. There are some 50 stones many of which are standing. There is also a later Bronze-Age barrow on the site.

Open: accessible at all reasonable times.
(AM)

ARBROATH
Tayside (Angus)   Map 12 NO64.
Arbroath Museum
Signal Tower, Ladyloan
Collection of local history from prehistoric times to the Industrial Revolution. Special features include the Bellrock Lighthouse, fishing and wildlife at Arbroath Cliffs.

℗ (0241) 75598.
Open: Apr-Oct, Mon-Sat 10.30-1, 2-5, Jul & Aug also Sun 2-5; Nov-Mar, Mon-Fri 2-5, Sat 10.30-1, 2-5.
♿ (ground floor only) ♫ (ex guide dogs).

ASHBURTON
Devon   Map 3 SX77.
Ashburton Museum
1 West Street
Exhibits include local antiquities, weapons, American Indian antiques, geology specimens.

℗ (0364) 53278.
Open: May-Sep, Tue, Thu, Fri, Sat 2.30-5
♫

ASHFORD
Kent   Map 5 TR04.
Intelligence Corps Museum
Templer Barracks
Items concerning the Corps from the two World Wars and other articles up to the present day.

℗ (0233) 25251 Ext 208.
Open: Mon-Fri by appointment only.
(Closed BH.)
♿ Shop ♫

ASH VALE
Surrey　　　　　　　　*Map 4 SU85.*
RAMC Historical Museum
Keogh Barracks
A collection of some 2,500 items, mainly of military interest but with many unusual items of general interest. Exhibits include a horse-drawn ambulance and a 1942 Austin K2 ambulance. There are three cases of items relating to the Falklands War and a display of a patient on an operating table.

✆ Aldershot (0252) 24431 Ext Keogh 5212.
Open: Mon-Fri 8.30-4. (Closed: Xmas, New Year & BH). Weekends & BH by appointment only.
♿ Shop ✗

ASTON ROWANT
Oxfordshire　　　　　*Map 4 SU79.*
Nature Reserve
(1½m W of Stokenchurch on unclass road off A40)
The Nature Reserve commands an excellent view over the Oxfordshire Plain and is located on the scarp slope of the Chiltern Hills. There are extensive beech woodlands, and scattered areas of juniper scrub among chalk grasslands. In summer, warblers, nightingales, kestrels and sparrowhawks can be seen. Violet helleborine, large white helleborine and wood barley are some of the unusual plants found in the wooded areas.

✆ Kingston Blount (0844) 51833
or Ickford (08447) 719.
Open: accessible at all reasonable times.
No picnicking ✗

AULDEARN
Highland (Nairn)　　　*Map 14 NH95.*
Boath Doocot
(off A96 at Auldearn, 2m E of Nairn)

A 17th-century doocot (as the Scots call a dovecote) stands on the site of an ancient castle where, in 1645, Montrose flew the standard of Charles I when he defeated an army of Covenanters. The plan of the battle is on display.

Open: accessible at all reasonable times.
(NTS)

AVEBURY
Wiltshire　　　　　　*Map 4 SU16.*
Stone Circle
The largest stone circle in Europe, measuring 1,400 ft across, consists of 100 sarsen stones, some of them about 20 ft high. Within the main circle there are traces of a smaller one. There is an enclosing bank of chalk, 20 ft high in places, and a chalk ditch. Leading away to the south east is an avenue of stones.

Open: accessible at all reasonable times.
(AM)

AVIEMORE
Highland (Inverness-shire)
　　　　　　　　　　Map 14 NH81.
Craigellachie National Nature Reserve
Aviemore Centre
Lying on the western edge of Aviemore, this 642-acre nature reserve rises to over 1,700 ft. One third of it is covered by birch woodlands, the remainder is moorland. The starting point of the mile-long nature trail is close to Loch Puladelern and from the trail there are some impressive views of the Cairngorm Mountains. The birch trees support several species of moth including the great brocade and the angle-striped sallow.

Open: accessible at all reasonable times.

AVON FOREST PARK
Dorset　　　　　　　*Map 4 SU10.*
(2m W of Ringwood off A31)
Three areas of heathland and pine woodland. North Park covers almost 300 acres and contains some fine Maritime, Corsican, and Weymouth Pines. Noble Fir and Redwood are among other interesting trees in the area. Thickly-wooded Matchams View is located close to the River Avon from which there are magnificent views of the Avon Valley. South Park includes an open area called Tumuli Hill from where there are good views. Much of this area was destroyed by fire in 1976. There are waymarked walks at all three sites. Visitors' Centre to be opened in the North Park in 1988.

✆ Ringwood (04254) 78082.
Open: accessible at all reasonable times.
♿ 🍴

AXBRIDGE
Somerset　　　　　　*Map 3 ST45.*
King John's Hunting Lodge
The Square
Restored early Tudor house with old photographs and exhibits of local interest. Town stocks and constables' staves also on show.

Open: Apr-Sep, daily 2-5.
(NT)

AXMINSTER
Devon　　　　　　　*Map 3 SY29.*
Axminster Carpets Ltd
Gamberlake
Visitors can see the complete process of making an Axminster carpet from winding the bobbins, weaving, and adding the latex backing to the finished product.

✆ (0297) 32244.
Open: Mon-Fri 9-12, 1.30-4.30 (Ex Spring Bank Hol

week, last week of Jul/first
week of Aug).
🔲 🕷

AYLESBURY
Buckinghamshire   Map 4 SP81.
Bucks County Museum
Church Street
Housed in former grammar
school built in 1720 and two
15th-century houses, which
were completely altered in
the mid 18th century. The
displays relate to the geology, natural history, archaeology and history of the county
and include costumes, Rural
Life Gallery and Aylesbury
Gallery. Temporary exhibitions.

✆ (0296) 82158 or 88849.
Open: Mon-Fri 10-5, Sat
10-12.30, 1.30-5. (Closed: Sun,
Good Fri, 25-26 Dec and New
Years day.)
Shop 🕷

AYLESFORD
Kent   Map 5 TQ76.
Kit's Coty House
(1½m NE off unclass road)
The best-preserved Neolithic
burial chamber in Kent, dating from about 3,500 BC.
Three upright stones are
capped by a fourth. The
covering mound of earth has
long since disappeared.

Open: accessible at all
reasonable times.
(AM)

Priory
The Friars
Restored 13th-to 14th-century
Carmelite house with fine
cloisters, conference centre
and place of pilgrimage and
retreat. Sculpture and ceramics by modern artists and
pottery. Restoration work in
progress on two 16th-century
barns

✆ Maidstone (0622) 77272.
Open: daily 9-dusk. Guided

tours by arrangement.
Shop, tea rooms and pottery
open: 10-12.45 & 2-4.30.
Donations
🖵 🔲 Shop.

AYR
Strathclyde (Ayrshire) Map 10 NS32.
Auld Kirk
Off High Street
Robert Burns was baptised in
the present church which
dates from 1654, when it replaced the 12th-century
church of St John. Inside are
the Merchants, Trades, and
Sailors Lofts. Around the
walls are the colours of various Scottish regiments, not-
ably those carried in the Cri-
mean War. Other items of
note are the Mort-Safe and
Mortification board. Monuments to various Burns characters in churchyard.

✆ (0292) 262938.
Open: Jun, Jly, Aug, Tue &
Thu evenings 7-8pm
(donation box)
🕷

**Maclaurin Art Gallery &
Rozelle House**
Rozelle Park
Monument Road
Contemporary and traditional art, decorative and applied. Nature trail in surrounding park with open air
sculpture; work by Henry
Moore on display. Local history and art exhibitions
based on permanent collections in mansion house. Small
military museum.

✆ Alloway (0292) 45447.
Gallery open: Mon-Sat 11-5,
Sun (Apr-Oct only) 2-5.
House open: Apr-Oct, Mon-
Sat 11-5, Sun 2-5.
🖵 🚻 🔲 (ground floor only)
🕷

AYSGARTH
North Yorkshire   Map 7 SE08.
National Park Centre

Visitor centre with interpretative display, maps,
walks, guides and local information available.

✆ (09693) 424.
Open: Apr-Oct daily mid
mornings to late afternoons.
🔲

BACONSTHORPE
Norfolk   Map 9 TG13.
Baconsthorpe Castle
A late 15th-century moated
and semi-fortified house, incorporating a gate-house, a
range of curtain walls and
towers.

Open: at all reasonable
times.
(AM) 🔲

BADBURY RINGS
Dorset   Map 3 ST90.
*(off B3082 4m NW of
Wimborne Minster)*
A massive Iron Age hill fort
comprising three concentric
rings, the centre of which is
thickly wooded. Four Roman
roads lead from the fort to
Dorchester, Old Sarum,
Poole Harbour and Bath. Also
of interest is the Roman post-
ing station of Vindogladia
which lies just outside the
fort.

Open: accessible at all
reasonable times.

BALLOCH
Strathclyde (Dunbartonshire)
*   Map 10 NS38.*
**Balloch Castle Country
Park**
Situated on the shore of the
loch, with large area of grassland suitable for picnics and
surrounded by extensive
woodlands. Views of the loch
from the castle terrace
(c 1808). Walled garden. Nature trail, tree trail. Countryside ranger service.

✆ Alexandria (0389) 58216.
Open: Visitor Centre; Apr &

Sep Sat, Sun 10-6. Country Park 8-dusk, garden 10-9 (4.30 winter).

⌂ ♿

BAMBURGH
Northumberland   *Map 12 NU13.*
Grace Darling Museum
Radcliffe Road
Pictures, documents and various relics of the heroine, including boat in which she and her father, keeper of Longstone Lighthouse, Farne Islands, rescued nine survivors from the wrecked 'SS Forfarshire' in 1838. 150th anniversary of wreck and rescue 7 Sep. Grace and her father rowed to the wreck at considerable risk to themselves.

Ø Seahouses (0665) 720037.
Open: 17 Apr, May, & Sep-mid Oct daily 11-6 and Jun-Aug daily 11-7.
♿ Shop ⚬

BAMFORD
Derbyshire   *Map 8 SK28.*
High Peak Garden Centre
This well-established garden centre in the heart of the Peak District offers much to attract all visitors, particularly gardeners. It is thoughtfully laid out with trees and shrubs in alphabetical order, a rose garden, rockery with fountain and a display of mature hedges and many other items. The centre is all on one level with good paths making it suitable for disabled visitors.

Ø Hope Valley (0433) 51484.
Open: Mon-Fri 9-5, Sat & Sun 10-5.30.
⌨ (Mar-Sep) ♿ ⚬

BANBURY
Oxfordshire   *Map 4 SP44.*
Banbury Museum
8 Horsefair, Marlborough Road
This small museum exhibits items of local history, archaeology and photography. Changing programme of temporary exhibitions and of local artists' work. Tourist Information Centre.

Ø (0295) 59855.
Open: Jan-Mar Tue-Sat 10-4.30; Apr-Sep, Mon-Sat 10-5; Oct-Dec, Tue-Sat 10-4.30.
⌨ ♿ Shop ⚬

BANCHORY
Grampian (Kincardineshire)
Map 15 NO69.
Banchory Museum
Council Chambers
Exhibition of local history and bygone days.

Ø Peterhead (0779) 77778.
Open: Jun-Sep daily (ex Thu) 2-5.20.
Shop ⚬ (ex guide dogs).

Dee Lavender Farm
(Ingasetter Ltd)
North Deeside Road
The Dwarf Munstead variety of lavender grows behind the factory on a five-acre site and is harvested during July and August. A film and short tour of the factory gives visitors the opportunity to see the processing of lavender from distillation to the making of a wide range of cosmetics. Dee Lavender and other Scottish fragrances can also be sampled.

Ø (0224) 580641.
Open: Mon-Fri 9-5.
♿ ⚬ Shop

BANFF
Grampian (Banffshire)   *Map 15 NJ66.*
Banff Museum
High Street
Exhibition of British birds set out as an aviary. Local history and armour also on show.

Ø Peterhead (0779) 77778.
Open: Jun-Sep, daily (ex Thu) 2-5.20.

♿ (ground floor only) shop ⚬ (ex guide dogs).

BANGOR
Gwynedd   *Map 6 SH57.*
Bangor Museum & Art Gallery (University College of North Wales)
Ffordd Gwynedd
The museum portrays history of North Wales, collections of furniture, crafts, costumes, maps, ceramics, and both Roman and prehistoric antiquities. Exhibitions illustrating history of the Menai Bridges and Conwy Bridge. Attendant always on duty to deal with enquiries. Art Gallery stages exhibitions of sculpture and paintings each year changing at approximately monthly intervals. If there is an exhibition in the gallery the Museum may be closed and if the Museum is open the gallery will generally be closed. From Apr-Sep both will normally be open.

Ø (0248) 353368.
Open: Tue-Sat. Art gallery open 10-4.30. Museum open normal daytime hours (but see above).
⚬ Shop exhibits works of art

BARDSEA
Cumbria   *Map 7 SD37.*
Bardsea Country Park
(½m S on A5087)
Overlooking Morecambe Bay, this strip of the Cumbrian coast combines woodland walks with fine coastal bird-watching country. The best times are in winter, when thousands of birds from northern Europe and Russia move here to feed, or in early spring and early autumn, when migrant birds pass through. At the south end of the country park is the 60-acre Sea Wood. About a mile to the north is Conishead Priory, the grounds of which offer three nature trails.

Open: at all reasonable times. (Conishead Priory nature trails open Apr-Sep, Sat & Sun 2-5, mid Jul-end Aug Wed & Thu 2-5.)
⌂

BARNARD CASTLE
Co Durham   *Map 12 NZ01.*
Egglestone Abbey
(1m SE)
Picturesque remains of Premonstratensian Abbey on right bank of River Tees.

Open: at all reasonable times. (AM) ♿

BARR, GREAT
West Midlands   *Map 7 SP09.*
Bishop Asbury Cottage
Newton Road
The boyhood home of Francis Asbury, the founder of Methodism in America. A small, mid 17th-century cottage containing furniture of the period of Asbury's home life.

✂ 021-569 2308.
Open: Mon-Fri 2-4. Other times by arrangement.
⨳ (ex guide dogs)

BARROW-IN-FURNESS
Cumbria   *Map 7 SD26.*
Furness Museum
Ramsden Square
Museum of Furness district with finds from late Stone Age sites. Also Vickers ship models and Lake District bygones. Various monthly exhibitions.

✂ (0229) 20650.
Open: Mon-Wed & Fri 10-5, Thu 10-1 & Sat 10-4.
(Closed: PH)
⨳

BARRY
South Glamorgan   *Map 3 ST16.*
Porthkerry Country Park
(2m W on coast)
Fossil-rich limestone cliffs rising to 150 ft, and a lofty

viaduct built in 1898 for the Vale of Glamorgan Railway, are dramatic features of the Park. Other links with the past include the remains of a kiln where lime was burned to make fertiliser, and a 19th-century sawmill overlooked by Mill Wood.

Open: at all reasonable times.
♿ 🍵 ⌂ Shop.

BASINGSTOKE
Hampshire   *Map 4 SU65.*
Willis Museum and Art Gallery
Old Town Hall, Market Place
The museum has recently moved and is now housed in the handsome Old Town Hall. New Town history gallery, natural history and aquarium. Exhibition gallery.

✂ (0256) 465902.
Open: Tue-Fri, 10-5. Sat 10-4.
Parties by arrangement.
Shop ⨳

BATH
Avon   *Map 3 ST76.*
Botanic Gardens (Royal Victoria Park)
Avenues of cherry trees (which blossom in spring) are only one of the thousands of different varieties of plants, trees and shrubs here. They come from all parts of the world, demonstrating what can be grown on local soil. The Gardens form part of some 50 acres of Royal Victoria Park, which offers good views of the Royal Crescent.

✂ (0225) 61111 ext 411 Mr. Littlewood
Open: daily, 8-sunset.
🍵 ♿

Victoria Art Gallery
Bridge Street
The museum contains a varied collection of 18th- to 20th-century British paint-

ings, watercolours and drawings, with the European Old Masters well represented. Also on display is the Carr collection of English glass and watches from the 18th and 19th centuries. There is a mixed programme of temporary exhibitions.

✂ (0225) 61111 Ext 418.
Open: Mon-Fri 10-6, Sat 10-5.
(Closed BH)
⨳

BATLEY
West Yorkshire   *Map 8 SE22.*
Art Gallery
Market Place
Permanent collection of British oil paintings, water colours, drawings and sculpture from mid 19th-century onwards. Temporary loan and special exhibitions throughout the year.

✂ Huddersfield (0484) 513808 ext 216
Open: Mon-Fri 10-6, Sat 10-4.
(Closed Sun & BH)
⨳

Bagshaw Museum
Wilton Park
A 19th-century building housing museum of local history, archaeology, geology, ethnography, oriental arts, natural history and folk life. (Best approached from Upper Batley Lane.)

✂ (0924) 472514.
Open: Mon-Sat 10-5, Sun 1-5.
♿ (ground floor and gardens only) Shop ⨳

BEACON FELL
Lancashire   *Map 7 SD54.*
Beacon Fell Country Park
(2½m NE of Inglewhite)
Opened in 1970, the Beacon Fell Country Park covers a wooded hilltop to the southwest of the Forest of Bowland. Around the perimeter there are a number of car

parks and many woodland paths lead to the summit (873 ft) which commands a good view across the Lancashire coastal plain. The wooded slopes are mostly coniferous and the home for many small mammals and a variety of birds. About half a mile south-east is the Carwags Information Centre which contains a small exhibition.

⌀ Chipping (09956) 235 or Preston (0772) 263896.
Open: Country Park; Accessible at any reasonable time. Information Centre Mar-Oct daily 1-5.
☐ (☞ most days, pm only)

BEARSDEN
Strathclyde (Dunbartonshire)
Map 11 NS57.
Roman Bath House
Roman Road
Considered to be the best surviving visible Roman building in Scotland the bathhouse was discovered in 1973 during excavations for a construction site. It was originally built for use by the Roman garrison at Bearsden Fort, part of the Antonine Wall defences.

Open: accessible at all reasonable times. (AM)

BECCLES
Suffolk
Map 5 TM49.
Beccles & District Museum
Newgate
Local industrial, rural and domestic displays, which include tools of the printing trade, a prominent industry in the town. A new addition is a needlework banner depicting scenes of the town.

⌀ (0502) 712628.
Open: Apr-Oct, Wed, Sat, Sun & BH 2.30-5; Nov-Mar, Sun only 2.30-5.
✗

BEDALE
North Yorkshire
Map 8 SE28.
Bedale Hall
On A684 (1½m W of A1 at Leeming Bar)
Grade 1 listed building with one of the most spectacular rooms of its period in the North of England, with stucco work by Cortese and the original floor. There is also a charming museum of local history containing archive material from the 17th century, Victoriana, costume and early toys. Tourist Information Centre.

⌀ (0677) 24604
Open: May-Sep, daily 10-4, Oct-Mar Tue only 10-4, other times by appointment.
☐ ✗ (ex guide dogs)

BEDFORD
Bedfordshire
Map 4 TL04.
Bedford Museum
Castle Lane
A local history and natural history museum with 19th-century room sets, displays on agriculture, Bedfordshire geology, archaeology, birds and mammals, fossils and minerals. Also a programme of temporary exhibitions.

⌀ (0234) 53323.
Open: all year, Tue-Sat 11-5 & Sun 2-5. (Closed: Mon, ex BH Mon afternoons, Good Fri & Xmas)
☐ (lift available on request)
Shop ✗

BEDWYN, GREAT
Wiltshire
Map 4 SU26.
Bedwyn Stone Museum
An open air museum that explains the ancient secrets of the freemason and how the carvings trace the behaviour of man in a language vastly different to that taught in school. Finest known sequence of carvings are to be found in the church adjacent.

⌀ Marlborough (0672) 870043.
Open: all year.
☐ garden centre.

BEMBRIDGE
Isle of Wight
See **Wight, Isle of**

BERKHAMSTED
Hertfordshire
Map 4 SP90.
Berkhamsted Castle
Remains of an 11th-century motte and bailey castle with later circular Keep. Former home of Black Prince and prison of King John of France.

Open: at all reasonable times.
(AM) ☐

BERWICK-UPON-TWEED
Northumberland
Map 12 NT95.
Castle and Town Walls
Remains of 12th-century stronghold incorporating three towers and west wall. Medieval town walls reconstructed during Elizabethan period.

⌀ (0289) 307881.
Open: at all reasonable times.
(AM)

BEVERLEY
Humberside
Map 8 TA03.
Art Gallery, Museum & Heritage Centre
Champney Road
Local antiquities, Victorian bygones and china, pictures by F W Elwell of Beverley and others, and bust of Sir Winston Churchill by Bryant Baker of New York. Various solo Art Exhibitions. Heritage Centre recently established.

⌀ Hull (0482) 882255.
Open: Mon-Wed & Fri 9.30-12.30, 2-5, Thu 9.30-12, Sat 9.30-4.
Shop ✗

Locks at Bingley

Lairgate Hall

Dates from 1710-80, now used as council offices. Interesting late 18th-century stucco ceiling, marble mantelpiece. Chinese room with hand-painted wallpaper.

⌖ Hull (0482) 882255.
Open: Mon-Thu, 8.45-5.30, Fri 9-4.
♿ ⚹

BEXLEY

Gt London   London plan 2: 38F2.

Hall Place

(Near Junction of A2 & A233)
15th-16th-century mansion. Grade I listed building and ancient monument with contrasting elevations of chequered flint and brick. Ornamental gardens with topiary in form of 'Queen's Beasts' roses, rock, water, herb, peat gardens, conservatory houses and recreation facilities.

⌖ Crayford (0322) 526574.
Open: House Mon-Sat 10-5, Sun 2-6 (summer); Mon-Sat 10-5 (winter); Gardens: Mon-Fri 7.30-dusk, Sat & Sun 9-dusk.
☕ (weather permitting)
♿ (gardens only) ⚹

BIDDENDEN

Kent   Map 5 TQ83.

Baby Carriage Collection

Bettenham Manor
A unique collection of 400 baby carriages (prams) of a bygone era. Exhibits portray the history of the pram up to the present day and include 18th-century stickwagons, perambulators and mailcarts, Edwardian bassinettes, Victorias and large coachbuilt prams of the twenties. The museum, in a Kentish oast house, adjoins a 15th-century moated manor house of historical and architectural interest and is set in a 15-acre garden.

⌖ (0580) 291343.
Open: all year (ex Xmas Day) by appointment only.
♿ (ground floor & garden only) ⚹

Biddenden Vineyards

Little Whatmans (1½m S off A262)
The present vineyard was established in 1969 and has now reached 18 acres. The varieties planted are mainly of German origin all of which produce fruity fragrant wines. Harvesting usually commences on 20 October when visitors can see the presses in operation. Visitors are welcome to stroll around the vines at leisure and to call at the shop for tasting of the wines, and cider etc.

⌖ (0580) 291726.
Shop open: all year Mon-Sat 11-5 (2pm Nov-Apr), Sun 12-5 (Closed Nov-Apr).
Parties by arrangement.
Shop.

BINGLEY

West Yorkshire   Map 7 SE13.

Bingley Five Rise Locks

(½m N of Bingley on canal towpath)
One of the wonders of the waterways. The lock staircase is situated on the Leeds and Liverpool Canal and was designed and built by John Longbotham of Halifax during the 1770s.

Open: Towpath accessible at all reasonable times.

BINHAM

Norfolk   Map 9 TF93.

Binham Priory

The Priory, or at least its extensive ruins, dates from the 12th century. The main fragment to survive intact is the western end of the monastic church which is now used as the parish church. Inside, there is a perpendicular, seven-sacrament font and the stalls have misericords.

Open: (Ruins) accessible at all reasonable times.
♿ (AM)

BIRKENHEAD

Merseyside   Map 7 SJ38.

Birkenhead Priory

Priory St

Founded in 1150, the Priory provided accommodation for a prior and 16 Benedictine monks. Most of the buildings were neglected after the Dissolution. A new interpretation centre traces the history and development of the site.

Open: 9.30-12.30. 1-4.
♿ (ground floor only)

Williamson Art Gallery & Museum

Slatey Road

Exhibits include: major collection of work by English water-colourists and Liverpool school of painters; sculpture; decorative arts; ceramics (English, Continental, Oriental wares); glass, silver and furniture. Also a large collection of paintings by P Wilson Steer, as well as approximately 25 special exhibitions throughout the year.

A local history and maritime museum containing model ships adjoins.

✐ 051-652 4177.
Open: Mon-Sat, 10-5; Thu, 10-9; Sun 2-5. (Closed: Xmas & BH.)
♿ Shop ⊘

BIRMINGHAM

West Midlands   Map 7 SP08.

City Museum & Art Gallery

Chamberlain Square

Fine and applied arts, Natural History, archaeology and local history exhibits. There is a fine collection of paintings from the 14th century to the present day, including a most important collection of Pre-Raphaelite paintings. Applied arts include costume, silver, ceramics and textiles; there are prehistoric, Egyptian, Greek and Roman antiquities, local history exhibits, an important coin collection and the famous Pinto Collection of wooden items. There are frequent lectures, temporary exhibitions, demonstrations and holiday activities for children.

✐ 021-235 2834.
Open: Mon-Sat 9.30-5, Sun 2-5. (Closed: Good Fri, Xmas & New Years Day.)
⌽ ♿ Shop ⊘ (ex guide dogs)

Museum of Science & Industry

Newhall Street (close to Post Office Tower)

Displays from the Industrial Revolution up to the present. Engineering hall was formerly a Victorian plating works and contains machine tools, electrical equipment, working steam, gas and hot air engines. Locomotive hall. Transport section. Science section. Pen room. Music room. In the aircraft section World War II Spitfire and Hurricane, and collection of aircraft engines. New James Watt building contains oldest working steam engine in the world, dated 1779. Steam weekends Mar and Oct. Traction Engine Rally in May. Engines steamed 1st and 3rd Wed each month.

✐ 021-236 1022.
Open: Mon-Sat 9.30-5, Sun 2-5. (Closed: Xmas & New Year's Day.)
♿ Shop ⊘ (ex guide dogs)

Selly Manor & Minworth Greaves

Sycamore Road, Bournville off A38

Two 13th- and early 14th-century half-timbered houses re-erected in Bournville. Collection of old furniture etc. and herb garden. Exhibitions.

✆ 021-472 0199.
Open: mid Jan-mid Dec, Tue-Fri 10-5 (ex BH). Open some weekends, phone for details. Parties & guided tours by arrangement with the curator.
🚼 (ground floor only) shop
🐾

BIRSAY

See **Orkney**

BLACKBURN

Lancashire   *Map 7 SD62.*
Lewis Museum of Textile Machinery
Noted for series of period rooms portraying continuous development of textile industry from 18th-century onwards. The gallery on the first floor has changing exhibitions.

✆ (0254) 667130.
Open: Tue-Sat 10-5. (Closed: Mon, Sun, Good Fri, Xmas, New Years Day & some BH.) (Booking 3 weeks in advance will enable a party to see machinery in operation.) Shop 🐾 (ex guide dogs).

Museum & Art Gallery
Library Street
Local history, militaria, coins, ceramics, fine books and manuscripts, paintings, icons, watercolours and Japanese prints. Time tunnel and children's corner.

✆ (0254) 667130.
Open: Tue-Sat 10-5. (Closed: Mon, Sun, Good Fri, Xmas, New Years Day & some BH.)
🚼 (ground floor only) shop
🐾 (ex guide dogs)

BLACKPOOL

Lancashire   *Map 7 SD33.*
Grundy Art Gallery
Queen Street
Established 1911, this gallery exhibits a permanent collection of paintings by 19th- and 20th-century artists. Also touring exhibitions, one man shows and group exhibitions.

✆ (0253) 23977.
Open: Mon-Sat 10-5. (Closed: BH.)
🐾 🚼 (ground floor only)

BLANDFORD FORUM

Dorset   *Map 3 ST80.*
Royal Signals Museum
Blandford Camp
Museum of history of army radio and line communications; paintings, uniforms, medals and badges.

✆ (0258) 52581 Ext 2248/2413.
Open: Mon-Fri 8.30-5. Wknds by appointment.
(Closed: BH.)
🐾

BLEAN WOODS

Kent   *Map 5 TR16.*
(A2 Dunkirk, NE to A291 at Herne Common. Clowes Wood, 1m S of Radfall)
Blean Woods complex combines a variety of woods and heaths. There are many acres of coppice, where trees are cut to the base on a 15-year cycle to produce a cluster of straight poles used for stakes, fencing and tools. Other areas of hazel, chestnut and oak are all rich in wildlife, and noted for interesting bird life including nightjars, redstarts, nightingales, warblers and woodpeckers. There is a forest walk at Clowes Wood. Bluebells may be seen here too.

Open: at all reasonable times. Generally restricted to footpaths on nature reserve and public rights of way.
🪧 (Clowes Wood)

BOLTON

Gt Manchester   *Map 7 SD71.*
Tonge Moor Textile Museum
Tonge Moor Library, Tonge Moor Road
Includes Arkwright's waterframe (1768), Crompton's spinning mule (1779) and Hargreave's spinning jenny.

℗ (0204) 22311 Ext 2195.
Open: Mon & Thu 2-7.30, Tue
& Fri 9.30-5.30, Sat 9.30-12.30.
(Closed: Sun & Wed.)
&

BO'NESS

Central (West Lothian)   Map 11 NS98.
Kinneil Museum & Roman Fortlet
Situated in the renovated
17th-century stable block of
Kinneil House. The ground
floor illustrates the industrial
history of Bo'ness. On the upper floor there is an interpre-
tive display on the history
and environment of the Kinneil Estate. Kinneil Roman
fortlet is open for viewing
near the museum.

℗ (0506) 824318.
Open: May-Oct, Mon-Sat 10-
12.30, 1.30-5; Nov-Apr, Sat
only 10-5.
& Shop

BOWES

Co Durham   Map 12 NY91.
Bowes Castle
(on A66)
Norman keep built between
1171 and 1187, in angle of Roman fort of 'Lavatrae'.

Open: at any reasonable
time.
(AM)

BRADFIELD WOODS

Suffolk   Map 5 TL95.
*(4½m SE of Bury St Edmunds,
off A134 between
Sicklesmere and Gedding)*
This nature reserve is one of
the finest examples in the
country of a woodland still
managed by the ancient
practice of coppicing. The
ground is extremely rich,
with over 370 species of plant
having been identified. The
coppicing of woodland also
provides suitable habitats for
a large variety of wildlife, including woodpeckers, tawny
owls and four types of deer.

℗ Bury St Edmunds (0284)
810379.
Open: all reasonable times,
along waymarked paths.
Visitor Centre Apr-Sep, Sun
1-5
(dogs on lead)

BRADFORD

West Yorkshire   Map 7 SE13.
Bolling Hall
Bowling Hall Road
A Yorkshire manor house
which dates from 15th century and contains fine furnishings including rare Chip-
pendale bed, heraldic glass
and 'ghost room'.

℗ (0274) 723057.
Open: Apr-Sep, Tue-Sun &
BH Mon 10-6; Oct-Mar, Tue-
Sun 10-5. (Closed: Good Fri,
Xmas Day & Boxing Day.)
& (ground floor & gardens
only) Shop (ex guide
dogs)

Cartwright Hall
Lister Park
Contains permanent collections of European and British
paintings, sculpture, drawings, modern prints and
ceramics. Also includes
varied and imaginative exhibition programme.

℗ (0274) 493313.
Open: Apr-Sep, Tue-Sun &
BH Mon 10-6; Oct-Mar, Tue-
Sun 10-5. (Closed: Mon ex
BH.)
& Shop (ex guide
dogs)

Industrial Museum
Moorside Road, Eccleshill
Features the growth of the
woollen and worsted textile
industry, transport and motive power galleries, and the
mill owner's house with temporary exhibitions.

℗ (0274) 631756.
Open: Tue-Sun & BH Mon 10-
5. (Closed: Mon ex BH.)
& Shop (ex guide dogs)

National Museum of Photography, Film & Television
Prince's Way
Incorporates displays, models and galleries that explore
photography in all its many
forms including press,
medical/scientific, moving
pictures, exhibitions and stu-
dios. Displays and talk-over
tapes make for realism and
visitor participation. In addition the only IMAX cinema in
Britain is housed in the
museum.

℗ (0274) 727488.
Open: Tue-Sun 11-6. (Closed
Mon ex BH.)
IMAX cinema, admission
charge.
(licensed) & Shop
(ex guide dogs).

The Colour Museum
82 Grattan Road
The headquarters of the
Society of Dyers and Colour-
ists. Housed on two floors, the
museum has 'The World of
Colour' exhibition on the first
floor, which is designed to increase visitors' awareness
and enjoyment of colour as a
factor of great importance in
their daily lives. 'The Science
of Colour' exhibition is
housed on the second floor
and shows how scientific
technology is employed in
making and using colouring
matters of all kinds, and the
methods by which they can
be tested and their colours
measured.

℗ (0734) 725138.
Open: Tue-Fri 2-5, Sat 10-4.
(ex PH).

BRADFORD-ON-AVON

Wiltshire   Map 3 ST86.
Barton Tithe Barn
14th-century building, once
the property of Shaftesbury
Abbey, since presented to

Wiltshire Archaeological Society.

Open: at any reasonable time.
(AM) ⬢

BRADGATE PARK & SWITHLAND WOOD ESTATE
Leicestershire   Map 8 SK51.
(6½m NE of Leicester off B5327)
Bradgate Park is an 850-acre country park. Natural parkland, woods, herds of red and fallow deer, with Old John Tower (1786). Ruins of Bradgate House, completed c 1510 by son of 1st Marquis of Dorset, and the birthplace of Lady Jane Grey (1537-54). There is a Visitor Centre, and of special interest is Swithland Wood-140 acres of ancient woodland.

✆ Leicester (0533) 871313 Ext 492 (The Ranger)
Open: all year to pedestrians during daylight hours. Bradgate ruins open Apr-Oct, Wed, Thu & Sat, 2.30-5; Sun 10-12.30. Parties by arrangement Apr-Oct. Registered disabled or permit holders issued by Bradgate Park Trust may drive through the park, Apr-Oct, Thu 2.30-7.30, Sun 9-11 am.
Also **Marion's Cottage**
Newton Linford
(visitor centre)
Newton Linford
Typical Charnwood Forest cottage offering selection of gifts, publications, etc. Information Point and Exhibition. Adjoins Newton Linford car park.

Open: Apr-Oct, Wed, Thu, Sat & Sun 2-6; Nov-Mar, Sat & Sun 2-5. Also BH Mon & Tue. Parties by arrangement.
⼌ ⬢ Shop.

BRAMBER
West Sussex   Map 4 TQ11.
Bramber Castle
Former home of the Dukes of Norfolk, this ruined Norman stronghold lies on a South Downs ridge with good views.

Open daily.
(NT)

BRAMHOPE
West Yorkshire   Map 8 SE24.
Golden Acre Park
The Park covers 137 acres of mature woodland and gardens, and incorporates an attractive lake, the home of many species of wildfowl. There is a collection of trees and shrubs as well as herbaceous and aquatic plants. Created features include rock gardens, a large Alpine house, a demonstration garden for vegetables and flowers, old shrub roses, rhododendrons and azaleas, an arboretum and a pinetum.

Open: daily, 11-5 (summer); 10-4 (winter).
⛾ ⼌ ⬢

BRANSGORE
Hampshire   Map 4 SZ19.
Macpenny's
One-time gravel pits have been converted into this large woodland garden and nurseries, with rare trees, shrubs, rhododendrons, azaleas, camellias and heathers.

✆ (0425) 72348.
Open: Mon-Sat 8-5; Sun 2-5 (collection box).
⼌ (NGS)

BRECON
Powys   Map 3 SO02.
Brecknock Museum
Captain's Walk
Archaeological and local historical exhibits, folk life, decorative arts and natural history.

✆ (0874) 4121.
Open: Mon-Sat (incl BH) 10-5
Shop ⬢ (ground floor only)
⚔

BRIDGEND
Mid Glamorgan   Map 3 SS97.
Newcastle
Small ruined 12th-century and later stronghold, with rectangular tower, richly carved Norman gateway to south side and massive curtain walls enclosing polygonal courtyard.

Opening details not confirmed for 1988. (AM. CADW)

BRIDGWATER
Somerset   Map 3 ST23.
Admiral Blake Museum
Blake Street
The Museum is housed in the birthplace of Admiral Robert Blake (1587-1657). Exhibits include an audio-visual of the Battle of Sedgemoor, industrial history of Bridgwater and its docks and the Archaeology of Bridgwater and District. In the Blake Room there is a diorama of the Battle of Santa Cruz, Blake's greatest victory over the Spaniards. Several of Blake's personal belongings are also on show.

✆ (0278) 456127.
Open: daily 11-5, Wed 11-8. Evenings open by arrangement.
⬢ Shop

BRIERLEY HILL
West Midlands   Map 7 SO98.
Royal Brierley Crystal
North Street
The company was founded in 1847 and every piece of its crystal is made and cut by hand. The 1½ hour factory tour shows the production of hand-made crystal and includes a visit to the site museum which contains some unique pieces.

⊘ (0384) 70161.
Open: Factory tours by appointment only. Mon-Thu 11, 12 & 1, Fri 11.
(Tours in the afternoon by arrangement).
Shop daily 9-4.30. ⊑

BRIGHOUSE
West Yorkshire   Map 7 SE12.
Brighouse Art Gallery
Halifax Road
Temporary exhibitions throughout the year of local artists work and of other modern works of interest.

⊘ (0484) 719222.
Open: Mon-Sat 10-5, Sun 2.30-5. (Closed: Sun, Oct-Mar; Xmas & New Year's Day.)
⌧ (ground floor only) ⚹

BRIGHTON
East Sussex   Map 4 TQ30.
Booth Museum of Natural History
194 Dyke Road
Contains British birds mounted in natural settings, butterfly gallery, also vertebrate evolution and 'Unnatural History' displays. Geology gallery. Temporary exhibitions; classroom available for use.

⊘ (0273) 552586.
Open: Mon-Sat (ex Thu) 10-5, Sun 2-5. (Closed: Good Fri, Xmas & New Year's Day).
⌧ (ground floor only) Shop ⚹

Museum & Art Gallery
Church Street
The collections include Old Master paintings, watercolours, Sussex archaeology, folklife and local history, ethnography and musical instruments. Also the Willett Collection of pottery and porcelain, and display of 20th-century fine and applied art, including Art Nouveau, Art Deco and 19th & 20th-century costume. Also various special exhibitions.

⊘ (0273) 603005.
Open: Tue-Sat 10-5.45, Sun 2-5. (Closed: Mon, Good Fri, 25-26 Dec & New Year's Day.)
⊑ (closed Sun) ⌧ (ground floor only) Shop ⚹

BRISTOL
Avon   Map 3 ST57.
For town plan, see pp. 22-3
Avon Gorge and Leigh Woods
*(off A369, 2m W of Bristol City Centre.)   Plan : **A3.***

Museum at Bridgwater

Leigh Woods is a nature reserve offering many delightful walks through deciduous woodland containing a wide variety of birds. The Avon Gorge, nearby, is two miles long and its fossil-rich limestone cliffs rise to 300 ft. The soil here suits some rare plants and the area is an attraction to botanists. In fact, the rare Bristol Whitebeam, found here, grows nowhere else in the world. The Avon Walkway is a recreational path which follows the southern bank of the River Avon through the Gorge.

Open: accessible at all reasonable times.
NT (part)

Blaise Castle House Museum
Henbury (4m NW of city, off B4057, not on plan)
18th-century mansion, now social history museum, situated in extensive grounds.

⊘ (0272) 506789.
Open: Sat-Wed 10-1 & 2-5. (Closed: 25-27 Dec & New Year's Day.)
Shop ⚹

Bristol Cathedral
*College Green.   Plan : **D3.***
Dating from the 12th century, the Cathedral was originally a monastic church but gained cathedral status in 1542. The Cathedral has been heavily restored and only the chapter house and adjoining buildings date from the original period. The nave has some unusual features which include the side aisles being as high as the central aisle, and a complex system of vaulting in the central aisle. The Lady Chapel contains some unique 'Stellar' tomb recesses found only in Bristol. The furnishing of stalls and misericords are of note.

✆ (0272) 24879 or 298567.
Open: daily 8-6 (donations).
⬤ (⬤ 10.30-3.30) ⊘

Bristol Industrial Museum
Prince's Wharf, Prince Street.   Plan : *D2.*
A converted dockside transit shed in the heart of Bristol, 400 yards from SS 'Great Britain'. Display of vehicles, horse-drawn and motorised from the Bristol area, locally built aircraft, aero-engines; railway exhibits include full-size industrial locomotive Henbury, steamed around once a month. Various kinds of machinery illustrating local trade and manufacturing. Display of history of the Port of Bristol.

✆ (0272) 299771 Ext 290.
Open: Sat-Wed 10-1 & 2-5.
(Closed: 25-27 Dec & New Year's Day).
⬤ Shop ⊘

City Museum & Art Gallery
Queen's Road.   Plan : *C4.*
Regional and world-wide collections, representing ancient history, natural sciences, fine and applied arts.

✆ (0272) 299771.
Open: Mon-Sat 10-5.
(Closed: Good Fri, May Day, Spring BH Mon, 25-27 Dec & New Year's Day)
⬤ (licensed) ⬤ Shop ⊘

Maritime Heritage Centre
Gas Ferry Road   Plan : *C2.*
The centre introduces the theme of 200 years of Bristol shipbuilding: with particular reference to Charles Hill & Son and their predecessor, James Hilhouse.

✆ (0272) 260680.
Open daily (ex 24 & 25 Dec) 10-5 (winter); 10-6 (summer). Tokens may be purchased for entry to S.S. Great Britain.
⬤ ⊘

Red Lodge
Park Row.   Plan : *D3.*
16th-century house altered in the early 18th century, with fine oak carvings and furnishings of both periods.

✆ (0272) 299771 Ext 236.
Open: Mon-Sat 10-1, 2-5.
(Closed: Good Fri, May Day, Spring BH Mon & 25-27 Dec & New Year's Day.)
⊘

St Mary Redcliffe Church
Redcliffe Way.   Plan : *E2.*
One of the largest churches in England and noted for its outstanding example of perpendicular architecture. The earliest part of the church dates from 1180, however much of it was constructed during the 13th century including the impressive hexagonal outer porch. In the 15th century the spire was struck by lightning and wasn't rebuilt until 1783. Rising to 295 ft the spire is a well known Bristol landmark. In 1574, Queen Elizabeth I reputedly described the church as 'the fairest, goodliest and most famous parish church in England'.

✆ (0272) 291487.
Open: daily 8-6, May-Aug Mon-Fri 8-8 (donations)
⬤

St Nicholas Church Museum
St Nicholas Street.   Plan : *E3.*
The history of Bristol from its beginning until the Reformation including Bristol church art and silver. Changing art exhibitions showing topographical features of the city mainly during the 18th and 19th century and the Hogarth altarpiece originally painted for St Mary Redcliffe. Brass rubbing centre.

✆ (0272) 299771 Ext 243.
Open: Mon-Sat 10-5.

(Closed: Good Fri, May Day, Spring BH Mon & Tue, 25-28 Dec & New Year's Day.)
⬤ (ground floor only) Shop ⊘

The Georgian House
7 Gt George St.   Plan : *C3.*
Georgian house with 18th-century furniture and fittings.

✆ (0272) 299771 Ext 237
Open: Mon-Sat 10-1, 2-5
(Closed: Good Fri, May Day, Spring BH Mon & 25-27 Dec & New Year's Day)
⊘

University Botanic Gardens
North Road.   Plan : *A3.*
The mature Gardens contain a wide range of plants, some labelled with their history. Many of the plants are tropical and include a collection from New Zealand. There is a small collection of regional fauna representing different British ecological situations. An arrowed route shows the way around the garden and staff are willing to answer questions.

✆ (0272) 733682.
Open: Mon-Fri 8.30-5
⬤ ⊘

BRIXHAM
Devon   Map 3 SX95.
Berry Head Country Park
Gillard Road
Occupying an exposed limestone promontory at the southern end of Tor Bay, the Country Park is rich in limestone-loving wild flowers such as rockrose and orchids. On the cliffs there is a wide variety of sea birds including guillemots, kittiwakes, shags, cormorants and several species of gull. Part of the area has been designated a nature reserve.

There are slight traces of an Iron Age promontory fort and in the past centuries a large area has been quarried.

✆ **Torquay (0803) 26244.**
Open: accessible at all reasonable times.
& (🚃 Apr-Sep daily 10-6)

BRIXWORTH

Northamptonshire   *Map 4 SP77.*
All Saints Church
Northern edge of village (signed from A508)
This is one of the best-preserved Saxon churches in the country and dates from the 7th century. The building

incorporates many Roman tiles and was monastic until 870. In the 14th century a belfry and spire were added to the Saxon tower.

✆ **(0604) 880286.**
Open: 9-6 summer months, 9-4 winter months (donations)

Bristol
© The Automobile Association

✗ Teas by arrangement; bookstall.

BROOK

Kent   Map 5 TR04.
Wye College Museum of Agriculture
(4m ENE of Ashford on unclass road)

An exhibition of old farm implements and machinery housed in a fine 14th-century tithe barn. Display of hop cultivation in old oast house.

✆ Wye (0233) 812401.
Open: May-Sep, Wed 2-5, Sat in Aug.

Parties by arrangement in writing to:
Hon. Curator, Museum, Wye College, Wye, Ashford, Kent TN25 5AH.
⛬ (ground floor only) ✗

BROUGHTON

Borders (Peeblesshire) Map 11 NT13.
Broughton Place
Built on the site of a much older house and designed by Sir Basil Spence in 1938 in the style of a 17th-century Scottish tower house. The drawing room and main hall are open to the public and contain paintings and crafts by living British artists for sale. The gardens, open for part of the summer, afford fine views of the Tweeddale hills.

✆ (08994) 234.
Gallery open: Apr-Sep daily 10.30-6 (ex Wed)
Donation for garden
⛬ (ground floor & gardens)
Shop ✗

BRUAR

Tayside (Perthshire)   Map 14: NN86.
Clan Donnachaidh (Robertson) Museum
Robes, uniforms, weapons, silver, glass, books and pictures associated with the Clan Donnachaidh, Bannockburn and the Jacobite risings. Clan gathering 20 & 21 Jun.

✆ Calvine (079683) 264.
Open: Apr-Oct, Mon-Sat 10-1 & 2-5.30, Sun 2-5.30. Other times by arrangement.
⛬ Shop ✗

BRYN-CELLI-DDU

Gwynedd   Map 6 SH57.
Bryn-Celli-Ddu Burial Chamber
(3m W of Menai Bridge off A4080)
Excavated in 1865, and again 1925-29, prehistoric circular cairn covering passage grave with polygonal chamber.

Open: accessible at all reasonable times.
(AM CADW)

BUCKHAVEN
Fife (Fife)   *Map 11 NT39.*
Museum
Above Buckhaven Library, College Street
A small museum depicting life in Buckhaven in the hey-day of its fishing industry. The museum includes old photographs, model boats, local history and a recon-struction of a fisherman's kitchen.

℘ (0592) 712192.
Open: all year Mon 2-7; Tue 10-12.30, 2-5;
Thu 10-12.30, 2-7; Fri 2-5; Sat 10-12.30.
⚹ Shop

BUCKIE
Grampian (Banffshire)   Map 15 NJ46.
Buckie Museum & Peter Anson Gallery
Maritime museum with dis-plays relating to the fishing industry including exhibits on coopering, navigation, life-boats and fishing methods. Selections from the Peter Anson watercolour col-lection of fishing vessels are on display.

℘ Forres (0309) 73701.
Open: all year (ex BHs) Mon-Fri 10-8, Sat 10-noon.
🖾 Shop ⚹

BURGH CASTLE
Norfolk   Map 5 TG40.
The Castle
(off A143)
Massive walls from former

3rd-century Roman fort, guarded by six pear-shaped bastions.

Open: accessible at any reasonable time.
(AM)

BURGHEAD
Grampian (Moray)   Map 15 NJ16.
Burghead Museum
16-18 Grant Street
Local history and temporary exhibitions.

℘ Forres (0309) 73701.
Open: Tue 1.30-5, Thu 5-8.30, Sat 10-noon.
🖾 ⚹

BURNLEY
Lancashire   Map 7 SD83.
Towneley Hall Art Gallery & Museum of Local Crafts & Industries
14th-century house with later modifications. Collection of oil paintings, early English water colours, period furni-ture, ivories, 18th-century glassware, archaeology and natural history. Nature trails. Loan exhibitions Apr-Sep.

℘ (0282) 24213.
Open: Mon-Fri 10-5, Sun 12-5.
(Closed: Sat & Xmas.)

Bury St Edmunds: Abbey Gate

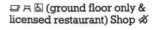

🖵 🍴 🖾 (ground floor only & licensed restaurant) Shop ⚹

BURTON AGNES
Humberside   Map 8 TA16.
Norman Manor House
Dates from 1170 and pre-serves original Norman piers and groined roof of a lower chamber. Upper room and an old donkey wheel.

Open: standard times, see page 4.
(AM)

BURY
Gt Manchester   Map 7 SD81.
Bury Art Gallery & Museum
Moss Street
Contains a fine collection of 19th-century British paintings including works by Turner, Constable and Landseer. The museum outlines the so-cial history of the town. Tem-porary exhibitions.

℘ 061-705 5881.
Open: Mon-Fri 10-6, Sat 10-5.
(Closed Sun & BH.)
🖾 ⚹

BURY ST EDMUNDS
Suffolk   Map 5 TL86.
Abbey Gardens & Ruins
Beautifully laid-out formal gardens form the centre-piece of the Abbey grounds and lead down to the 13th-century Abbots Bridge. A riverside path leads past a hexagonal dovecot to the ruins; little remains of the great Abbey which was once an important place of pil-grimage and held the Shrine of St Edmund. Stripped of its facing stone after the Dissolu-tion of the Monasteries, there are Tudor, Georgian and Victorian houses built into it, giving it the appearance of a folly.

℘ (0284) 64667 (May-Sep)
Open: daily, 7.30-dusk.

Angel Corner & The Gershom-Parkington Collection
Angel Hill
Queen Anne house containing fine Gershom-Parkington collection of clocks and watches.

⌀ (0284) 63233 Ext 2110.
Open: Mon-Sat 10-1, 2-5 (4pm Nov-Feb). (Closed: Good Fri, Etr Sat, May BH, Xmas & New Year.) Donation.
⋇ (NT)

Cathedral Church of St James
Of particular interest is the attractive hammerbeam roof with its painted angels holding shields with the insignia of St James, St Edmund and St George. The statue of St Edmund outside the south side is a bronze by the modern sculptress Elizabeth Frink. The tower, an outstanding example of Norman architecture, originally served as one of the gateways to the abbey precincts.

⌀ (0284) 4933.
Open: daily Jun-Jul-Aug 8-8 pm, Sep-May 8-5.30 (donation box)
⋇

Suffolk Regiment Museum
The Keep, Gibraltar Barracks, Out Risbygate
Exhibits include uniforms, weapons, medals, campaign souvenirs, documents and photographs.

⌀ (0284) 2394.
Open: all year (except PHs), Mon-Fri 10-12 & 2-4.
Shop ⋇

BUTE, ISLE OF

ROTHESAY
Isle of Bute, Strathclyde (Buteshire)
Map 10 NS06.
Ardencraig Gardens
Ardencraig Road, (1½m E off A844)

Overlooking the Firth of Clyde, fine floral displays can be seen in these gardens. Particular interest has been paid to improving layout and introducing rare plants into the garden. The greenhouse and walled garden produce plants for use in floral displays throughout the district. A variety of interesting fish are to be found in the ornamental ponds and the aviaries contain many foreign species of birds.

⌀ (0700) 4225
Open: May-Sep Mon-Fri 9-4.30, Sat & Sun 1-4.30.
⌑ 🚻

CADEBY
Leicestershire
Map 4 SK40.
Cadeby Light Railway
in grounds of Cadeby Rectory
Probably the smallest of Britain's narrow-gauge railways. Engine normally running is a 1919 steam saddle tank locomotive. Other exhibits include a 1927 Foster Traction Engine and two steam rollers from 1903 onwards. Exhibition model railway in 4mm scale representing the Great Western Railway in South Devon of about 1935. There is a Brass Rubbing Centre in Cadeby Church (50 facsimiles).

⌀ Market Bosworth (0455) 290462.
Open: all year on second Sat of each month 2-5.30.
🚻 🚻 (ground floor & gardens only) Shop

CAERNARFON
Gwynedd
Map 6 SH46.
Segontium Roman Fort and Museum
Branch archaeological gallery of the National Museum of Wales. Remains of Roman fort of 'Segontium' and museum of excavated relics.

⌀ (0286) 5625.
Open: Mar, Apr & Oct Mon-Sat 9.30-6, Sun 2-6, May-Sep Mon-Sat 9.30-6, Sun 2-6; Nov-Feb 9.30-4, Sun 2-4. (Closed: 24-26 Dec, 1 Jan, Good Fri & May Day.)
Shop ⋇ (AM CADW.)

CAERWENT
Gwent
Map 3 ST49.
Roman Town
(beside A48)
Complete circuit of town wall (in use from 1st to 4th centuries) together with excavated areas of houses, shops and temple.

Open: accessible at any time.
(AM)

CAISTER-ON-SEA
Norfolk
Map 9 TG51.
Roman Town
South gateway, town wall built of flint with brick bonding courses, part of what may have been a seaman's hostel.

Open: at all reasonable times.
(AM)

CALLANDER
Central (Perthshire)
Map 11 NN60.
Kilmahog Woollen Mill
A former woollen mill, famous for hand-woven blankets and tweed. An old water wheel has been preserved in working order. Showroom open for sale of woollens, tweeds and tartans.

⌀ (0877) 30268.
Open: summer months Mon 9-5.30, Sun 10-5.30. Winter months Mon-Sat 10-4, Sun 12-4.
⌑ ⋇ (ex guide dogs) Shop.

CALLANISH
Isle of Lewis, Western Isles
Ross & Cromarty
See **Lewis, Isle of**

Opening doors to the World of books

BOOK TOKEN

Book Tokens

Book Tokens can be bought and exchanged at most bookshops

CAMBRIDGE

Cambridgeshire   *Map 5 TL45.*
Ancient university city on the River Cam. Many of the colleges line the east bank overlooking the Backs; sweeping lawns set with willow trees, on the opposite side of the river transformed from rough marshland by Richard Bently (Master of Trinity College from 1669 to 1734). The colleges are open to the public on most days during daylight though there are some restrictions during term time.

(All free except Queens College, small admission charge.)

Clare College
These beautiful college gardens overlook the river and portray in their two acres many of English gardening's 20th-century ideas.

⌀ (0223) 358681.
Open: afternoons 2-4

Fitzwilliam Museum
Trumpington Street
Houses an extensive art and archaeological collection including Egyptian, Greek and Roman antiquities. European paintings, manuscripts and armour. European & Oriental decorative art. Special exhibitions throughout year.

⌀ (0223) 332900.
Open: Tue-Sat 10-5, Sun 2.15-5 plus Etr Mon, Spring & Summer BH (Closed Good Fri, May Day & 24 Dec-1 Jan). ⌑ (licensed) 🅰 Shop ✗ (ex guide dogs)

Kettles Yard
The house is converted from four 17th- and 18th-century cottages and has an extension with an adjoining exhibition gallery. A large collection of 20th-century paintings and sculptures are on display

and there is a continuous programme of modern art exhibitions, lectures, films and videos. A fascinating place to visit.

⌀ (0223) 352124.
Open: House, daily 2-4; Exhibition gallery Tue-Sat, 12.30-5.30 (7 on Thu evening); Sun 2-5.30 during exhibitions. Closed 24 Dec-4 Jan.

Kings College Chapel
One of the finest Gothic churches in England, the stained glass windows show the story of the New Testament beginning in the north-west corner and ending in the south-west corner. They are the most complete set of Renaissance windows to survive in this country. The intricately-carved screen and choir stalls are fine examples of Renaissance craftsmanship.

Open: weekdays 9-3.45; Sun 2-3 & 4.30-5.45. University holidays; weekdays 9-5; Sun 10.30-5.30. The chapel may be closed at certain times.

University Museum of Archaeology & Anthropology
Downing Street
New archaeology gallery covering man's development from the earliest times to civilisation throughout the world, and local archaeology up to the 19th century. New anthropology displays in preparation.

⌀ (0223) 337733.
Open: Mon-Fri 2-4, Sat 10-12.30. (Closed 24 Dec-2 Jan & 1 wk Etr.) 🅰 (ground floor only) Shop ✗

Scott Polar Research Institute
Lensfield Road

Contains relics and equipment relating to arctic and antarctic expeditions with special emphasis on those of Captain Scott. Includes Eskimo and general polar art collections and information on current scientific exploration.

⌀ (0223) 336540.
Open: Mon-Sat 2.30-4. (Closed: some public & university hols)
Shop ✗

University Botanic Garden
Cory Lodge, Bateman Street
Originally founded in 1762 and now covering 40 acres with fine botanical collections.

⌀ (0223) 336265.
Open: Mon-Sat 8-6 (dusk in winter). Sun, for non-ticket holders May-Sep 2.30-6.30. For ticket holders open all year 10-6.30. Glasshouses 11-12.30 & 2-4. (For ticket holders particulars from Director.)
🚻 🅰 Shop ✗ (ex guide dogs).

CANTERBURY

Kent   *Map 5 TR15.*

Canterbury Cathedral
Canterbury Cathedral has been regarded as the mother church of British Christianity since the 12th century. The famous and dramatic murder of Thomas Beckett took place here in 1170; from then on the Cathedral became the setting for the shrine of the martyr, attracting thousands of pilgrims. Dating from 1100, the crypt is the oldest part of the building, the nave is 15th century and Bell Harry tower, which dominates the exterior, dates from the 16th century.

⌀ (0227) 463135.
Open: daily, 8.45-6. Donations. 🅰

Canterbury Cathedral

Royal Museum, Art Gallery and Buffs Regimental Museum
High Street
The city's museum and art centre with a gallery for temporary exhibitions. Other galleries include local artist Thomas Sidney Cooper, RA; and the local regiment The Buffs. Also displays of fine porcelain, glass, clocks and watches, paintings; and east Kent archaeology with important Roman and Anglo-Saxon glass jewellery. Canterbury Festival exhibition Sep/Oct.

⌀ (0227) 452747.
Open Mon-Sat 10-5.
Shop ⌀

CAPEL DEWI
Dyfed　　　　*Map 2 SN44.*
Y Felin Wlan (Rock Mills)
This is one of the few remaining water-wheels in the country. Built in 1890 by the grandfather of the present owner, it has been in continuous operation since then. The water is supplied from the River Clettwr, a tributary of the Teifi.

⌀ Llandysul (055932) 2356.
Open: Mon-Fri 8.30-5,
Apr-Sep Sat 9-1pm.
Shop.

CARDIFF
South Glamorgan　　*Map 3 ST17.*
National Museum of Wales (Main Building)
Cathays Park
Collections and exhibitions in archaeology, geology, botany, zoology, industry and art.

⌀ (0222) 397951.
Open: Tue-Sat 10-5, Sun 2.30-5. (Closed: 24-26 Dec, New Year's Day, Good Fri & May Day.)
⌂ Ⓖ Shop ⌀

Welsh Industrial and Maritime Museum
Bute Street
A branch museum of the National Museum of Wales. Working exhibits tell the story of motive power and the roles played by a variety of machines over two centuries of intense industrial production and progress in Wales. Collection of boats, road and railway vehicles.

⌀ (0222) 481919.
Open: Tue-Sat 10-5, Sun 2.30-5. (Closed: Mon, Good Fri, May Day, 24-26 Dec & New Year's Day.)
Ⓖ Book shop ⌀

CARLISLE
Cumbria　　　*Map 12 NY45.*
Guildhall
Greenmarket
Renovated, half-timbered early 15th-century Guildhall with exposed timberwork and wattle and daub walls. Once the meeting place of Carlisle's eight trade guilds and retains much of the atmosphere of the period. Displays feature many items relating to these guilds, and other reminders of life in medieval Carlisle.

⌀ (0228) 34781.
Open: mid May-mid Sep,

afternoons only, telephone for details.
Shop ⌀

Museum and Art Gallery
Castle Street
At Tullie House – a fine Jacobean House (1689), with Victorian extensions – are comprehensive collections featuring the archaeology and natural history of Cumbria, English porcelain, costume, toys and musical instruments. Also temporary exhibitions in the Art Gallery.

⌀ (0228) 34781.
Open: Apr-Sep, Mon-Fri 9-6.45, Sat 9-5. Also Sun (Jun-Aug only) 2.30-5; Oct-Mar Mon-Sat 9-5.
Ⓖ (ground floor only) Shop ⌀

CARLOWAY
Isle of Lewis, Western Isles
Ross & Cromarty
See **Lewis, Isle of**

CARNASSERIE CASTLE
Strathclyde (Argyll)　*Map 10 NM80.*
(2m N of Kilmartin off A816)
Built in the 16th century by John Carswell, first Protestant Bishop of the Isles. It was taken and partly destroyed in Argyll's rebellion of 1685, and consists of a towerhouse with a courtyard built on to it.

Open: see page 4.
(AM)

CARRAWBROUGH
Northumberland　*Map 12 NY87.*
Roman Wall (Mithraic Temple)
(on B6318)
Remains of Mithraic temple measuring only 35 ft by 15 ft, dating from 3rd century but with later alterations. On line of Roman Wall near fort of 'Procolitia'. Excavations in 1960 revealed three dedica-

tory altars to Mithras and figure of the Mother Goddess.

Open: at all reasonable times.
(AM)

CASTLE TIORAM
Highland (Inverness-shire)   *Map 13 NM67.*
(3½m NW of Acharacle off A861)
A ruined but picturesque, 14th-century castle. It stands on a small grassy island connected to the mainland by a ribbon of sand which is covered in high spring tides. The Castle once belonged to the MacDonalds of Clanranald and was set alight in 1715 by the then chief, fearing it might be captured by his enemies, the Campbells.

Open: accessible at all reasonable times.

CAWTHORNE
South Yorkshire   *Map 8 SE20.*
Cannon Hall
(on A635)
Built circa 1765, mainly by John Carr of York, the museum set in 70 acres of parkland is owned by Barnsley Metropolitan Borough Council. Also Regimental Museum of the 13th/18th Royal Hussars (Queen Mary's Own).

⌾ Barnsley (0226) 790270.
Open: Mon-Sat 10.30-5 & Sun 2.30-5. (Closed: Good Fri & 25-27 Dec.)
⌕ (ground floor only) ⚹

CERNE ABBAS
Dorset   *Map 3 ST60.*
Cerne Giant
(on footpath ¼m NE of village)
The Cerne Giant can be seen clearly from the A352. It is an 18 ft high turf-cut figure on a chalk hillside of a naked man

bearing a club. It was associated with ancient fertility rites and is believed to date from Roman times.

Open: accessible at all reasonable times.
(NT)

CERRIGYDRUDION
Clwyd   *Map 6 SH94.*
Llyn Brenig Information Centre & Welsh Water Authority Estate
A 2,400 acre estate with a unique archaeological trail and 'round the lake' walk of 10 miles for which a completion certificate is available. Nature trail, and Nature Reserve includes a number of rare plants and birds. Access to bird hide, best viewing Nov-Mar. There are special fishing platforms, and an open day for disabled anglers. The Centre includes a bi-lingual exhibition on geology, archaeology, history and natural history.

⌾ (049082) 463.
Open: daily Apr-17 Oct 8-6; 18 Oct-Mar Mon-Fri 8-4.
(Access in the winter may be limited by snow; cross-country skiing is then available).
Charge for fishing, & watersports.
⌕ (wknds Apr-Jun & Sep, daily Jul-Aug ⌱ ⌕ Souvenir & fishing tackle shop (Apr-17 Oct)

Channel Islands
ST OUEN
Jersey   *Map 16*
Kempt Tower Interpretation Centre
Five Mile Road
This Martello tower has recently been converted into an interpretation centre displaying artifacts mostly relating to Les Mielles, Jersey's 'mini national park'. Ornithological walks are held on

most Sun afternoons around the adjacent Le Mielle de Morville area and nature walks on Thu pm (May-Sep); check local press for details.

⌾ Jersey (0534) 83651
Open: 31 Mar-28 Apr & 29 Sep-30 Oct, Thu & Sun only 2-5; May-25 Sep daily 2-5.
School parties by arrangement.

CHEDDLETON
Staffordshire   *Map 7 SJ95.*
Flint Mill
beside Caldon Canal, Leek Road
Two mills are preserved here with their low-breast wheels, one in working order. The original 17th-century south watermill ground corn but the 18th-century north mill was built to grind flint for the pottery industry. Museum collection includes examples of motive power (100hp Robey steam engine and model Newcomen engine) and transport (restored 70 ft horse-drawn narrow boat 'Vienna' moored on the Caldon Canal) and a haystack boiler of about 1770.

⌾ Barlaston (078139) 2561.
Open: Sat & Sun afternoons.
⌕ (ground floor only)

CHELMSFORD
Essex   *Map 5 TL70.*
Chelmsford and Essex Museum
Oaklands Park, Moulsham Street
Prehistoric and Roman Essex, coins, costumes, paintings, British birds and mammals, glass, ceramics, geology and local industries display. Also Victorian room, Tunstill collection of glass and temporary exhibition programme. Incorporates Essex Regiment Museum brought here from Warley.

∅ (0245) 353066, Essex Regiment Museum (0245) 260614.
Open: Mon-Sat 10-5, Sun 2-5. (Closed: Good Fri, 25-26 Dec plus other days as may be advertised.)
⬒ (ground floor only) Shop ⚹

CHELTENHAM
Gloucestershire   Map 3 SO92.
Art Gallery & Museum
Clarence Street
Contains nationally important Arts and Crafts Movement collection; notable 17th-century Dutch and 17th-20th century British paintings. Also a large collection of English and Oriental ceramics, pewter, social history and archaeological material relating to the area. Temporary exhibitions are held throughout the year.

∅ (0242) 239431.
Open: Mon-Sat 10-5.30. Exhibitions close 5.15. (Closed Sun & BH)
⬒ Shop ⚹

Gustav Holst Museum
4 Clarence Road, Pittville
The composer's birthplace containing rooms with period furnishings and working Victorian kitchen. Holst personalia and reference collection.

∅ (0242) 524846.
Open: Tue-Fri noon-5.30, Sat 11-5.30. (Closed Sun, Mon, BH)
Shop ⚹

CHEPSTOW
Gwent   Map 3 ST59.
Stuart Crystal
Bridge Street
Visitors can view craftsmen applying decoration to handmade crystal; included in the tour is a museum section dis-playing past and present Stuart crystal produced over 150 years. A video of the techniques used in present day manufacture can also be seen.

∅ (02912) 70135.
Open: factory tours Mon-Fri 10, 11, noon & 1.30, 2.30, 3.30, 4.30 (parties of 12 or more by appt.). Shop daily 9-8 May-Sep; 9-5 Oct-Apr
⬒ ⌂

CHERTSEY
Surrey   Map 4 TQ06.
Chertsey Museum
33 Windsor Street
A late Georgian house, The Cedars, containing Matthews collection of costumes and accessories, local history collection, including a 10th-century Viking sword, silver, glass, dolls and collection of Meissen porcelain figures. Also various exhibitions throughout the year and the 'Black Cherry Fair' 9 July.

∅ (09328) 65764.
Open: Tue & Thu 2-5, Wed, Fri & Sat 10-1 & 2-5. (Closed Xmas).
⬒ (ground floor & garden only) Sales point.

CHESTER
Cheshire   Map 7 SJ46.
Grosvenor Museum
27 Grosvenor Street
One of the finest collections of Roman remains in Britain, including special Roman Army gallery and many inscribed and sculptured stones excavated in Chester. Natural History gallery and art gallery. Period house with Victorian and Georgian rooms. Temporary exhibitions.

∅ (0244) 313858.
Open: Mon-Sat 10.30-5, Sun 2-5. (Closed: Good Fri & Xmas.)
⬒ (ground floor only) Shop ⚹

CHESTERFIELD
Derbyshire   Map 8 SK37.
Peacock Information and Heritage Centre
Low Pavement
A medieval timber framed building, thought to have been a guildhall. First floor is now used as an exhibition room. Audio visual on history of Chesterfield available for showing on request. Special medieval market in July.

∅ (0246) 207777.
Open: Mon-Sat. Information centre 9-5.30; Heritage centre noon-5.
⌂ ⬒ (ground floor only) Shop.

CHICHESTER
West Sussex   Map 4 SU80.
District Museum
29 Little London
Housed in a former 18th-century corn store with displays of local history, archaeology and geology. Temporary exhibitions programme.

∅ (0243) 784683.
Open: all year, Tue-Sat 10-5.30. (Closed BH & PH.)
⬒ (ground floor only) Shop ⚹ (ex guide dogs).

Guildhall Museum
Priory Park
Branch of District Museum in medieval Greyfriars church, later used as City Guildhall, containing archaeological finds from district. The small public park contains mound of Norman Castle.

∅ (0243) 784683.
Open: Jun-Sep, Tue-Sat 1-5; Other times by appointment; Park open daily.
⬒ Shop ⚹ (except guide dogs)

CHRISTCHURCH

Dorset   *Map 4 SZ19.*

Christchurch Castle and Norman House
Rare example of ruined Norman house c. 1160; stands in bailey of 11th-century house.

Open: at all reasonable times.
(AM)

CHURCH CROOKHAM

Hampshire   *Map 4 SU85.*

Gurkha Museum
Queen Elizabeth's Barracks
Contains a record of the Gurkha's service to the Crown from 1815.

℘ Fleet (0252) 613541 Ext 63.
Open: all year, Mon-Sat 9.45-4.30 & BH. Open Sun 10-12 by appointment only.
🛇 Shop ✗

CLAPHAM

North Yorkshire   *Map 7 SD76.*

Yorkshire Dales National Park Centre
Visitor Centre with interpretative display on 'The Limestone Dales'. Audiovisual theatre. Maps, walks, guides and local information available.

℘ (04685) 419.
Open: daily Apr-Oct mid morning-late afternoon.
🚻

CLAVA CAIRNS

Highland (Inverness-shire)
     Map 14 NH74.
(6m E of Inverness)
Situated on the south bank of the River Nairn, this group of burial cairns has three concentric rings of great stones.

Open: at all reasonable times.
(AM)

CLAWDD-NEWYDD

Clwyd   *Map 6 SJ05.*
Bod Petrual Visitor Centre
(on B5105 3m W)

On the southern edge of Clocaenog Forest, with waymarked walks. The centre is in a converted keepers cottage and has an exhibition on the history and ecology of the forest.

℘ (08245) 208.
Open: Visitor Centre, daily end Apr-Sep 9-6.
🚻

CLUN

Shropshire   *Map 7 SO28.*
Clun Town Trust Museum
Situated in the town hall, the original court house to Clun Castle; court was moved to market square in 1780. Flint tools, maps of earthworks etc, domestic and family relics. There are also exhibits of local geological and mineralogical interest.

℘ (05884) 247.
Open: Etr-Nov, Tue-Sat 2-5 and BH weekends Sat, Mon & Tue 11-1 & 2-5.
Other times by request, school parties welcome.
Enquiries *Mrs F Hudson, Florida Villa.*
(Donations)

COLCHESTER

Essex   *Map 5 TL92.*
Hollytrees Museum
High Street
Fine Georgian house, dating from 1718, with collection of costume, toys, etc.

℘ (0206) 712481/2.
Open: Mon-Sat 10-1, 2-5 (4pm Sat, Oct-Mar). (Closed Sun, Good Fri & 24-27 Dec.)
Shop ✗

Museum of Social History
Holy Trinity Church, Trinity Street
Historical displays of country life and crafts, with some industrial exhibits.

℘ (0206) 712481/2.
Open: Mon-Sat 10-1 & 2-5

On show at Colchester's Museum of Social History

4pm Sat, Oct-Mar). (Closed: Sun, Good Fri & 24-28 Dec.)
🛇 (ground floor only) Shop ✗

Natural History Museum
All Saints Church, High Street
Formerly 15th-century All Saints Church, with flint tower. Features the Natural History of Essex with special reference to the area.

℘ (0206) 712481/2.
Open: Mon-Sat 10-1 & 2-5 (4pm Sat, Oct-Mar). (Closed: Sun, Good Fri & 24-28 Dec.)
🛇 (ground floor only) Shop ✗

COLLIESTON

Grampian (Aberdeenshire)
     Map 15 NK03.
Slains Castle
(1m NE)
Spectacular but fragmentary Keep on a rocky headland, home of the Hays of Erroll for three centuries. Nearby are two cannons salvaged from the Spanish galleon *Santa*

Caterina, wrecked in 1594. A coastal path from Collieston leads to the castle.

**Open: accessible at all reasonable times.
(AM)**

COLONSAY
Strathclyde (Argyllshire)
                          Map 10 NR39.
Kiloran Gardens
(2m N of Scalasaig)
Set close to Colonsay House, these peaceful gardens and woodlands are a maze of colour during the Spring, and are noted for their fine display of rhododendrons and shrubs, including embothriums and magnolias. The Gulf Stream encourages plants not normally found at this latitude.

Open: daily, dawn to dusk.

COMPTON
Surrey   *Map 4 SU94.*
Watts Picture Gallery
Down Lane
Memorial gallery with a collection of about 150 paintings by G F Watts who is buried by the nearby Art Nouveau Watts Mortuary Chapel.

✆ **Guildford (0483) 810235.
Gallery Open: Fri-Wed 2-6 Apr-Sep & 2-4 Oct-Mar; also 11-1 Wed & Sat. Chapel open daily.**
⟐ (ground floor only) ✗

CORFE CASTLE
Dorset   *Map 3 SY98.*
Corfe Castle Museum
Tiny rectangular building, partly rebuilt in brick after fire in 1680. Small museum with old village relics and dinosaur footprints 130 million years old. Council chamber accessible by staircase at one end, the Ancient Order of Marblers meet here each Shrove Tuesday (open by appointment only).

✆ **(0929) 480346.
Open: daily, Etr-Sep 8-7, Oct-Etr 8-5 (times are approximate).**
⟐ (ground floor only)

CORRIESHALLOCH GORGE
Highlands (Ross and Cromarty)
                          Map 14 NH27.
(On A835 14m SE of Ullapool)
Spectacular canyon a mile long and 200 ft deep, varying in width from 50 ft to 150 ft. The Abhainn Droma plunges 150 ft over the Falls of Measach; a suspension bridge spans the gorge giving breathtaking views. The gorge is a special habitat for plant life, with high humidity and poor light.

**Open: accesible at all reasonable times.
(NTS)**

CORRIS
Gwynedd   *Map 6 SH70.*
Railway Museum
In village, 300 yds from A487
Museum in century-old railway building with photographs of operation of Corris narrow-gauge railway from 1890–1948. Items connected with railway are constantly added, and some old wagons are on show, half mile of track between museum and old engine shed at Maespoeth has now been reinstated. Passengers not carried. Children's playground nearby.

✆ **(05473) 343.
Open: BH periods & Mon-Fri 11 Jul-2 Sep 10.30-5, also 5-8 Apr; 31 May-1 Jul & 5-9 Sep 12-5, and as advertised locally during holiday season.**
⟐ (ground floor only) Shop

COVENTRY
West Midlands   *Map 4 SP37.*
Coventry Cathedral
7 Priory Row
Symbol of the rebirth of the city after the ravages of the Blitz, the splendid modern cathedral, designed by Sir Basil Spence, was consecrated in 1962.
Inside are many outstanding works of art, including the Sutherland altar tapestry and windows by John Piper. There is also a Visitors' Centre (admission charge).

✆ **(0203) 27597
Open: daily, summer 9.30-7.30; winter 9.30-5.30 (ex during services)**

Herbert Art Gallery and Museum
Jordan Well
Collections include social history, archaeology, folk life, industry, natural history, visual arts. Of special interest are the collection of Graham Sutherland's studies for the 'Christ in Glory' tapestry in Coventry Cathedral, and the Frederick Poke collection of fine 18th-century English furniture and silver. Also a permanent exhibition of Coventry's history, and the Natural History live animal display.

✆ **(0203) 833333 Ext 2315.
Open: Mon-Sat 10-6, Sun 2-5. (Closed: Good Fri & part Xmas.)**
⟐ Shop ✗

St Mary's Guildhall
Between Bayley Lane and Earl Street
Medieval guildhall, with minstrels' gallery, restored hall with portraits and Flemish tapestries and Caesar's watchtower.

✆ **(0203) 833333 Ext 2874.
Open: Etr, then May-Oct, Mon-Sat 10-5, Sun 12-5 (subject to civic requirements—enquiry advised before visiting.)**
⟐ (ground floor only) ✗

COWES
Isle of Wight
See **Wight, Isle of**

COXWELL, GREAT
Oxfordshire   Map 4 SU29.
Great Coxwell Barn
Stone-built   13th-century
barn. Possibly finest in Eng-
land, with fine roof timbers.

Open: at all reasonable
times.
(NT)

CRANBROOK
Kent   Map 5 TQ73.
Cranbrook Windmill
Seventy foot high smock mill
with sided three storey
brick base and a four-storey,
fixed wooden tower. The mill
was built in 1814 by the mill-
wright Humphrey for Henry
Dobell. Wind powered, and
now fully restored to working
use for milling, it is main-
tained by the Cranbrook
Windmill Association.

✆ (0580) 712256.
Open: Etr-Sep Sat & BH 2.30-5
(Donation box) Shop

CRASTER
Northumberland   Map 12 NU22.
Kipper Curing (L Robson &
Son Ltd.)
Haven Hill
Curing kippers has been carried out in this original
smokehouse building since
1856,   using   traditional
methods which visitors can
see.

✆ Embleton (066 576) 223.
Open: Jun-mid Sep (ex BH),
Mon-Fri 9.30-5, Sat 9.30-12
🖵 🅰 ⚒ Shop

CRATHIE
Grampian (Aberdeenshire)
              Map 15 NO29.
Crathie Church
Built in 1893 this small build-
ing is the parish church

where the Royal Family
worships when in residence
at Balmoral.

✆ (03384) 208.
Open: Apr-Oct, 9.30-5.30.
(Donations)
🅰

CRESWELL
Derbyshire   Map 8 SK57.
**Creswell Crags Visitor
Centre**
(off Crags Road 1m E off
B6042)
Limestone Gorge which was
once the home of early man.
Picnic site and a visitor centre,   which   explains   the
archaeological   significance
of the site with an exhibition
and audio-visual programme
which shows what life was
like for our ancestors.

✆ Worksop (0909) 720378.
Open: Feb-Oct, Tue-Sun &
BH Mons 10.30-5; Nov & Jan
Suns only 10.30-5.
🍴 🅰 Shop.

CRICKLEY HILL
COUNTRY PARK
Gloucestershire   Map 3 SO91.
(off A436)
On the extreme edge of the
Cotswold scarp, 62 acres of
countryside and scenery, the
steep grassy slopes rich in
flowers and butterflies. From
the edge of the hill there are
views to the Malverns, Forest
of Dean, mountains of South
Wales and the Severn Val-
ley.

✆ Gloucester (0452) 863170.
Open: daily.
🍴

CRIEFF
Tayside (Perthshire)   Map 11 NN82.
Stuart Strathearn Glass
Muthill Road
Handmade lead crystal in-
cludes vases, rose bowls,
honey pots, decanters and
whisky glasses. The range is
engraved with a wide variety
of flowers and Scottish game.
Self-conducted tours enable
the visitor to see at close
hand all stages of manufacture. Video on glassmaking
and   decoration.   Children's
playground.

✆ (0764) 4004.
Open: Factory daily 9-5;
Shop Mon-Sat 9-5, Sun 10-5
(extended hours Jun-Sep).
🍴 ⚒

*Glass from the Strathearn
Collection, at Stuart
Strathearn Glass, Crieff*

CROMER
Norfolk   *Map 9 TG24.*
Lifeboat Museum
Situated in No 2 boathouse at
the bottom of The Gangway.
Covers both local lifeboat
and general RNLI history.
Also **Lifeboat Station** on
pier.

✆ (0263) 512503.
Open: daily May-Sep 10-5.
Other times by arrangement.
Parties by arrangement.
🖫 Shop.

CULROSS
Fife (Fife)   *Map 11 NS98.*
Culross Abbey
Cistercian monastery, founded by Malcolm, Earl of Fife in
1217. The choir is still used as
the parish church and parts
of the nave remain. Fine central tower, still complete.

Open: See page 4.
(AM)

CUSWORTH
South Yorkshire   *Map 8 SE50.*
Cusworth Hall Museum
(2m NW Doncaster)
18th-century house with fine
chimney pieces and chapel
in south-west wing. Museum
of South Yorkshire life and
sections of interest to children. Temporary exhibitions
and many annual events.
Also extensive grounds
which are open all year, with
fishing in ponds, cricket and
football pitches. Children's
study base, and research
facilities.

✆ Doncaster (0302) 782342.
Open: Mar-Oct, Mon-Thu &
Sat 11-5, (4pm Nov-Feb), Sun
1-5 (4pm Nov-Feb). (Closed:
Xmas.)
🖫 (ground floor & gardens
only) Shop ⚫ (ex in park)

DANBY
North Yorkshire   *Map 8 NZ70.*
The Moors Centre
Lodge Lane
The former shooting lodge
offers full information and
countryside interpretation
service to visitors to the
North York Moors National
Park. The grounds include
riverside meadow, woodland
and terraced gardens, children's play area and brass
rubbing centre. Slides shown
daily, and also an exhibition
about the North York Moors.
Bookshop information desk.

✆ Castleton (0287) 60654.
Open: daily Apr-Oct 10-5;
Nov-Mar Sun 12-4. Guided
walks Jul-Aug (Sun only).
Parties by arrangement.
🖵 🍴 🖫 (ground floor) Shop
⚫

DANEBURY RING
Hampshire   *Map 4 SU33.*
(off unclass road 2½m NW of
Stockbridge)
A fine Iron Age fort rising to
469 ft, much of it thickly
wooded with beech trees.
Extensive excavations have
been carried out since 1969.
There is a nature trail and
leaflets are available at the
site.

Open: accessible at all
reasonable times.

DARLINGTON
Co Durham   *Map 8 NZ21.*
Art Gallery
Crown Street
Contains a permanent collec-
tion of pictures but also has
temporary loan exhibitions
throughout the year.

✆ (0325) 462034.
Open: Mon-Fri 10-8, Sat 10-
5.30. (Closed: Sun & all
weekends BH).
⚫

Darlington Museum
Tubwell Row
Local social and natural
history, archaeology and
bygones. Observation bee-
hive and beekeeping ex-
hibits, approx May-Sep, each
year.

✆ (0325) 463795.
Open: all year Mon-Wed &
Fri 10-1 & 2-6; Thu 10-1; Sat
10-1 & 2-5.30. (Closed: Good
Fri, May Day, Xmas & New
Year's Day).
🖫 (ground floor only) Shop
⚫ (ex guide dogs)

DARTMOUTH
Devon   *Map 3 SX85.*
Agincourt House
Lower Ferry
A wealthy medieval mer-
chants' house, built 1380 and
restored in 1968 by the present owner. Two of the four
storeys are open to the public and have an antique gallery, with notable boudoir
grand piano in working
order.

✆ (08043) 2472
Open: Mon-Fri 10-5.30, Sat
10-5, Sun 2.30-5. (Donations)
🖵 ⚫

Bayard's Cove Castle
Low, circular ruined stronghold, built by townspeople in
1537, with gunposts as at
Dartmouth Castle.

Open: accessible at all
reasonable times.
(AM)

DEDDINGTON
Oxfordshire   *Map 4 SP43.*
Deddington Castle
Mainly earthworks from
outer bailey and inner ward.
Excavations have revealed
portions of a 13th-century
chapel.

Open: at all reasonable
times.
(AM)

DEERHURST
Gloucestershire   *Map 3 SO82.*
Odda's Chapel
(off B4213 near River Severn)
Rare Saxon chapel, dating back to 1056 and erected originally by the Lord of the Manor. Attached to the old house.

Open: at all reasonable times.
(AM)

DENMEAD
Hampshire   *Map 4 SU61.*
Denmead Pottery & Woodland Park
In a woodland setting, a pottery manufacturers where the latest ceramic plant and technology processes are used. Visitors may walk around the production area. For children, the park has a lake, pets enclosure and adventure playground.

✆ Waterlooville (0705) 261942.
Open: Factory tours Mon-Fri 9-4; shop daily 9-5.30.
🛏

DERBY
Derbyshire   *Map 8 SK33.*
Derby Museum & Art Gallery
Antiquities, social and natural history, militaria. Bonnie Prince Charlie room (1745 rebellion), and also temporary exhibitions. There are paintings by Joseph Wright of Derby (1734-1797). Derby porcelain and costumes. Many temporary exhibitions are held.

✆ (0332) 29311 ext 782.
Open: Tue-Sat 10-5.
(Closed: Sun, Mon & BH.)
Shop ✗ (ex guide dogs)

Industrial Museum
Silk Mill, off Full St
Housed in an early 18th-century silk mill substantially rebuilt in 1910. The collection of Rolls-Royce aero-engines occupies the ground floor gallery, alongside the history of aviation from the Wright Brothers to the present day. 'An introduction to Derbyshire Industries' occupies the first floor gallery. Temporary exhibitions are held.

✆ (0332) 293111 ext 740.
Open: Tue-Fri 10-5, Sat 10-4.45. (Closed: BH.)
🛗 Shop ✗ (ex guide dogs)

DEVIZES
Wiltshire   *Map 4 SU06.*
Caen Hill Lock Flight
(½m W off A361)
An impressive flight of locks under restoration on the Kennet and Avon Canal, engineered by John Rennie and completed by 1810. In the space of only two miles there are 29 locks of which 17 are placed close together down Caen Hill. At the side of the locks large ponds were built to act as reservoirs. A good towpath runs along the southern bank of the canal; it is hoped to open the locks by 1990.

✆ (0380) 71279.
Open: accessible by foot at all reasonable times.

DINAS MAWDDWY
Gwynedd   *Map 6 SH81.*
Meirion Mill
In the Dyfi Valley, at the southern end of the Snowdonia National Park, is this working woollen weaving mill and retail shop in rural estate. Pack-horse bridge (AM). Field-walk on trackbed of Old Mawddwy Railway. Gardens and children's playground. Dog exercise area.

✆ (06504) 311.
Open: Apr-Oct daily including BH. Enquire for winter opening.
🍴 (licensed) 🛏 🛗 Shop.

DONCASTER
South Yorkshire   *Map 8 SE50.*
Museum & Art Gallery
Chequer Road
Prehistoric and Romano-British archaeology, British natural history, local history and costumes. British and European Art Collection, paintings, sculpture, ceramics, glass and silver. Historical collection of the Kings Own Yorkshire Light Infantry. Temporary exhibitions.

✆ (0302) 734287.
Open: all year, Mon-Thu & Sat 10-5, Sun 2-5. (Closed: Xmas Day New Years Day & Good Friday.)
🍴 (pre booked parties)
🛗 (ground floor only)
Shop ✗

DONINGTON-LE-HEATH
Leicestershire   *Map 8 SK41.*
Donington-le-Heath Manor House
(near Coalville)
Medieval manor house of c.1280 with very few alterations.

✆ Coalville (0530) 31259.
Open: 30 Mar-2 Oct, Wed-Sun, also BH Mon & Tue, 1-6.
🍴 🛗 (ground floor & gardens only) Shop ✗ (ex guide dogs).

DORCHESTER
Dorset   *Map 3 SY69.*
Maiden Castle
(1m SW)
Prehistoric earthworks, the name being derived from Celtic 'Mai-Jun' (the stronghold by the plain). Huge, oval, triple-ramparted camp, with extensive plateau on summit. Complicated defensive system of ditches and ramparts.

Open: at all reasonable times.
(AM)

Old Crown Court
The court is contained in the Old Shire Hall, dating from 1796-97, and was the scene of the trial of the six Tolpuddle Martyrs in 1834 who were sentenced to transportation to Botany Bay in Australia for demanding a wage increase. The building is now a Tolpuddle Memorial.

✆ (0305) 251010.
Open: all year Mon-Fri 9-1 & 2-4. Guided tour of cells 11am & 3pm. (Closed: PH & Tues following Spring & Aug BH.) Other times only by arrangement at adjacent West Dorset District Council.
🚫🐕

DORCHESTER-ON-THAMES

Oxfordshire *Map 4 SU59.*

Dorchester Abbey and Museum
Archaeological finds from the Bronze Age through to Anglo-Saxon times with maps showing layout of village during Roman times and later, and a display of Roman material from Roman town of 'Dorocina'. The Abbey Church of SS Peter and Paul is the only remaining part of the Augustinian Abbey founded in 1140, enlarged in 13th and 14th centuries and 200 ft long. Of note are the fine Norman lead font and the Jesse Window in the north aisle which represents the Tree of Jesse.

✆ Museum, Oxford (0865) 340056; Abbey, Oxford (0865) 340007.
Open: Museum Etr-Apr Sat, Sun; May-Sep Tue-Sat & BH, 10.30-12.30 & 2-6, Sun 2-6; Abbey daily 9-7 or sunset if earlier.
Museum shop (☕ Summer only Wed-Sun 3-5.30)
Abbey ⛩ 🚫🐕

DORNOCH

Highland (Sutherland) *Map 14 NH78.*

Dornoch Cathedral
Founded in the 13th century by Gilbert, Archdeacon of Moray and Bishop of Caithness and largely destroyed by fire in 1570 but restored between the 18th and 20th centuries. Burial place for 16 Earls of Sutherland with at the western end a fine statue by Chantey of the first Duke of Sutherland.

Open: daily dawn-dusk.
♿ 🚫🐕

Dornoch Craft Centre
Situated in the town jail, visitors can observe the weaving of tartans on Saurgr power looms. There is also kilt and soft toy making. The jail cells have a small exhibition.

✆ (0862) 810555.
Open: Mon-Fri (Nov-Mar) Apr-Oct Mon-Sat 9-5; Sun Jul & Aug 12-5.
☕ ♿ (ground floor only) Shop

DOUGLAS

Isle of Man
See **Man, Isle of**

DOUNBY

See **Orkney**

DOVER

Kent *Map 5 TR34.*

Dover Museum
Ladywell
The museum, founded in 1836, contains exhibits of local history, archaeology, ceramics, coins, natural history and geology. Monthly programme of temporary exhibitions.

✆ (0304) 201066.
Open: Mon, Tue & Thu-Sat 10-4.45
♿ Shop. 🚫🐕

DOWLISH WAKE

Somerset *Map 3 ST31.*

Perry's Cider Mills
A long established family-run firm using traditional methods of cidermaking. The museum, which is housed in a modern thatched barn, includes wagons and carts and a fine collection of small farm tools. Also on display are photographs of cidermaking and nostalgic pictures of village life around 1900.

✆ Ilminster (04605) 2681.
Open: Mon-Fri 9-1, 2-5.30; Sat & Spring & Summer BH 9.30-1, 2-4.30 & Sun 9.30-1.
Shop.

DRUMCOLTRAN TOWER

Dumfries and Galloway (Kirkcudbrightshire) *Map 11 NX86.*

(7m NE of Dalbeattie)
A 16th-century tower house, three-storeys in height and built to an oblong plan, with a projecting tower or wing.

Open: standard times, see page 4. (AM)

DRYSLWYN

Dyfed *Map 2 SN52.*

Dryslwyn Castle
Ruined, 13th-century, native Welsh stronghold on a lofty mound, important for its part in the struggles between the Welsh and English in the 13th century.

Open: accessible at any time. (AM)

DUDLEY

West Midlands *Map 7 SO99.*

Museum & Art Gallery
St James's Road
Includes the Brooke Robinson collection of fine and decorative art. Geological Gallery and a wide variety of temporary exhibitions throughout the year.

Perry's Cider Mills at Dowlish Wake

✆ (0384) 55433 Ext 5530.
Open: Mon-Sat 10-5.
(Closed: BHs).
🛇 (ground floor only) ⚥

DUFFTOWN
Grampian (Banffshire)   Map 15 NJ33.
Dufftown Museum
The Tower, The Square
Small local history museum
featuring Mortlach Kirk
material. Temporary dis-
plays.

✆ Forres (0309) 73701.
Open: 13-25 Apr, 11-31 May,
1-17 Oct, Mon-Sat 10-5.30; Jun
& Sep Mon-Sat 10-6, Sun 2-6;
Jul & Aug Mon-Sat 9.30-6.30,
Sun 2-6.30. Details not
confirmed for 1988.
🛇 Shop ⚥

Glenfiddich Distillery
(N of town, off A941)
Situated by Balvenie Castle
in the heart of Speyside
country, the distillery was
founded in 1887 by Major
William Grant. A visitor's reception centre houses a bar
and a Scotch whisky
museum. The theatre offers a
programme in six languages
covering the history of Scotland and Scotch whisky.

✆ (0340) 20373.
Open: all year Mon-Fri 9.30-
4.30, also 14 May-16 Oct Sat
9.30-4.30, Sun 12-4.30.
(Closed: Xmas & New Year).
🎨 🛇 (ground floor & gardens
only) Shop. ⚥

DUFFUS
Grampian (Moray)   Map 15 NJ16.
Duffus Castle
(off B9012)
Motte and bailey castle, with
8-acre bailey surrounding rebuilt 15th-century hall and
14th-century tower, now
broken into two halves.

Open: at all reasonable
times.
(AM)

DUMFRIES
*Dumfries & Galloway
(Dumfriesshire)   Map 11 NX97.*
Robert Burns Centre
Old Town Mill, Mill Road
Interpretation Centre and ex-
hibition on the life of the poet,
Robert Burns. Also audio-
visual (admission charged).

✆ (0387) 64808.
Open: Apr-Sep Mon-Sat 10-8,
Sun 2-5; Oct-Mar Tue-Sat
10-1, 2-5.
🛇 ⌨ Shop.

Dumfries Museum
The Observatory, Church St
Large collection of local history, archaeology, geology,
local birds and animals. The
Old Bridge House (on the
Old Bridge) contains period
rooms portraying the local
way of life in former times.
Nearby is the 13th-century
bridge built by Devorgilla,
wife of Robert Balliol.

Open: Museum all year, Mon-
Sat 10-1 & 2-5. Closed Sun &
Mon Oct-Mar. Old Bridge
House, Apr-Sep.
🛇 Shop.

Old Town Mill
Mill Road
Burns interpretation centre
with exhibition of 'Robert
Burns and Dumfries'.

✆ (0387) 64808.
Open: all year Tue-Sat 10-8,
also Apr-Sep Mon 10-8, Sun
2-5.
Shop.

DUNBAR
Lothian (East Lothian)   Map 12 NT67.
John Muir Country Park
(W off A1087 & A198)
An attractive stretch of coastline forms this country park
named after John Muir, a
pioneer of conservation. The
park, includes Belhaven Bay
and Ravensheugh Sands,
with waymarked paths and a
clifftop nature trail giving
good views to the Bass Rock
and the Isle of May. A wide
variety of wildlife reflects the
diversity of habitats, which
include cliff, dunes, salt-
marsh, woodlands, scrub and
grassland.

Open: accessible at all
reasonable times.

DUNBLANE
Central (Stirlingshire)   Map 11 NN70.
Dunblane Cathedral
The Cathedral mostly dates from the 13th century but incorporates a 12th century tower. After the Reformation it became a ruin but was restored 1892-95.

 (0786) 823388.
Open: daily Apr-Sep, 9.30-12.30, 1.30-7; Oct-Mar, 9.30-12.30, 1.30-4.

DUNDEE
Tayside (Angus)   Map 11 NO43.
Barrack Street Museum
Barrack Street
Museum of Natural History; Scottish Wildlife of Lowlands and Highlands. Skeleton of Great Tay Whale. Some changes in displays may be caused by redevelopment.

 (0382) 23141.
Open: Mon-Sat 10-5.
Shop

Broughty Castle Museum
Broughty Ferry (4m E)
15th-century castle rebuilt as estuary fort in 19th century. Displays of arms and armour, seashore wildlife, Dundee's former whaling industry and history of former Burgh of Broughty Ferry.

 (0382) 76121 or 23141.
Open: Mon-Thu & Sat 10-1 & 2-5. Sun 2-5 (Jul-Sep only).
 Shop

McManus Galleries (Dundee Art Galleries & Museums)
Albert Square
Major Art Gallery with changing exhibitions of local and national interest. Important Scottish and Victorian collections. Local history displays cover Archaeology, Trade and Industry, Social and Civil History. McManus Galleries is one of Dundee's finest Victorian buildings by Sir Gilbert Scott. Lectures and guided walks.

 (0382) 23141.
Open: Mon-Sat 10-5.
 Shop

Mills Observatory
Balgay Park, Glamis Road
Observatory, built in 1935, with fine Victorian 10-inch Cooke refracting telescope and other instruments. Gallery displays on astronomy and space exploration, and small planetarium. Regular side shows.

 (0382) 67138 or 23141.
Open: Apr-Sep Mon-Fri 10-5, Sat 2-5; Oct-Mar, Mon-Fri 3-10, Sat 2-5.
Parties booked in advance.
 Shop

DUNFERMLINE
Fife (Fife)   Map 11 NT08.
Andrew Carnegie Birthplace Museum
Junction of Moodie Street and Priory Lane.
The cottage in which the great philanthropist was born in 1835. New displays tell the exciting story of the weaver's son who gave away 350 million dollars and how the Carnegie Trust still spend his money for the good of mankind.

 (0383) 724302.
Open: all year daily. Apr-Oct Mon-Sat 11-5, Sun 2-5; Nov-Mar 2-4. Other times by arrangement.
 (ground floor only) Shop (ex guide dogs)

Dunfermline Abbey
Pittencrieff Park
Benedictine house founded by Queen Margaret. The foundations of her church remain beneath the present Norman nave. The site of the choir is now occupied by a modern parish church, at the east end of which are remains of St Margaret's shrine dating from the 13th century. King Robert the Bruce is buried in the choir and his grave is marked by a modern brass. Guest house was a royal palace where Charles I was born.

Open: standard times, see page 4.

Dunfermline District Museum
Viewfield Terrace
Interesting and varied displays of local history, domestic bygones and damask linen. The Small Gallery has monthly changing art and craft exhibitions. Periodic special exhibitions.

 (0383) 721814.
Open: all year, Mon-Sat 11-5. (Closed: Sun & PH).
Shop

Pittencrief House Museum
Pittencrief Park
Situated in a rugged glen, with lawns, hothouses and gardens, overlooked by the ruined 11th-century Malcolm Canmore's Tower. Fine 17th-century mansion house, with galleries displaying local history, costumes and temporary exhibitions.

 (0383) 722935 or 721814.
Open: 1 May-3 Sep & Mon, Wed-Sun 11-5
 (ground floor & gardens only). Shop

DUNGENESS
Kent   Map 5 TR01.
'A' Nuclear Power Station
Building open throughout the year for organised group tours by pre-arrangement any weekday and to the general public on Wed, 10-4.

Children must be accompanied by an adult.

⌀ Lydd (0679) 20461 Ext 238.
⌷ (by arrangement) ⋇

DUNKELD
Tayside (Perthshire)   Map 11 NO04.
Dunkeld Cathedral
High Street
The present building dates from the 13th century. The nave is now a roofless ruin but the choir has been restored and is used as the parish church. The nave arcade is supported on heavy drum columns reminiscent of an earlier period.

⌀ (03502) 601.
Open: Apr-Sep, Mon-Sat 9.30-7, Sun 2-7; Oct-Mar, Mon-Sat 9.30-4. Sun 2-4. (Donations)
⌷ ⋇

Hermitage
(2m W, off A9)
A tree garden was created here by the Second Duke of Atholl in the 18th century. Today, there is a wide variety of trees including a Douglas Fir over 180 ft tall. Among the wildlife is the red squirrel. Two follies, Ossian's Hall and Ossian's Cave, can be visited on the nature trail.

⌀ Pitlochry (0796) 3233.
Open: accessible at all reasonable times.
⌷ (NTS)

Little Houses
Dating from after the Battle of Dunkeld in 1689. Trust display of photographs of the restoration scheme and an audio-visual show are in the Tourist Information Centre.

⌀ (03502) 460.
Open: Apr-May & Sep-23rd Dec, Mon-Sat 10-1, 2-4.30, Jun-Aug, Mon-Sat 10-6, Sun 2-5.
Shop (NTS)

Loch of The Lowes Wildlife Reserve
Variety of wildlife. Great crested grebes and other waterfowl in natural surroundings can be watched through high-powered binoculars from observation hide. There is an exhibition and slide programme in the visitor centre.

⌀ (03502) 337.
Open: daily Apr-Sep 10-7 (Jun-Aug open until 8.30pm). (Times subject to change.) Hide open at all times. Special arrangements for parties booked in advance.
⌷ (ground floor only) Shop ⋇

DUNOON
Strathclyde (Argyllshire)   Map 10 NS17.
Scottish White Heather Farm
(5m SW of Dunoon)
Extensive gardens, including azaleas, white heathers, sprays, coloured heather and conifers for sale.

⌀ Toward (036987) 237.
Open: all year 9-6. Visitors advised to phone in advance during winter months.
⌷

DUNWICH
Suffolk   Map 5 TM47.
Dunwich Museum
St James Street
Contains the history and relics of the ancient city of Dunwich. Also flora and fauna of the area.

⌀ Westleton (072873) 358.
Open: Apr-Oct, Sat & Sun 2-4.30. Also Tue & Thu, May-Sep & daily in Aug. (Subject to availability of volunteers.)
Shop ⋇

DURHAM
Co. Durham   Map 12 NZ24.
Durham Cathedral

One of the most outstanding examples of Romanesque architecture in Europe, begun in 1093 by Bishop William of St Calais. Much of the original building remains. The nave shows the first use of ribbed vaulting on an extensive scale in a church. Also of note are the Chapel of Nine Altars, the Lady Chapel, the tomb of Venerable Bede, 8th-century illuminated manuscripts and the Sanctuary Door Knocker.

⌀ 091-3862367.
Open: daily, May-Sep 7.15-8; Oct-Apr, Mon-Sat 7.15-6.15, Sun 7.15-5 (Donations). (Treasury: Admission charge, Mon-Sat 10-4, Sun 2.30-4.) (Tower: Admission charge, Mon-Sat 10-3.30.)
⌷ (⌗ Mon-Sat 9.30-5 Sun 1-5)
Shop Museum

St Aidan's College Grounds
Windmill Hill
The College was designed by Sir Basil Spence, and built in the early sixties. The spacious and well-stocked grounds, landscaped by Professor Brian Hackett, are at their best during July, when the shrub beds are in flower. Features include a laburnum walk and a reflecting pool, well stocked with aquatic plants and fish. From the garden there are fine views of Durham Cathedral.

⌀ 091-3865011.
Open: all year, daily from 9-dusk.
Donations to NGS.
⌗ (by prior arrangement)
⌷ (ground floor only) ⋇ (garden only)

University Botanic Garden
A teaching and research garden with specific collections of tropical and arid zone plants, as well as specimens

from Scandinavia and the Himalayas.

✆ 091-3864971 Ext 657.
Open: daily. ✗

EASTBOURNE
East Sussex   Map 5 TV69.
Lifeboat Museum
Grand Parade
The museum displays details of the work carried out by the various lifeboats which have been on station at Eastbourne. There are also displays illustrating the work of the RNLI, a selection of lifeboat models, the original sails and oars from the last sailing lifeboat at the station, various types of gear worn by lifeboat men, together with descriptions and accompanying photographs of notable rescues.

✆ (0323) 30717.
Open: Jan-Mar weekends only, Apr-Dec daily 9.30-6. ⌂ ⅏ ✗ Shop.

Towner Art Gallery & Local History Museum
Manor Gardens, High Street, Old Town
Georgian manor house (1776) with later alterations set in pleasant gardens. Large collection of 19th- and 20th-century British art. Frequent temporary exhibitions. Museum traces the history of Eastbourne.

✆ (0323) 21635 or 25112.
Open: all year Mon-Fri 10-5 & Sun 2-5. (Closed: Mons in winter, Good Fri, Xmas Day and New Years Day).
⅏ (ground floor & gardens only) Shop ✗

EAST FORTUNE
Lothian (East Lothian)   Map 12 NT57.
Museum of Flight
East Fortune Airfield
The National Museums of Scotland. The former airship base now displays the history of aircraft and rockets and has working exhibits which visitors may operate. Exhibits include a Supermarine Spitfire Mk 16. De Havilland Sea Venom, Hawker Sea Hawk and Comet (4c).

✆ 031-225 7534.
Open: July & Aug Mon-Sat 10-5, Sun 11-5, plus open days.
⅏ Shop ✗

EASTHAM
Merseyside   Map 7 SJ38.
Eastham Country Park
Ferry Road
Seventy-six-acre country park with a fine nature trail, unique views across the Mersey estuary and historical features that include a bear pit and the site of an ancient river crossing, "Job's Ferry", originally operated by a brotherhood of monks.

✆ 051-327 1007.
Open: Park, at all reasonable times; Visitor Centre, Apr-Sep Sat, Sun & BH 11-6; Oct-Mar, Sat, Sun & BH (ex Xmas Day) 12-4.
⅏ ⊡ ⌂

ECCLES
Gt Manchester   Map 7 SJ79.
Monks Hall Museum
Wellington Road
16th-century building with later additions, housing a small toy museum and material of local interest including a Nasmyth steam hammer. There are frequent temporary exhibitions.

✆ 061-789 4372.
Open: Mon-Fri 10-12.30, 1-5, Sun 2-5, (Closed: Good Fri, Xmas & New Year's Day.) ⅏ (most parts) Shop ✗

Edinburgh: an Acheson House craft design

EDINBURGH
Lothian (Midlothian)   Map 11 NT27.
Acheson House (Scottish Craft Centre).
140 Canongate.   Plan : F4.
This beautiful mansion, built 1633 and restored in 1937 by R Hurd is now the headquarters of the Scottish Craft Centre. There is a changing display of crafts from ceramics to silverware.

✆ 031-556 8136/7370.
Open: Mon-Sat 10-5.30.
⅏ (ground floor only) ✗

Calton Hill and Parthenon
Regent Road.   Plan : F6.
Rising to 335 ft it offers an impressive view of the city centre and Firth of Forth. On the top is a collection of monuments, including the National monument (1882), a partly completed copy of the Greek Parthenon, dedicated to the Scottish dead in the Napoleonic wars. Also the Nelson monument (1807), the Playfair (1826) and Dugald Stewart (1832) monuments.

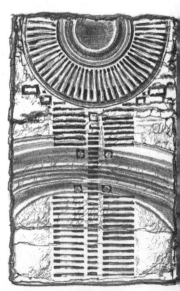

Open: at all reasonable times.
(Nelson monument: Admission charge.)

City Art Centre
2 Market Street   Plan : **F4**
The Art Centre houses the City's permanent fine art collection comprising 3,000 paintings, drawings, prints and sculptures mostly by Scottish artists, dating from 17th century to the present. There is also a diverse programme of temporary exhibitions drawn from the UK and abroad.

✆ 031-225 2424 Ext 6650.
After 5pm & weekends 031-225 1131.
Open: Mon-Sat 10-5 (10-6 Jun-Sep) & Sun 2-5 during Edinburgh Festival.
⌂ (licensed) 🅰 Shop ✗

Clan Tartan Centre
James Pringle Woollen Mill, 70-74 Bangor Road, Leith (1m N), Not on plan
The Clan Tartan Centre offers the opportunity to find out (on the Pringle Archive Computer) if your name is linked to any of the Clans. A 15-minute film tells the history and development of the tartan. The shop sells a range of Pringle knitwear.

✆ 031-553 5161.
Open: daily Apr-Dec, 9-6; Jan-Mar, Mon-Sat 9-5.30.
🅰 ⌂ ✗ Shop.

Fruit Market Gallery
29 Market Street.   Plan : **E4**
A fine arts gallery with changing programme of exhibitions including contemporary art, paintings, sculpture, photographs and architecture.

✆ 031-225 2383.
Open: Tue-Sat, 10-5.30.
✗ ⌂ Shop.

General Register House
(East end of Princes Street).
    Plan : **E5**.
Designed by Robert Adam, it was founded in 1774. Headquarters of the Scottish Record Office and the repository for National Archives of Scotland. Changing historical exhibitions. Historical and Legal Search Rooms available to visitors engaged in research.

✆ 031-556 6585.
Open: all year Mon-Fri 9-4.30.
Exhibitions Mon-Fri 10-4.
(Closed: Certain PH.)
🅰 (ground floor only) ✗

George Heriot's School
Lauriston Place.   Plan : **D3**.
Dates from 1628 and was founded by George Heriot, the 'Jingling Geordie' of Scott's 'Fortunes of Nigel'.

✆ 031-229 7263.
Open: Jul-Aug Mon-Fri 9.30-4.30.
🅰 (ground floor only) ✗

Huntly House
142 Canongate.   Plan : **F4**.
Dating from 1570 and housing the City Museum of local history. Includes collections of silver, glass, and pottery.

✆ 031-225 2424 Ext 6689 (031-225 1131 after 5pm & weekends).
Open: Mon-Sat, Jun-Sep 10-6; Oct-May 10-5. (During Festival period only Sun 2-5).
🅰 (ground floor only) Shop ✗

Lady Stair's House
Off Lawnmarket.   Plan : **D4**.
A restored town house dating from 1622, containing a museum of literary relics of Robert Burns, Sir Walter Scott and Robert Louis Stevenson.

✆ 031-225 2424 Ext 6593 (031-225 1131 after 5pm & weekends)
Open: Mon-Sat, Jun-Sep 10-6; Oct-May 10-5. (During Festival period only Sun 2-5).
Shop ✗

Museum of Childhood
42 High St (Royal Mile).
    Plan : **E4**.
A wonderful collection of childhood memories for all ages.

✆ 031-225 2424 Ext 6645.
Open: Mon-Sat 10-6 & Sun 2-5 during Festival; Oct-May 10-5. (Closed: Xmas).
🅰 (3 floors) Shop ✗

National Gallery of Scotland
The Mound.   Plan : **D4**.
One of the most distinguished of the smaller galleries in Europe, containing collections of Old Masters, Impressionists and Scottish paintings including: Raphael's Bridgewater Madonna, Constable's Dedham Vale, and masterpieces by Titian, Velasquez, Raeburn, Van Gogh and Gauguin. Drawings, water-colours and original prints by Turner, Goya, Blake etc (these items are shown on request Mon-Fri 10-12 & 2-4.30).

✆ 031-556 8921.
Open: Mon-Sat 10-5, Sun 2-5; winter lunchtime closure (Oct-Mar) 12-1 West Gallery, 1-2 East Gallery and New Wing. (Mon-Sat 10-6, Sun 11-6 during Festival).
🅰 Shop ✗

National Library of Scotland
George IV Bridge.   Plan : **D4**.
Founded in 1682, this is one of the four largest libraries in Great Britain with nearly four and a half million books. There is an extensive collection of manuscripts, together

with 19th-century music, Caxton bible and a map collection.

✆ 031-226 4531.
Open: Reading room Mon-Fri 9.30-8.30, Sat 9.30-1;

Exhibition room Mon-Fri 9.30-5, Sat 9.30-1, Apr-Sep Sun 2-5. ⅃ ✗

Parliament House
East of George IV Bridge.

Plan : **D4.**

Dates from 1639, but façade was replaced in 1829. The Hall has a fine hammer-beam roof. The Scottish Parliament met here before the Union of 1707. Now the seat of Supreme Law Courts of Scotland.

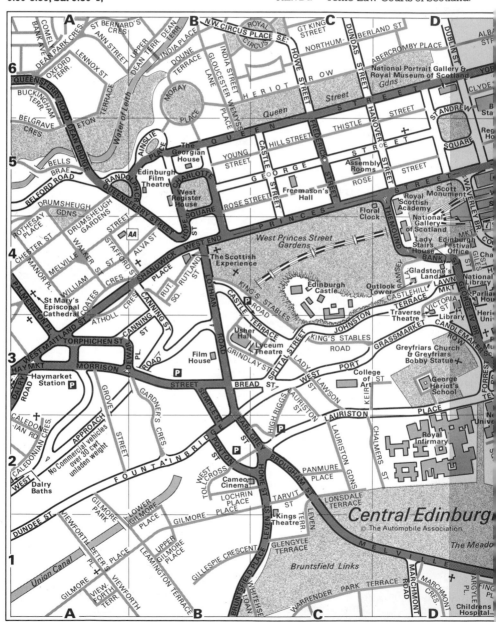

✆ 031-225 2595.
Open: Mon-Fri 10-4.
🚻 ♿ (ground floor only)
🐕 (ex guide dogs)

Royal Botanic Garden
Inverleith Row. Not on plan

Famous garden, noted especially for the rhododendron collection, rock garden, plant houses and exhibition hall.

✆ 031-552 7171 Ext 260.
Garden open all year (ex Xmas Day and New Year's Day). Mar-Oct Mon-Sat 9-1 hr before sunset, Sun 11-1 hr before sunset; Oct-Mar Mon-Sat 9-sunset, Sun 11-sunset. Plant houses, exhibition hall & Inverleith House Visitor Centre open Mon-Sat 10-5, Sun 11-5 (from 10am during festival period).
🚻 Apr-Sep ♿ Shop 🐕 (ex guide dogs)

Royal Museum of Scotland
1 Queen Street
Extensive collections and national treasures from earliest times to the present day, illustrating everyday life and history.

✆ 031-225 7534 Ext 279.
Open: Mon-Sat 10-5, Sun 2-5.
♿ Shop 🐕

Royal Museum of Scotland
(formerly Royal Scottish Museum)
Chambers Street.   Plan : E3.
The most comprehensive display in Britain under one roof comprising the decorative arts of the world and ethnography, natural history, geology, technology and science. Lectures, gallery talks and films at advertised times.

✆ 031-225 7534.
Open: Mon-Sat 10-5, Sun 2-5.
🚻 ♿ Shop 🐕

Scottish National Gallery of Modern Art
Belford Road. Not on plan
New home of the national collection of 20th-century painting, sculpture and graphic art. Among many modern masters represented are Derain, Picasso, Giacometti, Magritte, Henry Moore, Barbara Hepworth, Lichtenstein and Scottish painting. Some sculpture is displayed. The gallery print room and library are also open to the public by appointment.

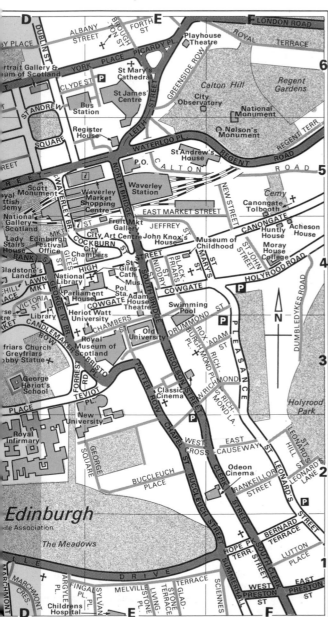

⏍ 031-556 8921.
Open: all year. Mon-Sat 10-5
& Sun 2-5 (During Festival
Mon-Sat 10-6, Sun 11-6).
⏏ (licensed) ⬓ Shop ⚹

Scottish National Portrait Gallery

Queen Street.   **Plan : D6.**
Striking red Victorian building containing portraits of
men and women who have
contributed to Scottish history. The collection includes
such popular figures as Mary
Queen of Scots, James VI and
I, Burns, Sir Walter Scott and
Ramsay MacDonald. Many
other artists, statesmen, soldiers and scientists are por-
trayed in all media, including
sculpture. Collections also
illustrate the development of
Highland dress. There is an
extensive reference section
of engravings, and photo-
graphs.

⏍ 031-556 8921.
Open: all year daily, Mon-Sat
10-5 & Sun 2-5 (Closed:
lunchtime 12-30-1.30 in
winter). (During Festival
Mon-Sat 10-6, Sun 11-6).
⬓ Shop ⚹

Talbot Rice Art Centre

*(Old University), South
Bridge.*   **Plan : E3.**
Two main exhibition areas,
one housing the university's
permanently displayed Tor-
rie Collection of 16th- and
17th-century European paintings and bronzes. The centre
also promotes Scottish artists
and has touring exhibitions.

⏍ 031-667 1011 Ext 4308.
Open: Mon-Sat 10-5.
⬓ ⚹

West Register House

Charlotte Square.   **Plan : B5.**
The former St George's
Church, designed by Robert
Reid in the Greco-Roman
style in 1811. Now an auxili-

ary repository for the Scottish
Record Office and housing
an exhibition '800 years of
Scottish History'. Search
Room available to resear-
chers.

⏍ 031-556 6585.
Open: Mon-Fri 9-4.45.
Exhibitions 10-4 (Closed:
some PHs).
⬓ ⚹

EDNASTON

Derbyshire   **Map 8 SK24.**
Ednaston Manor
A Lutyens house with garden
of botanical interest. Large
collection of shrubs, shrub
roses, clematis and unusual
plants.

⏍ Ashbourne (0335) 60325.
Open: Etr-Sep, Mon-Fri
1-4.30 & Sun 2-5.30. House not
open.
⬓ ⏏ garden centre ⚹

EDWINSTOWE

Nottinghamshire   **Map 8 SK66.**
**Sherwood Forest & Visitor
Centre**
(½m N on B6034)
Probably the most famous
forest in Britain but now consisting of scattered areas of
woodland. The Visitor Centre has an exhibition on
Robin Hood with information
on forest wildlife found in the
forest and walks, including
one to the Major Oak, which
lies about half a mile west.

⏍ Nottingham (0602) 824215
Ext 2.
Open: Forest accessible at all
reasonable times; Visitor
Centre permanent exhibition
open all year. Mar-Sep 10.30-
5; Oct-Feb 10.30-4.30. Tourist
Information office, cafe and
shop open Apr-Sep 11-5; Oct,
Tue-Sun 11.30-4; Nov & Dec,
Tue, Wed, Thu, Sat & Sun
11.30-4. Shop open wknds
Jan & Feb.
⬓ ⏏ ⎓

ELCOT

Berkshire   **Map 4 SU36.**
Elcot Park Hotel
(5½m W of Newbury off A4)
16-acre garden overlooking
the Kennet Valley with extensive views. Mainly lawns
and woodland laid out by Sir
William Paxton in 1848.
Magnificent display of daffodils, rhododendrons and
other shrubs in Spring.

⏍ Kintbury (0488) 58100.
Open: all year, daily 10-6.
(Charged on NGS Sun.)
⏏ (Licensed Restaurant)
⬓ (NGS)

ELGIN

Grampian (Moray)   **Map 15 NJ26.**
Pluscarden Abbey
(6m SW on unclass road)
The original monastery was
founded by Alexander II in
1230. Restoration took place
in the 14th and 19th centuries, and the Abbey has been
re-occupied by the Benedic-
tines since 1948.

⏍ Dallas (034389) 257.
Open: daily, 5am-8.30pm.
⬓ (ground floor & gardens
only) Shop

ELLISLAND FARM

*Dumfries and Galloway
(Dumfriesshire)*   **Map 11 NX98.**
(6m NW of Dumfries off A76)
In this farm on the west bank
of the Nith, Robert Burns
lived from 1788 to 1791 and
composed Tam O'Shanter
and other poems and songs.
Material associated with the
poet is on display.

⏍ Dumfries (0387) 74426.
No restriction on times of
visiting, but visitors are
advised to telephone in
advance.
⬓ (ground floor & gardens
only) ⚹

ENFIELD

Gt London   *see page 77.*
Forty Hall
Forty Hill.   *London plan 2 : 39 E5.*
Built in 1629 for Sir Nicholas Raynton, Lord Mayor of London, the Mansion was modified in the early 18th century. Contemporary plaster ceilings and screen, 17th- and 18th-century furnishings and paintings, ceramics and glass. Also temporary exhibitions.

✆ 01-363 8196.
Open: all year Tue-Fri 10-6 (5pm Oct-Etr). Sat & Sun 10-6 (5pm Oct-Etr).
🚗 ⛱ 🚻 (ground floor only) Shop ⚋

EPPING FOREST AND CONSERVATION CENTRE

Essex   *Map 5 TL40.*
Over six thousand acres of ancient woodland, grassland, heath, open water and marsh where the nightingale still sings in spring and early summer, given special protection by the 1878 Epping Forest Act for recreational and wildlife value. The Conservation Centre provides an interpretative and information service for the public and a base for ecological research.

✆ 01-508 7714. (Conservation Centre).
Open: Forest, at all times.
Conservation Centre, Etr-Oct Wed-Sat 10-12.30 & 2-5, Sun & BH 11-12.30 & 2-5; Nov-Etr weekends only, Sat 10-12.30 & 2-5 (dusk if earlier), Sun 11-12.30 & 2-5 (dusk if earlier).
Location between Chingford and Epping off A1069, A104 and B1393. 🚗

EWELL

Surrey   *see page 76.*
Bourne Hall Cultural Centre
Spring Street.
    London plan 2 : 40 C1.
18th-century house replaced by cultural centre, comprising museum, art centre, library, theatre hall and banqueting rooms. Collections embrace the human and natural history of the Epsom and Ewell area, and include costumes, dolls, toys and early photography. The Art Gallery has a continuous temporary exhibition programme. Other services include the identification of objects brought in by visitors.

✆ 01-393 9573 Ext 3.
Open: all year Mon-Sat; Mon Wed & Thu 10-5 (8pm Tue & Fri) & 9.30-5 on Sat.
🚗 🚻 ⚋

EWLOE

Clwyd   *Map 7 SJ26.*
Ewloe Castle
(NW of village on A55)
Remains of native Welsh castle in Ewloe woods near where Henry II was defeated in 1157.

Open: accessible at all reasonable times.
(AM CADW)

EXETER

Devon   *Map 3 SX99.*
Devonshire Regimental Museum
Wyvern Barracks, Barrack Road
The exhibits cover the history of the Devonshire Regiment from its formation in 1685 to 1958 when the Regiment amalgamated with the Dorset Regiment. Exhibits include uniforms, weapons, medals, historical documents and military souvenirs collected by the Regiment over the years.

✆ (0392) 218178.
Open: all year Mon-Fri 9-4.30. (Closed: Sat, Sun & BHs.)
(Donations)
🚻 (ground floor only) Shop ⚋

Guildhall
High Street
Dates from 1330, partially rebuilt 1446, arches and façade, added 1592-5, fine displays of oil paintings, Guild Crests and civic silver and regalia.

✆ (0392) 77888.
Open: all year Mon-Sat 10-5.15 (ex when used for Civic functions).
🚻 (ground floor only) ⚋

Royal Albert Memorial Museum
Queen Street
Founded in 1865, and extended several times. Large permanent displays of fine and applied art, natural history and ethnography and local industry. Of particular interest are collections of Devon paintings, Exeter silver, glass, lace, local and foreign natural history. Programme of temporary exhibitions.

✆ (0392) 265858.
Open: all year Tue-Sat 10-5.30.
🚻 (by arrangement ground floor only) ⚋ (ex guide dogs)

Spacex Gallery
45 Preston Street
The largest public fine art gallery in Devon. There is a continuous programme of the contemporary visual arts, plus regular film screenings, performances and poetry readings.

✆ (0392) 31786.
Open: all year, Tue-Sat 10-5.
🚻 ⚋

Tuckers Hall
Fore Street
Old Hall of the Weavers, Ful-

lers and Shearmen, occupied since 1471 by their incorporation which was granted Royal Charter in 1479-81. Wagon-roof and panelling of 1638.

⌀ (0392) 36244.
Open: Jun-Sep Tue, Thu & Fri 10.30-12.30; Oct-May Fri only 10.30-12.30.
⊀

EXMOUTH
Devon.   *Map 3 SY08.*
Exmouth Museum
Sheppards Row
In the early stages of development with items from the town's past and present. Eventually to include a typical local kitchen of one hundred years ago and shipbuilding exhibits.

Open: Mon-Sat 10-12.30 and 2-4.30.

FAIRBURN INGS
West Yorkshire   *Map 8 SE42.*
(2 miles N of Ferrybridge, off unclass road W of A1)
Nature reserve and haven for small birds all year round. In spring and autumn, common, Arctic and more exotic black terns are regularly seen. Late summer and early autumn bring a large roost of swallows to the waterside vegetation. Colder months are noted for bringing an influx of wintering wildfowl.

Open: all year. Information centre and hide open weekends (one mile west of Fairburn village).

FAIRFORD
Gloucestershire   *Map 4 SP10.*
St Mary's Church
Glorious stained glass: 28 windows installed at the beginning of the 16th century have, despite the ravages of the Reformation and the Civil War, for once been preserved intact.

⌀ Cirencester (0285) 712467.
Open: daily 9.30-5.
⌖

FALKIRK
Central (Stirlingshire)   *Map 11 NS87.*
Falkirk Museum
District history exhibition with displays tracing the development of the area from earliest times to the present.

⌀ (0324) 24911 Ext 2472.
Open: Mon-Sat 10.30-12.30 & 1.30-5.
⌖ (ground floor only) Shop
⊀

Rough Castle
One of the most remarkable forts on the Antonine Wall built by the Roman army in the 140's AD. The site covers one acre with double ditches and defensive pits.

Open: accessible at all reasonable times.
(AM)

FARNHAM
Surrey   *Map 4 SU84.*
Farnham Museum
38 West Street
Geology, archaeology, local history and art housed in Willmer House, a fine example of Georgian brickwork.

⌀ (0252) 715094.
Open: Tue-Sat 11-5, BH Mons 2-5. Also open by prior arrangement only May-Aug Wed evenings. (Closed: 25 & 26 Dec).
⌖ (ground floor & garden only) Shop ⊀

FENCE
Lancashire   *Map 7 SD83.*
Lake District Green Slate Co
Visitors can see slate from Coniston and Elterwater being cut with diamond saws and made up into fancy goods and gifts.

⌀ Nelson (0282) 66952.
Open: Workshop and Shop Mon-Fri 8-4.30, Sat 8-4. (Closed: Xmas.)

FILKINS
Oxfordshire   *Map 4 SP20.*
Cotswold Woollen Weavers
(¾m off A361)
In a splendid 18th-century barn, with traditional machinery to bring the Industrial Revolution to life. Exhibition gallery shows weaving processes and the history of wool in the Cotswolds.

⌀ (036786) 491.
Open: Mon-Sat 10-6, Sun 2-6. (Coach parties by arrangement).
⌷ ⌗ ⊀ Shop.

FINDON
West Sussex   *Map 4 TQ10.*
Cissbury Ring
(1 mile E)
Well preserved 60-acre Iron Age fort — the largest on the South Downs. It was occupied between the 5th and the 1st centuries BC and again in the 4th century AD. Extensive excavations have revealed flint mines, ploughing patterns and sites of huts. There are good views from the ramparts.

Open: accessible at all reasonable times.
(NT)

FINSTOWN
See **Orkney**

FLAMBOROUGH HEAD & BEMPTON CLIFFS
Humberside   *Map 8 TA17.*
(4m NE of Bridlington off B1259, B1255 & B1229
Great chalk cliffs rising high above the North Sea between Flamborough Head and Bempton where the largest breeding colony of seabirds in England includes

gannets and kittiwakes. The cliffs are extremely dangerous and visitors should keep to footpaths and observation points. A good place for wildflowers.

Open: accessible at all times by public footpath.

FLINT
Clwyd   *Map 7 SJ27.*
Flint Castle
Ruined late 13th-century castle, erected by Edward I, with circular detached keep originally surrounded by moat.

Open: accessible at all reasonable times.
(AM, CADW)

FLIXTON
Suffolk   *Map 5 TM38.*
Norfolk & Suffolk Aviation Museum
A collection of aircraft and aviation spanning the years from the Wright Brothers to present day. There are sixteen aircraft on static display outside a large specially converted barn containing the smaller items relating to the history of flight.

✆ Brooke (0508) 50614.
Open: Apr-Oct, Sun & BH 10-5; Jun-Aug, Sun Wed & Thu 7pm-9pm; also Jul & Aug Thu 11-5. Parties at other times by prior arrangement.
🔊 (Assistance required)
Shop ✄ (in museum).

FOCHABERS
Grampian (Morayshire)   *Map 15 NJ35.*
Baxters Visitor Centre
The Visitor Centre tells the story of how Baxters first began over 100 years ago up to present day, now supplying customers in over 60 countries throughout the world. There is a guided tour of the factory, an audio-visual show a Victorian kitchen and

the 'old shop' where it all began.

✆ (0343) 820393.
Open: Mar-23 Dec Mon-Fri 10-5, 14th May-11 Sep, Sat & Sun 11-6.
🖵 🚻 🔊 (ground floor only)
Shop ✄

FOLKESTONE
Kent   *Map 5 TR23.*
Museum & Art Gallery
Grace Hill
Local history, archaeology and natural science. Temporary art exhibitions.

✆ (0303) 57583.
Open: all year, Mon, Tue, Thu & Fri 9-5.30, Wed 9-1 & Sat 9-5. (Closed: BH). ✄

FORRES
Grampian (Moray)   *Map 14 NJ05.*
Falconer Museum
Tolbooth Street
Displays of local history, wildlife, geology, ethnography and archaeological finds from Culbin.

✆ (0309) 73701.
Open: all year (ex PH) mid Oct-mid May Mon-Fri 10-4.30; mid May-mid Oct Mon-Sat 10-6 (6.30 in Jul & Aug), also Sun 2-6.30 Jul & Aug only.
🔊 (ground floor only) Shop ✄

Suenos' Stone
A notable 20ft-high Dark Age monument with a sculptured cross on one side and groups of warriors on the reverse.

Open: accessible at all reasonable times.
(AM)

FORT AUGUSTUS
Highland (Inverness-shire)   *Map 14 NH30.*
Great Glen Exhibition
Canal Side
History of the Great Glen from Pict to modern Scot.

The Clans, battles and general history. Exhibits include rare antiques and weapons smithy. Mock forestry exhibition and information on the canal and railway.

✆ (0320) 6341.
Open: Etr-Nov 9-5.
🚻 🔊 Shop

FORTROSE
Highland (Ross & Cromarty)   *Map 14 NH76.*
Fortrose Cathedral
Partly dismantled by Cromwell for a fort at Inverness: the surviving portions of the 14th-century cathedral include the south aisle with vaulting and fine detail.

Open: accessible at all reasonable times. (AM)

FORT WILLIAM
Highland (Inverness-shire)   *Map 14 NN17.*
Inverlochy Castle
A well-preserved example of a 13th-century and later stronghold, noted for the famous battle fought nearby in 1645, when Montrose defeated the Campbells.

Under repair and interior not accessible. Can be viewed from outside.
(AM)

FOVANT
Wiltshire   *Map 4 SU02.*
Regimental Badges
(¾m SE on footpath)
The Regimental Badges line the scarp slope of Fovant Down and were cut into the chalk by regiments encamped in the area during the First World War. The badges can be viewed from the A30 east of Fovant or from the footpath which runs between Fovant and Chiselbury Hill Fort.

Open: accessible at all reasonable times.

FOWEY
Cornwall   *Map 2 SX15.*
St Catherine's Castle
Ruined stronghold erected in 16th century by Henry VIII to defend coast and restored in 1855.

Open: all year, daily any reasonable time.
(AM)

FOXTON
Leicestershire   *Map 4 SP68.*
Foxton Locks
Constructed by Benjamin Bevan between 1810 and 1814 to raise the Grand Union Canal 75 feet. Arrranged in two 'staircases', each with a series of five locks. At the halfway point is a passing pond. Nearby Foxton Barge Lift was completed in 1900 to raise boats up an inclined plane in 12 minutes, thus saving the passage through the locks. Dismantled in 1928, but partially restored and now an ancient monument.

Open: accessible at all reasonable times.
Shop.

GALASHIELS
Borders (Selkirkshire) Map 12 NT43.
Nether Mill (Peter Anderson Ltd),
Huddersfield St
Opened in 1983, the museum brings aspects of the town's past to life by the clever use of early photographs and captions. A central unit displays artifacts of the town's involvement with the woollen trade and also every day items in common use in days gone by. Conducted mill tours are organised lasting approximately 40 minutes.

✆ (0896) 2091.
Open: Apr-Oct, Mon-Sat 9-5, (Jun-Sep, Sun 12-5); Mill Tours Mon-Fri between 10.30-2.
⅃ (ground floor only) Shop

GILLING EAST
North Yorkshire   *Map 8 SE67.*
Gilling Castle
14th-, 16th-, and 18th-century house now preparatory school for Ampleforth College, with Elizabethan great chamber noted for panelling, painted glass and ceilings (rest of house not open to public). Fine gardens.

✆ Ampleforth (04393) 238.
Open: Great chamber & hall weekdays 10-12 & 2-4.
Garden only
Jul-Sep Mon-Fri (Closed: Xmas & New Years Day.)
Admission charge to gardens. ✗

GLASGOW
Strathclyde (Lanarkshire)
                    Map 11 NS56.
Bellahouston Park
Sports Centre
171 acres of parkland only 3 miles from the city centre. Site of the Empire Exhibition of 1938. Sunken garden, walled garden and rock garden. Multi-purpose Sports Centre situated at west end of park, with adjacent all-weather Athletic Centre. Glasgow show.

✆ 041-427 4224
041-427 5454 Sports Centre.
Open: daily end Apr-Aug 8-10, Sep-Apr 8-5 (times approximate).
⌨ (sports centre) ⅃

Botanic Garden
(off Great Western Rd)
Established in 1817, it contains an outstanding collection of plants. The Kibble Palace is a unique glasshouse with, among others, a famous collection of tree ferns. The main glasshouse contains numerous tropical and exotic plants. The 40 acres of gardens include systematic and herb gardens, and a chronological border.

✆ 041-334 2422.
The Kibble Palace. Open: daily 10-4.45 (4.15 in winter).

Glasgow Museums & Art Galleries

Art Gallery & Museum	The Burrell Collection	The People's Palace	Pollok House
Kelvingrove	2060 Pollokshaws Road	Glasgow Green	2060 Pollokshaws Road
Glasgow G3 8AG	Glasgow G43 1AT	Glasgow G40 1AT	Glasgow G43 1AT
Tel: 041-357 3929	Tel: 041-649 7151	Tel: 041-554 0223	Tel: 041-632 0274
Museum of Transport	Haggs Castle	Provand's Lordship	Rutherglen Museum
1 Bunhouse Road	100 St Andrews Drive	Castle Street	Rutherglen
Glasgow G3 8DP	Glasgow G41 4RB	Glasgow G4 0RB	Glasgow G73 1DQ
Tel: 041-357 3929	Tel: 041-427 2725	Tel: 041-552 8819	Tel: 041-647 0837

Open all year except Christmas Day and New Year's Day   Mon-Sat: 10am-5pm Sun: 2-5pm Admission Free

The main glasshouse,
Open: Mon-Sat 1-4.45 (4.15 in winter) Sun 12-4.45 (4.15 in winter). Gardens, Open: daily 7-dusk.
🔲 (garden only)

The Burrell Collection

Pollok Country Park (2½m SW). Not on plan.

The Burrell Collection was opened to the public by HM the Queen on 21 October 1983 in an award-winning gallery, which makes the most of its superb natural setting. The Collection was formed by Sir William and Lady Burrell and comprises more than 8,000 items. These include Chinese ceramics, bronzes and jades, Near Eastern rugs and carpets. Turkish pottery and artefacts from the ancient civilisations of Iraq, Egypt, Greece and Italy. European medieval art is represented by metalwork, sculpture, illuminated manuscripts, ivories and two of the most important museum collections in the world of stained glass and tapestries. The paintings range from the 15th to the early 20th centuries and include works by Memling, Bellini, Cranach, Rembrandt, Courbet, Millet, Boudin, Degas, Manet and Cezanne. There are also important collections of British silver and needlework.

✆ 041-649 7151.
Open: Mon-Sat 10-5, Sun 2-5. (Closed: 25 Dec & 1 Jan).
🖵 🅿 🔲 Shop ✗ (ex guide dogs)

Cathedral

Castle Street.   Plan : **F3.**
The most complete medieval Cathedral surviving on the Scottish mainland, dating mainly from the 13th and 14th centuries.

Open: standard times, see page 4.
(AM)

City Chambers

George Square.   Plan : **E2.**
Opened by Queen Victoria in 1888, this impressive building, designed by William Young, occupies the eastern side of George Square and is the headquarters of Glasgow District Council. The building was built in Italian Renaissance style and is noted for its loggia, marble staircase and banqueting hall.

✆ 041-221 9600.
Open: Guided tours Mon-Wed, Fri 10.30 & 2.30. (Closed: BH) (Telephone in advance.) 🔲 ✗ (ex guide dogs)

Collins Gallery

University of Strathclyde Richmond Street.   Plan : **E2.**
A modern exhibition hall with a varied programme of temporary exhibitions of mainly visual arts and paintings and sometimes historical subjects.

✆ 041-552 4400 Ext 2682/2416.
Open: all year, Mon-Fri 10-5 & Sat 12-4. (during exhibition) (Closed: BH.)

Glasgow Art Gallery & Museum

Kelvingrove Park (¼m NW). Not on plan
The finest civic art collection in Great Britain. All schools and periods of European painting with emphasis on Dutch 17th century, French 19th century and Scottish art from 17th-century to the present day. Collections of pottery, porcelain, silver, sculpture, arms and armour, also archaeology, ethnography and natural history.

✆ 041-357 3929.
Open: Mon-Sat 10-5, Sun 2-5. (Closed: Xmas day & New Years day.)
🖵 🔲 Shop ✗ (ex guide dogs)

Haggs Castle

100 St Andrews Drive, (2m SW). Not on plan
Built in 1585, the castle houses a museum for children. The emphasis is on the exploration of history through activities and a 'hands on' approach to the displays. These include a 16th-century kitchen, 17th-century bedroom and a Victorian nursery. There are also regular temporary exhibitions and children's activities.

✆ 041-427 2725.
Open: Mon-Sat 10-5, Sun 2-5. (Closed: Xmas Day & New Years Day.)

Glasgow: Museum of Transport

Guided tours only if booked in advance.
🚗 🖥 (ground floor & workshops only) Shop ⊗ (ex guide dogs)

Hunterian Museum

The University of Glasgow (¼m NW). Not on plan
The museum is named after the 18th-century physician, Dr William Hunter, who bequeathed his own collections to the University. The geological, archaeological, ethnographical, numismatic and historical collections are exhibited in the main building of the University. Temporary exhibition programme.

✆ 041-330 4221 Ext 4221.
Open: Mon-Fri 10-5, Sat 9.30-1.
(Please telephone for details of PH closures.)
🖥 🖥 (ground floor. Lift by prior arrangement) Shop ⊗

Hutcheson's Hall

158 Ingram St
A 19th-century building, de-

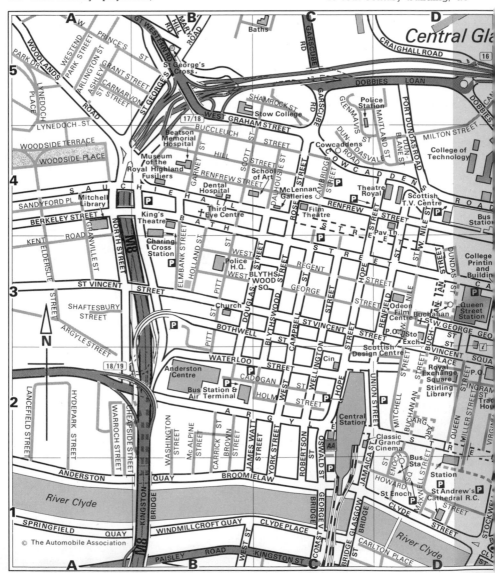

© The Automobile Association

signed by David Hamilton. Acquired by the National Trust for Scotland in 1982 for use as their West Regional offices and shop.

✆ 041-552 8391.
Visitor centre open Mon-Fri 9-5, Sat 10-4. Shop Mon-Sat 10-4
(NTS)

Linn Park
Cathcart (southern outskirts of Glasgow)
Not on plan
Comprises more than 200 acres of pine, deciduous woodland and riverside walks. Britain's first public park nature trail, (1965) features many varieties of flowers, trees, and insects. A

children's zoo and a collection of British ponies and Highland cattle. There is also a ruined 14th-century castle.

✆ 041-637 1147.
Open: daily 7-dusk.

Mitchell Library
Kent Road.   Plan : **A4.**
The largest public reference library in Europe with more than a million volumes, founded in 1874, and named after Stephen Mitchell, a Glasgow tobacco manufacturer. There is a special collection on Robert Burns and Scottish Poetry.

✆ 041-221 7030.
Open: all year, Mon-Fri 9.30-9 & Sat 9.30-5.

Museum of Transport
Kelvin Hall, 1 Bunhouse Road (Not on plan)
This new museum tells the history of transport with displays of Glasgow trams and buses, Scottish-built cars and other vehicles, railway locomotives and horse drawn vehicles.
There is also a large display of ship models and a reconstruction of a typical Glasgow side street of 1938.

✆ 041-357 3929
Open: due to open in Spring 1988.
Shop

People's Palace Museum
Glasgow Green, off London Road (¼m SE). Not on plan
Contains a fascinating visual record of the history and life of the City. Exhibits include Medieval Glasgow, interesting relics of Mary, Queen of Scots, the Battle of Langside, the Tobacco Lords of the 18th century, and the history of the music hall. Fine exam-

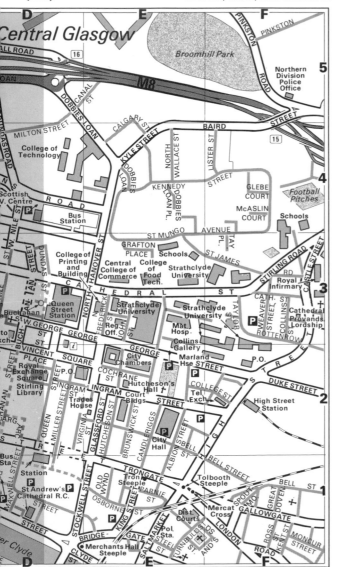

Central Glasgow

ples of Glasgow crafts-manship, particularly pottery and special displays illustrating social and domestic life, including women's suffrage, temperance and the two world wars. A wide range of pictures of noteworthy people and places. Winter gardens with adjoining tropical house.

℡ 041-554 0223.
Open: Mon-Sat 10-5, Sun 2-5. (Closed: Xmas Day & New Years Day).
⌨ ♿ (ground floor only)
Shop
✗ (ex guide dogs)

Pollok Country Park
Formerly a private estate, there are 361 acres of land containing an extensive collection of flowering shrubs and trees in a natural setting. There is a herd of 50 Highland cattle, a display rose garden, nature trails and jogging track. Demonstrations held fortnightly on Sat mornings.
Ranger service. Countryside Rangers Interpretation Centre.

℡ 041-632 9299 or 041-649 0331.
Park always open.
Demonstration and display garden open: daily Mon-Thu 8-4, Fri 8-3; Weekends 8-6.30 (Winter 8-4).
д ♿

Also **Pollok House**
Situated within the grounds, a neo-Palladian building first constructed in 1752, with Edwardian additions containing the famous Stirling Maxwell Collection of Spanish paintings, furniture, etc.

℡ 041-632 0274.
Open: Mon-Sat 10-5, Sun 2-5. (Closed: Xmas Day & New Years Day.)

⌨ ♿ (ground floor only)
Shop. ✗ (ex guide dogs)

Provand's Lordship
3 Castle Street Plan : **F3**
Built in 1471 as a manse serving the Cathedral and St Nicholas Hospital, this is the oldest house in Glasgow. Mary Queen of Scots is reputed to have stayed in the house, which now has period displays from 1500 onwards and a fine collection of 17th century Scottish furniture. Latterly a confectioner's shop, the machines which made the sweets can also be seen.

℡ 041-552 8819.
Open: Mon-Sat 10-5 & Sun 2-5. (Closed: Xmas Day & New Years Day.)
♿ (ground floor only) Shop
✗ (ex guide dogs)

Provan Hall
Auchinlea Road (6½m E. off B806). Not on plan
Well restored 15th-century house considered most perfect example of a simple pre-Reformation house remaining in Scotland, set in Auchinlea Park. In the adjacent grounds are formal and informal gardens including garden for the blind.

℡ 041-771 6372.
For information on opening hours please telephone the above number.
♿

Regimental Museum of the Royal Highland Fusiliers
518 Sauchiehall Street. Plan : **B4**
The history of the Highland Light Infantry, The Royal Highland Fusiliers and the Royal Scots Fusiliers from 1678 to the present day. Exhibits include medals, pictures, uniforms, weapons, mementoes and records.

℡ 041-332 0961.
Open: all year, Mon-Thu 9-4.30 & Fri 9-4.
(Closed: BH's.)
✗

Ross Hall Park
Crookston (5m W on A736). Not on plan
Beautifully kept gardens with artificial ponds, featuring a variety of aquatic plants and stocked with fish. Extensive heather and rock gardens and woodland nature trails.

℡ 041-882 3554.
Open: Apr-Sep daily 1-8, Oct-Mar daily 1-4.
♿

Rouken Glen Park
Thornliebank (4¾m S on A726). Not on plan
Fine park with lovely walks through the glen. Waterfall at head of the glen is a noted beauty spot. Large walled garden. Boating on picturesque loch.

℡ 041-638 1101.
Open: daily dawn-dusk.
⌨ (in garden centre) ♿
Shop and garden centre.

Scottish Design Centre
72 St Vincent Street. Plan : **D3.**
Scottish made goods and craft items are on sale here. There is also an exhibition centre with changing displays.

℡ 041-221 6121.
Open: all year, Mon-Fri 9.30-5 & Sat 9-5.
⌨ ♿

The Stock Exchange
69 St George's Place. Plan : **D3.**
Dating from 1877 this Venetian Gothic building is by John Burnet (Sen). Recently it has been rebuilt within the external walls. There is a visitors viewing gallery.

℡ 041-221 7060.
Open: all year, Mon-Fri 10-4.

Victoria Park
Whiteinch (2½W on A814).
Not on plan
This park has the best known fossilized tree stumps of the prehistoric Coal Age period, discovered in 1887 and housed in the Fossil Grove building. The park has extensive carpet bedding depicting centennial events.

℗ 041-959 1146.
Fossil Grove building open: Mon-Fri 8-4, Sat, Sun pm only. Park open: daily 7am-dusk.
ℼ 🅰

GLASTONBURY
Glastonbury Tor
(¾m E of town centre off A361)
Rising to 521 ft, legend-rich Glastonbury Tor is also an excellent viewpoint, overlooking the Somerset levels. Crowning it is a 14th-century tower, the remains of a chapel destroyed in a landslip in 1271; near the foot is the Chalice Spring. Footpaths climb to the summit.

Open: accessible at all reasonable times.
(NT)

GLENDRONACH
Grampian (Aberdeenshire)
Map 15 NJ64.
Glendronach Distillery
(junc of B9001 & B9024)
Owned by William Teachers and Son Limited. Visitors can see the complete process of whisky making, including the malting barley rooms and distilling of spirits. Whisky has been made on the premises for over 160 years.

℗ Forgue (046682) 202.
Open: Guided tours Mon-Fri 10 & 2. (Other times by special arrangement.)
⍋ Shop

GLENLIVET
Grampian (Banffshire)   Map 15 NJ12.
The Glenlivet Distillery Reception Centre
(off B9008 10m N of Tomintoul)
The reception centre contains an exhibition of ancient artefacts used in malting, peat cutting and distilling. Distillery tour. Free whisky sample.

℗ Glenlivet (08073) 427 & 301 (Winter).
Open: Etr-Oct, Mon-Sat 10-4.
Details not confirmed for 1988.
💬 🅰 (ground floor only)
Shop ⍋ (ex Guide dogs)

GLENMUICK AND LOCHNAGAR
Grampian (Aberdeenshire)
Map 15 NO28.
Glenmuick and Lochnagar Nature Reserve
(9m SW of Ballater on unclass road)
The nature reserve occupies a wild and remote area south of the River Dee. There are a variety of walks from the visitor centre at the Spittal of Glenmuick, including paths along Loch Muick and up to the summit of Lochnagar (3786 ft) where a variety of alpine plants can be seen. Visitors are requested to keep to footpaths. Weatherproof clothing and sturdy footwear are essential on all the walks.

℗ Ballater (0338) 55434.
Open: Visitor Centre daily, all year 10-5 (weather permitting).
ℼ

GLOUCESTER
Gloucestershire   Map 3 SO81.
Gloucester Cathedral
Norman in origin with extensive rebuilding in the Perpendicular style. Two of its many treasures are the tomb of Edward II and the great east window.

℗ (0452) 28095.
Open: daily 7.30-6 (ex during services).

City East Gate
Eastgate Street
Roman and medieval gatetowers and moat in an underground exhibition chamber.

℗ (0452) 24131.
Open: May-Sep, Wed & Fri 2.15-5, Sat 10-12 & 2.15-5.
Shop ⍋

City Museum & Art Gallery
Brunswick Road
The Marling bequest of 18th-century walnut furniture, barometers and domestic silver. Paintings by Richard Wilson, Gainsborough, Turner, etc, supplemented by art exhibitions throughout the year. Local archaeology including Roman mosaics and sculptures, natural history including a freshwater aquarium.

Gloucester Docks

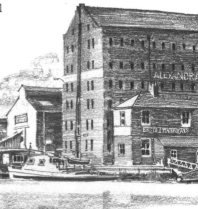

⌀ (0452) 24131.
Open: Mon-Sat 10-5.
⌖ Shop ⌗

Folk Musuem
99-103 Westgate Street
A group of half-timbered
houses, (Tudor and Jaco-
bean), furnished to illustrate
local history, domestic life
and rural crafts. Civil War
armour, Victorian toys,
Severn fishing tackle,
wooden ploughs, etc. Reconstructed Double Gloucester
dairy and wheelwright's
shop. Pin factory with 18th-
century forge.

⌀ (0452) 26467.
Open: Mon-Sat 10-5.
⌖ (ground floor only) Shop
⌗

Gloucester Docks
An inland Victorian port still
preserved virtually intact in
the heart of Gloucester, now
being redeveloped as a major regional tourist, cultural
and commercial centre.
Famous as the location for
filming the *Onedin Line*, the
area has many listed buildings. Principle attractions are
the National Waterways
Museum (due to open 1st Apr
1988); Robert Opie Museum,
Gloucester Antiques Centre.
Permission is needed to en-
ter the docks.

⌀ Information Centre (0452)
421188 (Leisure Services
Dept) or 25524 (Regional
British Waterways Board).
Open: Vantage points at all
times, contact British
Waterways Board,
Commercial Road,
Gloucester GL1 2ES.
Guided tours available.

**House of the Tailor of
Gloucester — Beatrix
Potter Museum**
9 College Court
A museum in miniature,

housed in the building featured by Beatrix Potter in
'The Tailor of Gloucester'.
The tailor's kitchen has been
recreated and there is a
working model of mice creat-
ing the waistcoat. On the
ground floor, a bookshop
sells Beatrix Potter books.

⌀ (0452) 422856.
Open: Mon-Sat 9.30-5.30.
Shop

GODALMING
Surrey
Godalming Museum
109A High Street
Local history displays. Gardens in Jeykll and Lutyens
style.

⌀ (04868) 4104.
Open: Tue-Sat 10-5.
Shop ⌗

GOLSPIE
Highland (Sutherland)   Map 14 NH89.
**Golspie Burn Gorge and
Waterfalls**
*(½m E of A9, ½m along
unclass road signed Backies)*
Waymarked paths, including
one which follows the Golspie Burn towards Backies,
running through the spec-
tacular narrow gorge and
climbing past waterfalls and
deep dark pools. The gorge
and surrounding area are
heavily wooded with many
interesting woodland plants.
Display boards are sited at
various locations (summer
only).

Open: accessible at all
reasonable times. ⌤

GOMERSAL
West Yorkshire   Map 8 SE22.
Red House
Oxford Road
Off M62 (junc 26)
Built in 1660 of red brick,
which because of its rarity at
that time gave rise to its name.
Associations with the Brontës,

particularly Charlotte, who
often spent weekends here
with her schoolfriend Mary
Taylor. She immortalised it in
her novel 'Shirley' where it is
described under the name of
'Briarmains'.

⌀ Cleckheaton (0274)
872165.
Open: all year, Mon-Sat 10-5,
Sun 1-5.
⌖ (ground floor & gardens
only) Shop ⌗ in house

GRASSINGTON
North Yorkshire   Map 7 SE06.
National Park Centre
Colvend, Hebden Road
Visitor centre featuring interpretative display on 'Walking
in Wharfedale'. Audio-visual
programme, maps, guides
and local information.

⌀ (0756) 752748.
Open: Apr-Oct daily from
mid morning to late
afternoon.
⌤ ⌖

GRAYS
Essex   Map 5 TQ67.
Thurrock Museum
Orsett Road
Local history, agriculture,
trade and industrial collec-
tions. Also Palaeolithic to
Saxon archaeology.

⌀ Grays Thurrock
(0375) 33325.
Open: all year, Mon-Fri 10-8
& Sat 10-5 (Closed: BH's.)
⌖ Shop ⌗

**Great Cumbrae Island
MILLPORT**
Strathclyde (Bute)   Map 10 NS15.
Museum of the Cumbraes
Garrison House
The museum tells the story of
life on and around the Cumbraes and features many old
photographs, including some
of steamers which achieved
fame on the Millport run.

(0475) 530741.
Open: Jun-Sep Tue-Sat
10-4.30
&

GREENFIELD
Clwyd   *Map 7 SJ17.*
Greenfield Valley Heritage Park
Sixty acres of lakeside and wooded walks including 5 reservoirs, a farm and farm museum, monuments and Basingwerk Abbey remains. A nature and industrial heritage trail goes past the remains of cotton and wire mills.

Holywell (0352) 714172.
Open: all year 10-5.
(Admission charge to farm)
& ⊓ (visitor centre)

GREENOCK
Strathclyde Renfrewshire
                     Map 10 NS27.
McLean Museum & Art Gallery
9 Union St
The museum displays exhibits relating to local history, ethnography, natural history, geology and shipping, including river paddle steamers and cargo vessels. Also relics of James Watt. The Inverclyde Biennial is held here 23 May-18 Jun.

(0475) 23741.
Open: Mon-Sat 10-12 & 1-5.
(Closed: Sun & PH's.)
& (ground floor only) Shop
⌀

GREENSTED-JUXTA-ONGAR
Essex   *Map 5 TL50.*
St Andrews Church
(1m W of Chipping Ongar on unclass road)
The only surviving wooden Saxon church in Britain with walls of solid oak which are believed to date from the 9th century. In 1013 the body of King Edmund rested here on its way to Bury St Edmunds.

Ongar (0277) 364694.
Open: daily, 9-dusk
(Donations)

GRIMSBY
Humberside   *Map 8 TA20.*
Welholme Galleries
Welholme Road
Collection of Napoleonic and later 19th-century ship models, marine paintings and fine china from Doughty Bequest. Folk-life collections and photographs of Lincolnshire life from collection of the late W.E.R. Hallgarth.

(0472) 242000 Ext 1385/6.
Open: all year Tue-Sat 10-5.
(Closed: Xmas day & BH's.)
& Shop ⌀ (ex guide dogs)

GROSMONT
Gwent   *Map 3 SO42.*
Grosmont Castle
(on B4347)
Ruined Marcher stronghold, rebuilt in 13th century by Hubert de Burgh, on hill above Monnow Valley. One of three 'tri-lateral' castles of Gwent.

Open: at all reasonable times.
(AM, CADW)

GUILDFORD
Surrey   *Map 4 SU94.*
Guildford Castle
Castle Street
Early 12th-century rectangular three-storeyed keep affording fine views. The castle ditch has been transformed into a flower garden, seen at its best throughout the summer. Brass rubbing display. Open air theatre during summer.

(0483) 505050.
Grounds open: daily 8.30-dusk. (Closed: Xmas day.)
Keep open Apr-25 Sep 10.30-6. Admission charge to keep.
& (gardens only) Shop ⌀

Guildford House Gallery
155 High Street
Built in 1660, timber-framed building containing richly carved elm and oak staircase and finely decorated plaster ceilings. Monthly, temporary art exhibitions, including paintings sculpture and craftwork.

(0483) 503406 Ext 3531.
Open: Mon-Sat 10.30-4.50.
(Closed: a few days prior to each exhibition). For details of exhibitions please apply for leaflet.
& (ground floor only) Shop ⌀

Guildford Museum
Castle Arch, Quarry Street
Local history, archaeology and needlework.

(0483) 503497.
Open: Mon-Sat 11-5.
(Closed: on certain PH.)
& (ground floor only) Shop ⌀

HADDINGTON
Lothian (East Lothian) *Map 12 NT57.*
St Mary's Pleasance and Church
Sidegate
Sixteenth-century restored gardens belonging to Haddington House including rose, herb, meadow, cottage and sunken gardens. Nearby the Pleached Alley leads to St Mary's Gate and the large medieval church of St Mary's, restored in 1973. Guided tours are available.

(062082) 3738. Church's phone number (062082) 5111.
Open: Apr-Sep Mon-Sat 10-4 & Sun 1-4.
(Donations)
& ⊟ Shop.

Cloth was sold in the 315 rooms of Halifax Piece Hall

HADLEIGH
Essex   Map 5 TQ88.
Hadleigh Castle
Founded in 1231 by Hubert de Burgh and rebuilt by Edward III in the 14th century. The walls are of Kentish rag and the castle retains two of its original towers.

Open: accessible at any reasonable time.
(AM)

HADLEIGH
Suffolk   Map 5 TM04.
Wolves Wood
(2m E on A1071)
An RSPB reserve located in an ancient woodland, one of the four surviving fragments of the vast forests that once covered this area. Interesting plants and birds to be seen, including five species of orchid. Can be quite muddy.

✆ Norwich (0603) 615920.
Open: accessible at all times.
✗

HADRIAN'S WALL
Cumbria/Northumberland
Map 12 NY77.
Stretching 73 miles between Bowness on Solway and Newcastle upon Tyne, Hadrian's Wall was built from 122AD to separate the Romans from the Barbarians. Originally about 15ft high and 10ft wide it had milecastles at every Roman mile (1620 yards) and two equidistant turrets between them. Seventeen forts for up to 1000 soldiers each were built along the wall, and running parallel to the south of Hadrian's Wall is the Vallum, a ditch with mounds on either side.
The best places to see the wall are between Banks in Cumbria and Chollerford in Northumberland.

The following places are accessible at all reasonable times:
BIRDOSWALD, off B6318, 1¼m W of Gilsland. Roman fort of Camboglanna visible and section of wall.
GILSLAND, W of village, Milecastle 48 and Willowford Roman bridge.
CARVORAN, ¾m E of Greenhead. Fine section of wall running along crest of ridge.
CAWFIELDS, 2m N of Haltwistle on unclass road. Remains of Milecastle 42 and sections of wall.
BROCOLITIA, 4m W of Chollerford on B6318. Remains of Roman Fort and traces of the ditch Vallum. (Admission charges to Chester's Roman Fort and Housesteads Roman Fort).

HALIFAX
West Yorkshire   Map 7 SE02.
Bankfield Museum & Art Gallery
Boothtown Road, Akroyd Park
Built by Edward Akroyd in the 1860s, this Renaissance-

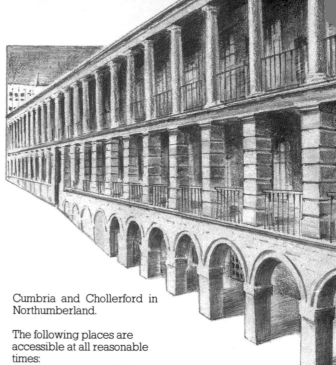

style building, set in the centre of parkland on a hill overlooking the town, contains one of the finest and most representative collections of costume and textiles from all periods and all parts of the world. There are new galleries of costume and toys. There are also displays of local natural history and the museum of the Duke of Wellington's Regiment. The Museum mounts regular temporary exhibitions, both from its collection, and also travelling art exhibitions.

✆ (0422) 54823 & 52334.
Open: Mon-Sat 10-5, Sun 2.30-5. (Closed: Xmas & New Year's day).
♿ (ground floor & park only)
Shop ✗

Piece Hall
Unique and outstanding 18th-century cloth hall, restored and converted; museum, exhibition galleries; antique,

craft and souvenir shops. Tourist information. Open market Fri-Sat.

✆ (0422) 68725 & 58087.
Open: daily 10-5. (Closed: Xmas & New Year's day). Individual facilities vary. ⌨ ♿ (ground floor only) Shop.

HALNAKER
West Sussex   Map 4 SU90.
Halnaker Mill
(1½m NE off A285)
Standing on Halnaker Hill (416ft) the windmill is a local landmark and has been partially restored. Built in 1740, it is the oldest tower mill in Sussex.

Open: accessible at any reasonable time.

HAMILTON
Strathclyde (Lanarks)   Map 11 NS75.
Hamilton District Museum
129 Muir Street
Local history museum in a 17th-century coaching inn with original stable and 18th-century Assembly Room with musicians gallery. Displays include prehistory, art, costume, natural history, agriculture and local industries of the past. Transport museum and reconstructed Victorian kitchen.

✆ (0698) 283981.
Open: Mon-Sat 10-5. (Closed 12-1 on Wed & Sat). ♿ (ground floor only) Shop ✗

The Cameronians (Scottish Rifles) Regimental Museum
Mole Hill, off Muir Street
Medals, banners, uniforms, documents and silver.

✆ (0698) 283981.
Open: Mon, Tue, Wed, Fri & Sat 10-1 & 2-5.
♿ ✗

HAMPTON COURT
Gt London   see page 76
Bushey Park
(off A308)   London plan 2: 41 B2.
Less formal than its neighbour Hampton Court Park, with herds of deer roaming free. Mile-long Chestnut Avenue is ideal for horse riding close to the Hampton Court end, and the Diana Fountain marks the junction with an avenue of limes, a formal highway through an otherwise wild part of the park. North of the limes is the Longford River.

✆ 01-977 1328.
Open: all year 6.30-mdnt. ⌨

HARDKNOTT CASTLE ROMAN FORT
Cumbria   Map 7 NY20.
On Hardknott Pass above Eskdale, 375ft square fort with three double gateways enclosing walled and ramparted area of almost three acres. Situated above western end of steep and narrow pass (maximum gradient 1 in 3), fort was occupied in mid-2nd century.

Open: accessible at all reasonable times.
(AM)

HARLOW
Essex   Map 5 TL41.
Harlow Museum
Passmores House, Third Avenue
The exhibits cover various aspects of local history from Roman to modern and also natural history and geology. Housed in an early Georgian building, set in gardens; part of the medieval moat from the earlier house can be seen.

✆ (0279) 446422.
Open: Tue & Thu 10-9, Wed, Fri, Mon 10-5.

(Closed: 12.30-1.30, Sat & Sun & Xmas).
♿ (ground floor & gardens only) Shop ✗

Mark Hall Cycle Museum & Gardens
Muskham Road, off First Avenue
History of the bicycle 1819-1980s, with 60 machines on display from an 1819 hobby horse to a 1982 plastic machine. Three walled period gardens, Tudor herb garden and cottage garden.

✆ (0279) 39680.
Open: daily 10-5 (dusk in winter). (Closed: Xmas).
♿ Shop ✗

HARTLEPOOL
Cleveland   Map 8 NZ53.
Gray Art Gallery & Museum
Clarence Road
Permanent collection of pictures. Museum collections feature local history, archaeology, engineering, Indian idols, porcelain, British birds, working blacksmith's shop in museum grounds. Monthly temporary exhibitions.

✆ (0429) 66522 Ext 259.
Open: Mon-Sat 10-5.30, Sun 2-5. (Closed: Good Fri, Xmas & New Year's Day).
♿ (ground floor only) Shop ✗

Maritime Museum
Northgate
Collections feature the maritime history of the town and its shipbuilding industry. Also reconstructed fisherman's cottage, a ship's bridge and an early lighthouse lantern.

✆ (0429) 272814.
Open: Mon-Sat 10-5. (Closed: Good Fri, Xmas & New Year's Day).
Shop ✗

HASTINGS

East Sussex *Map 5 TQ80.*

Fishermen's Museum

Rock a Nore Road

Former fishermen's church, now museum of local interest, including the last of Hastings luggers built for sail.

✆ (0424) 424787.
Open: last wk May-last Sun Sep Mon-Fri 10.30-12 & 2.30-6, Sun 2.30-5.
♿ (ground floor only) 🚫🐕

Hastings Country Park

Main entrance off Coastguard Lane S of Fairlight Road

Opened in 1974 and covering 600 acres, the country park occupies 5 kilometres of the most attractive stretch of the Sussex coast, with several fine walks and several nature trails. Much of the area is well wooded. Visitors Centre near Fairlight.

✆ (0424) 722022.
Open: Country Park accessible at all reasonable times. Interpretative Centre: Etr-Sep, Sat, Sun, BH 2-5
⛺ (🚫🐕 in Visitors Centre).

Hastings Museum & Art Gallery

Cambridge Road

Collections of natural history of Hastings, archaeology and history of Hastings and neighbouring areas. Sussex ironwork and pottery. Fine and applied art. Durbar Hall (Indian Palace). Extensive collection of pictures, and a special Exhibition Gallery.

✆ (0424) 721202.
Open: Mon-Sat 10-1 & 2-5, Sun & BH 3-5. (Closed: Good Fri & Xmas).
♿ (ground floor only) 🚫🐕

HAVANT

Hampshire *Map 4 SU70.*

Havant Museum

East Street

The museum shares this late 19th-century building with a flourishing Arts Centre. Local history displays can be seen in two rooms off the main exhibition gallery. A display of firearms and their history, formed by C.G. Vokes, is on the first floor of the museum.

✆ (0705) 451155.
Open: Tue-Sat 10-5.
♿ (ground floor only) Shop

HAWES

North Yorkshire *Map 7 SD89.*

National Park Centre

Station Yard

Interpretative display relating to farming in the Yorkshire Dales. Audio-visual programme, maps, guides and local information available.

✆ (09697) 450.
Open: daily Apr-Oct, mid morning-late afternoon.
♿

HAWICK

Borders (Roxburghshire) *Map 12 NT51.*

Trowmill Woollen Mill

(2½m NE on A698)

There has been a mill here since the 1750s. Trowmill ground meal until about 1880 when it changed to woollen manufacture. The mill was powered by water until 1965 and by electricity until 1977. Visitors can see the various processes and stages of tweed being made at the new automated factory.

✆ (0450) 72555.
Open: daily 9-5.
♿ ☕

HAWORTH

West Yorkshire *Map 7 SE03.*

St Michael's Church

The tower is all that remains of the church in which Patrick Brontë (father of the celebrated writers Charlotte, Anne and Emily) preached, demolished by his successor the Reverend John Wade. In the crypt the Brontë family lie beneath an inscribed stone and commemorative plaque (except for Anne, who lies at Scarborough). The memorial chapel contains many documents associated with the family's life. In the churchyard are the graves of Martha Brown and Tabitha Aykroyd, servants of the Brontë household.

✆ (0535) 42329.
Open: daily 10-5.
(Donation box).

HEBDEN BRIDGE

West Yorkshire *Map 7 SE02.*

F Walkley Clogs Ltd

(¾m SE on A646)

The firm was founded by Mr F Walkley at Huddersfield in 1946. This is the only surviving clog mill in Britain and visitors can see the complete process of clog-making, from the 100-year-old method to the modern methods used to make the latest leisure footwear.

✆ (0422) 842061.
Open: daily 8.30-5, (ex 25, 26 Dec, 1 Jan).
☕ Mill Shop

HECKINGTON

Lincolnshire *Map 8 TF14.*

Craft/Heritage Centre

Station Rd

Ten crafts represented include pottery, a silversmith's, toymaking, spinning and weaving, fabric painting, wood and leather work and silk flowers. There are also Heritage displays and exhibitions of work by Lincolnshire craftsmen. Tourist Information Centre.

Open: Jul & Aug Mon-Sat & BH Mon 10-5; Sun 12-5; Jan-Jun & Sep-Dec, Tue-Sat 10-1,

2-5, Sun 2-5, BH Mon 12-5,
Closed: 24-31 Dec.
🚗 (fr. Jul) 🔲 (ground floor
only) Shop ⊗

HELSTON
Cornwall   *Map 2 SW62.*
Helston Folk Museum
Old Butter Market
Folk museum covering local
history and articles from The
Lizard Peninsula. Various
summer exhibitions are reg-
ularly held.

✆ (03265) 61672.
Open: Mon, Tue, Thu-Sat
10.30-12.30 & 2-4.30, Wed
10.30-noon. Touring schools
and visiting groups welcome.
🔲 Shop ⊗

HENLEY-IN-ARDEN
Warwickshire   *Map 4 SP16.*
Guildhall
High Street
Gabled, timber framed
building of 1448, restored in
1915, with outside staircase
leading from Dutch-style garden to hall with impressive
roof timbering.

✆ (05642) 2309.
Open: at any reasonable time
on application to Caretaker,
Guild Cottage.
(Donations)
⊗

HEREFORD
Hereford and Worcester Map 3 SO54.
**Hereford Museum & Art
Gallery**
Broad Street
Roman tessellated pave-
ments, natural history, bee
keeping display with
observation hive, English
watercolours, local geology
and county's archaeology,
also folk life and folklore
material. The exhibitions at
City Art Gallery are changed
every month.

✆ (0432) 268121 Ext 207.
Open: Tue, Wed & Fri 10-6,

Thu 10-5, Sat 10-5. Oct-Mar
Sat 10-4 (Closed: Mon ex
BH's).
🔲 Shop ⊗

HERTFORD
Hertfordshire   *Map 4 TL31.*
Hertford Castle & Gardens
The original castle was built
by William the Conqueror;
the walls and motte preserve
the plan of his structure. The
Edward IV gatehouse still remains, with wings added in
the 18th and 20th centuries.
The grounds are open to the
public and band concerts are
held on the open days.

✆ (0992) 552885.
Open: 1st Sun in each of the
months of May-Sep 2.30-4.30.
🔲 (ground floor & gardens
only).

HIGHDOWN
West Sussex   *Map 4 TQ00.*
Highdown
*(N off A259 halfway between
Worthing & Litttlehampton)*
Gardens laid out in chalk pit
on Highdown Hill, with rock
plants, flowering shrubs and
daffodils, as well as excellent
views.

✆ Worthing (0903) 501054.
Open: all year Mon-Fri
10-4.30; weekends & BH's
Apr-Sep 10-8.
🚗 ⊓ 🔲

HIGH WYCOMBE
Buckingshamshire   *Map 4 SU89.*
Wycombe Chair Museum
*Castle Hill House, Priory
Avenue*
Fine house set in gardens
and museum of chairs, old
tools, and chair-making
apparatus.

✆ (0494) 23879.
Open: Mon-Sat (ex Wed) 10-1
& 2-5. (Closed: Sun & BHs).
🔲 (ground floor only) Shop
⊗

HIMLEY
Staffordshire   *Map 7 SO89.*
Himley Hall
*(6m S of Wolverhampton off
A449 4m N of Stourbridge)*
Extensive parkland with 9-
hole golf course, model village, trout and coarse fishing
(extra charge). Hall **not** open
to the public.

✆ Dudley (0384) 55433 Ext
5414.
Grounds open: daily 8-8 or
½hr before dusk.
🚗 ⊓ 🔲

HITCHIN
Hertfordshire   *Map 4 TL12.*
**Hitchin Museum & Art
Gallery**
Paynes Park
Contains local and natural
history collections, costume
and Victoriana. Regimental
Museum of the Hertfordshire
Yeomanry. Special tempor-
ary exhibitions changed
monthly. Good collection of
watercolours, especially
those by local Quaker artist
Samuel Lucas Snr 1805-1870.

✆ (0462) 34476.
Open: Mon-Sat 10-5.
(Closed: BH's.)
🔲 (ground floor only) Shop
⊗

HOLYHEAD
Gwynedd   *Map 6 SH28.*
**South Stack Cliffs (Nature
Reserve)**
(2m W on unclass road)
Covering 800 acres of an exposed headland with
thousands of sea birds including guillemots, razorbills
and puffins. There are two
areas of maritime heathland;
Holyhead Mountain and Pen-
rhos Feilw Common. A flight
of 403 steps lead down to the
South Stack Lighthouse
which is reached by crossing
a suspension bridge. In clear
weather, Ireland can be seen

from the summit of Holyhead Mountain (722ft).

✆ (0407) 2522.
Open: accessible at all reasonable times; information centre Apr-Sep.

HOLY ISLAND (Lindisfarne)
Northumberland   *Map 12 NU14.*
Lindisfarne Liqueur Company
St Aidan's Winery
Visitors, although not allowed into the working area because of Customs and Excise restrictions, are welcomed into the winery showrooms where manufacturing of Lindisfarne Mead is explained (the recipe is a closely guarded secret). Products are on sale. Mead sampling sometimes possible.

(0289) 89230.
Open: Etr-Sep daily; Oct-Mar Mon-Fri.
Opening hours depend on tide. Holy Island is accessible at low tide across a causeway with tide tables posted at each end. Shop.

HONITON
Devon   *Map 3 ST10.*
Honiton Pottery
30-34 High Street
Visitors can tour the pottery at leisure and see the several stages of the craft during normal working hours.

✆ (0404) 2106.
Pottery open: Mon-Thu 9-12 & 2-4.30, Fri 4. Shop Mon-Sat 9-5.
☕ (small coffee shop) Shop & Showroom

HORSHAM
West Sussx   *Map 4 TQ13.*
Horsham Museum
9 The Causeway
16th-century timbered house with walled garden planted with herbs and English cottage garden flowers. Displays include: costume and accessories, toys, early cycles, domestic life, Sussex rural crafts, local history, archaeology and geology. Regular temporary exhibitions throughout the year.

✆ (0403) 54959.
Open: Oct-Mar Tue-Fri 1-5, Sat 10-5. Apr-Sep Tue-Sat 10-5.
♿ (ground floor & garden) Shop &

HOVE
East Sussex   *Map 4 TQ20.*
Museum and Art Gallery
New Church Road
The museum contains local history, dolls, toys, coins and medals, a notable collection of British ceramics as well as an exhibition of 18th-century pictures, furniture and decorative arts. A large collection of 20th-century paintings and drawings are also on display.

✆ Brighton (0273) 779410.
Open: Tue-Fri 10-5, Sat 10-4.30. Sun afternoons May-Sep.
♿ (ground floor only) &

HOY
See **Orkney**

HUDDERSFIELD
West Yorkshire   *Map 7 SE11.*
Art Gallery
Princess Alexandra Walk
Contains a permanent collection of British oil paintings, watercolours, drawings, sculpture from mid 19th century onwards. Temporary loan exhibitions throughout the year.

✆ (0484) 513808 Ext 216.
Open: Mon-Fri 10-6, Sat 10-4. (Closed: Sun & BH's)
♿ &

Tolson Memorial Museum
Ravensknowle Park
Geology, natural history, archaeology, folk life, toys, development of cloth industry and collection of horse-drawn vehicles.

✆ (0484) 530591.
Open: Mon-Sat 10-5, Sun 1-5. (Closed: Xmas).
♿ Shop &

HULL
Humberside   *Map 8 TA02.*
Ferens Art Gallery
Queen Victoria Square
Contains collection of works by European Old Masters; 19th-century marine paintings from Humberside; 20th-century English art and a regular programme of visiting exhibitions.

✆ (0482) 222750.
Open: Mon-Sat 10-5, Sun 1.30-4.30. (Closed: Good Fri, 25 & 26 Dec & 1 Jan).
☕ (ex Sun) Shop ♿ (ground floor only) &

Town Docks Museum
Queen Victoria Square
Displays include 'Whales and Whaling', 'Fishing and Trawling', 'Hull and the Humber', 'Ships and Shipping', plus Victorian Court Room.

✆ (0482) 222737.
Open: Mon-Sat 10-5, Sun 1.30-4.30. (Closed: Good Fri, 25 & 26 Dec & 1 Jan).
☕ (ex Sun) ♿ (ground floor only) Shop &

Transport & Archaeological Museum
36 High Street
Development of road transport through the ages. Archaeology of Humberside and Roman mosaics, including the Horkstow Pavement.

✆ (0482) 222737.
Open: Mon-Sat 10-5, Sun 1.30-

4.30. (Closed: Good Fri, 25 & 26 Dec & 1 Jan).
🔲 (ground floor only) Shop ✗

Wilberforce House
23-25 High Street
Early 17th-century mansion, where William Wilberforce was born, with Jacobean and Georgian rooms and slavery displays. Secluded garden.

✆ (0482) 222737.
Open: Mon-Sat 10-5, Sun 1.30-4.30. (Closed: Good Fri, 25 & 26 Dec & 1 Jan).
🔲 (ground floor only) Shop ✗

HUNTERSTON
Strathclyde (Ayrshire)   Map 10 NS15.
Hunterston Power Station
Nuclear Power Station of advanced gas-cooled reactor (AGR) type. Guided parties of about 32 taken on tours of the premises and also see video presentation on nuclear power generation.

✆ West Kilbride (0294) 823668.
Open: May-Sep Mon-Sat at 10, 11.30, 2 & 3.30, Sun 2 & 3.30 (by telephone appointment only). (Children accepted if accompanied by an adult). ✗

HUNTINGDON
Cambridgeshire   Map 4 TL27.
Cromwell Museum
Grammar School Walk
Restored Norman building, once a school where Oliver Cromwell and Samuel Pepys were taught, now Museum of Cromwellian relics.

✆ (0480) 425830.
Open: Apr-Oct, Tue-Fri 11-1 & 2-5, Sat & Sun 11-1 & 2-4; Nov-Mar, Tue-Fri 2-5, Sat 11-1 & 2-4, Sun 2-4. (Closed: BH's ex Good Fri).
Shop ✗

HUNTLY
Grampian (Aberdeenshire)
Map 15 NJ53.
Huntly Museum
The Square
Local history and changing special exhibitions every year. Governed by North East of Scotland Library Committee.

✆ Peterhead (0779) 77778.
Open: all year, Tue-Sat 10-12 & 2-4.
Shop ✗ (ex guide dogs).

ILKLEY
West Yorkshire   Map 7 SE14.
Manor House Museum
Castle Yard, Church Street
Elizabethan manor house, built on site of Roman fort, showing exposed Roman wall, collections of Roman material, archaeology and 17th- and 18th-century farmhouse parlour/kitchen furniture. Exhibitions by regional contemporary artists and craftsmen.

✆ (0943) 600066.
Open: Apr-Sep, Tue-Sun 10-6; Oct-Mar 10-5. Also open BH Mon. (Closed: Good Fri & Xmas.)
🔲 (ground floor only) Shop ✗

White Wells
Wells Road
Built on the site of a natural spring when Ilkley was a fashionable spa town. The present building (1756, restored 1972) has two plunge baths, and a display on Ilkley Moor subjects.

✆ (0943) 600066.
Open: Apr-Sep, Sat, Sun & BH's, 11-12 & 2-5.

INGLISTON
Lothian (Midlothian)   Map 11 NT17.
Scottish Agricultural Museum (National Museums of Scotland)
Royal Highland Showground
Displays of original farming tools, equipment and models showing how the land was worked and the living conditions of agricultural workers and their families in rural Scotland.

✆ 031-225 7534
Open: May-Sep, Mon-Fri 10-5, Sun 11-5.
🖵 🔲 Shop ✗ (ex guide dogs)

INVERFARIGAIG
Highland (Inverness-shire)
Map 14 NH52.
Farigaig Forest Centre
(on B852, 2½m NE of Foyers)
Set on the wooded eastern shore of Loch Ness, and housed in a converted stone stable, this Forestry Commission interpretation centre shows the development of the forest environment in the Great Glen. There are plenty of woodland walks nearby.

Hunterston 'B'

⌀ Inverness (0463) 791575.
Open: daily Apr-Oct 9.30-6.
🖾 ⩗

INVERKEITHING
Fife (Fife)   *Map 11 NT18.*
Inverkeithing Museum
The Old Friary (founded in 1384) is home of the town museum. Exhibits show the history of the Old Royal Burgh with military, industrial, religious and domestic items.

⌀ (0383) 413344.
Open: all year Wed-Sun, 11-5. ⩗

INVERNESS
Highland (Inverness-shire)
     Map 14 NH64.
Museum and Art Gallery
Castle Wynd
Museum of the Highlands' social and natural history, archaeology and culture with a very good collection of Jacobite relics, bagpipes and Highland silver. Art gallery has interesting pictures of old Inverness and frequently changing exhibitions.

⌀ (0463) 237114.
Open: all year, Mon-Sat 9-5 (ex 25 & 26 Dec & 1 & 2 Jan).
🖾 (ground floor only)
⌑ (10-4) ⩗ (ex guide dogs)

INVERURIE
Grampian (Aberdeenshire)
     Map 15 NJ72.
Inverurie Museum
Town House, The Square
Thematic displays changing at four- or six-monthly intervals. Permanent local history and archaeology exhibition. Established in 1884, this museum is now governed by the North East Scotland Library Service Committee.

⌀ Peterhead (0779) 77778.
Open: all year Mon, Tue, Thu & Fri 2-5, Sat 10-12.
Shop ⩗ (ex guide dogs)

IONA
Strathclyde (Arygll)   *Map 10 NM22.*
Iona Abbey
This tiny island became an important Christian centre when St Columba brought Christianity from Ireland in 563AD, and it is still a place of pilgrimage. On the site of St Columba's monastery is a 13th-century abbey restored during the early part of the 20th century with more rebuilding and excavations since then.

⌀ (06817) 404.
Open: accessible at all reasonable times.
(Donations)
Shop ⌑ (Mar-Oct 10-4.30) ⩗
⩗ (in abbey and other buildings)

IPSWICH
Suffolk   *Map 5 TM14.*
Christchurch Mansion
Soane Street (South side of Christchurch Park)
16th-century town house with period furnished rooms, up to 19th century. Art gallery attached with Suffolk artists collection and temporary exhibitions.

⌀ (0473) 53246 or 213761.
Open: all year (ex Xmas, Good Fri and some BH), Mon-Sat 10-5, Sun 2.30-4.30 (dusk in winter).
Guided tours by written request to Director of Recreation & Amenities, Civic Centre, Civic Drive, Ipswich.
🖾 (ground floor & gardens only) Shop ⩗

The Museum
High Street
Local geology. Prehistoric to medieval archaeology in eastern counties, and natural history collection. Asia, Africa, America and Pacific gallery with commentary plus a Roman gallery. Temporary exhibition programme.

⌀ (0473) 213761 or 263550.
Open: Mon-Sat 10-5.
(Closed: Sun, Xmas, Good Fri & some BH.)
🖾 (ground floor only) Shop ⩗

IRVINE
Strathclyde (Ayrshire)   *Map 10 NS34.*
Eglinton Castle & Gardens
Irvine Road, Kilwinning
Late 18th-century castle, built for 13th Earl of Eglinton. Castle ruin set in a 12-acre garden. Site of the famous Eglinton Tournament of 1839.

⌀ (0294) 74166.
Open: all year during daylight hours.
⌑ ⩗ 🖾

ISLE OF BUTE
Strathclyde *Bute*
See **Bute, Isle of**

ISLE OF LEWIS
Western Isles *Ross & Cromarty*
See **Lewis, Isle of**

ISLE OF MAN
See **Man, Isle of**

ISLE OF WIGHT
See **Wight, Isle of**

KEIGHLEY
West Yorkshire   *Map 7 SE04.*
Cliffe Castle Museum
Spring Gardens Lane (NW of town on A629)
Mansion of c.1878 given by Sir Bracewell Smith. Contains collections of natural and local history, dolls, ceramics, geological gallery, craft workshops, and interesting exhibitions programme. Play area and aviary in adjacent park. French furniture from Victoria and Albert Museum.

☏ (0274) 64184.
Open: Apr-Sep, Tue-Sun
10-6; Oct-Mar, Tue-Sun 10-5.
Also open BH Mons.
(Closed: Good Fri & Xmas).
⌨ Shop ✗ (ex guide dogs)
♿ (ground floor only)

KEITH
Grampian (Banffshire)   Map 15 NJ45.
Strathisla Distillery, Chivas Bros Ltd
Station Road
Claimed to be the oldest established distillery in Scotland, dating from 1786. Visitors are given a tour through various parts and shown a film. Whisky sampling may be available to visitors.

☏ (05422) 7471.
Open: Jun-early Sep, Mon-Fri 9-4.30 (other times by arrangement). Parties over 10 in number not accepted.
⌨ ✗

KELSO
Borders (Roxburghshire)
*   Map 12 NT73.*
Kelso Abbey
Little but the abbey church remains, and that only in imposing fragments which seem to consist almost wholly of Norman and Transitional work.

Open: standard times, see p4.
♿ (AM)

KESWICK
Cumbria   Map 11 NY22.
Castlerigg Stone Circle
(1½m E on unclass road)
Dating from neolithic and post neolithic periods these 38 standing stones are thought to have been constructed for religious or otherwise ceremonial meetings. A further 10 stones nearby form a rectangle.

Open: accessible at all reasonable times.
(AM)

KETTERING
Northamptonshire   Map 4 SP87.
Alfred East Art Gallery
Sheep Street
Approximately 12 exhibitions visit the gallery each year, each lasting for about three weeks.

☏ (0536) 85211.
Open: Mon-Sat 10-5. ♿ ✗

KEYHAVEN
Hampshire   Map 4 SZ39.
Keyhaven, Pennington and Hurst (Nature Reserve)
Area of mudflats, marshes and old salterns notable for its breeding seabirds including little, common and sandwich terns and also the black-headed gull. Golden samphire, yellow horned poppy and sea kale are among the shingle plants. Visitors must keep to the sea wall footpath (Solent Way) during the breeding season. Access at Keyhaven and at Lymington.

Open: accessible at all reasonable times.

KILMARNOCK
Strathclyde (Ayrshire)   Map 10 NS43.
Dick Institute
Elmbank Avenue
Exhibits of geology (including fossils), small arms, shells, ethnography, numismatics, and archaeological specimens. Also art gallery, (paintings and etchings) and library containing Ayrshire and Burns printed books.

☏ (0563) 26401.
Open: May-Sep; Mon, Tue, Thu & Fri 10-8, Wed & Sat 10-5; Oct-Apr Mon-Sat 10-5.
Details not confirmed for 1988.
♿ ✗

John Walker & Sons Limited
Hill Street
Home of the world's largest selling Scotch whisky. Tour begins with visit to Barleith to see the blending of whiskies from all over Scotland, and repair of oak casks by coopers, followed by a tour through the bottling halls at Kilmarnock.

☏ (0563) 23401.
Open: Mon-Fri; tours 10.15 & 2 ex Fri 1.45pm (ex company holidays). Minimum age 14 years, telephone in advance if more than family.
✗

KILMARTIN
Strathclyde (Argyll)   Map 10 NR89.
Dunadd Fort
(3m S, off A816)
A prehistoric hillfort incorporating walled enclosures. It was once the capital of the ancient Scots kingdom of Dalriada.

Open: at all reasonable times.
(AM)

KILMUN
Strathclyde (Argyll)   Map 10 NS18.
Kilmun Arboretum & Forest Plots
(on A880 1m from junc with A815)
A large collection of conifer and broadleaved tree species planted in plots and specimen groups. Established by the Forestry Commission in 1930 and now extending to 200 acres on a hillside overlooking the Holy Loch. Guidebooks available at the nearby Forestry Commission Office.

☏ (036984) 666.
Open: all year

KILSYTH
Strathclyde (Stirlingshire)
*   Map 11 NS77.*
Colzium House & Estate
Partly a museum, with attractive walled garden. Ice

house and old castle associated with Montrose's victory over the Covenanters in 1645.

℘ (0236) 823281.
House open: Etr weekend-Sep, Mon-Fri 9-5, Sun 10-6. (Closed when booked for private functions). Grounds open at all times, Museum open Wed 2-8.
☐ ⊼ 🖰 (ground floor & gardens only) ⚹ (in house)

KINGSTON ST MARY
Somerset   *Map 3 ST23.*
Fyne Court
(3m N)
Nature reserve for associated species of plants, with nature trails, guided walks, arboretum and countryside interpretation centre. Events through the summer, mostly free.

℘ Kingston St Mary (082345) 587.
Open: daily 9-6.
⚹

KINGUSSIE
Highland (Inverness-shire)
                   Map 14 NH70.
Ruthven Barracks
(½m SE of Kingussie)
The best preserved of the four infantry barracks built by the Hanovarian Government in the Highlands following the Jacobite uprising of 1715.

Open: at any reasonable time.
(AM)

KIRKCALDY
Fife (Fife)   *Map 11 NT29.*
Museum & Art Gallery
War Memorial Grounds (next to Kirkcaldy Station)
A unique collection of fine Scottish paintings, historical displays and a full programme of changing art, craft and local history exhibitions. Temporary exhibitions throughout the year.

℘ (0592) 260732.
Open: Mon-Sat 11-5, Sun 2-5. (Closed local Hols).
⊼ 🖰 (ground floor only) Shop ⚹

John McDouall Stuart Museum
Rectory Lane, Dysart
Set in the National Trust restored 18th-century house which was the birthplace of John McDouall Stuart (1815-1866) the first explorer to cross Australia. The award winning display describes his journeys and the Australian wilderness.

℘ (0592) 260732.
Open: Jun-Aug daily 2-5.
Shop ⚹

KIRKHILL
Highland (Inverness-shire)
                   Map 14 NH54.
Moniack Castle (Highland Winery)
Seven miles from Inverness on the A862 Beauly road
Once a fortress of the Lovat chiefs and their kin, it is today the centre of an enterprise unique in Scotland – that of commercial wine making. The winery produces a wide range of wines including "country wines" such as Elder Flower and Silver Birch, also two liqueurs, mead and sloe gin. An additional feature is the Wine Bar/Bistro.

℘ Drumchardine (046383) 283.
Open: Mon-Sat 10-5.
☐ (licensed) ⊼ Shop.

KIRKWALL
See **Orkney**

KNOCKANDO
Grampian (Moray)   *Map 15 NJ14.*
Tamdhu Distillery
Visitors are able to see the complete process of whisky being made.

℘ Carron (03406) 221.
Open: Etr-May, Mon-Fri 10-4. Jun-Sep, Mon-Sat 10-4. Details not confirmed for 1988.
🖰 (ground floor only) Shop

KNOWLTON
Dorset   *Map 4 SU01.*
Knowlton Circles
(3¼m SW of Cranborne on B3078)
Three large henge circles lying in a row, the eastern one is disected by the B3078 and measures 800ft across. The ruinous Norman Knowlton Church stands in the middle of the centre circle. There are several round barrows nearby.

Open: accessible at all reasonable times.
(AM)

LAKE VYRNWY
Powys   *Map 6 SJ01.*
(SE of Bala on B4393)
Large artificial lake with an interesting dam. Focal point for a Royal Society for the Protection of Birds reserve covering 16,000 acres, with two RSPB nature trails and 3 hides. Wildlife display at Visitor Centre at the southern end of the lake, plus information on the area before and after the lake was formed.

℘ Llanwddyn (069173) 278.
Visitor Centre open: Weekdays 12-6. Sun 11-6.
⊼ 🖰 (spinal-disabled bird watching look-out.) (Visitor Centre)

LAMB HOLM
See **Orkney**

LANCASTER
Lancashire   *Map 7 SD46.*
City Museum
Market Square
Georgian building with archaeology, history collec-

tions and Museum of the King's Own Royal Lancaster Regiment.

∅ (0524) 64637.
Open: daily Mon-Fri 10-5, Sat 10-3. (Closed: Xmas & New Year).
🔲 (ground floor only) Shop
🐕

LEAMINGTON SPA
Warwickshire   Map 4 SP36.
Warwick District Council Art Gallery & Museum
Avenue Road
The art gallery specialises in British, Dutch and Flemish paintings and watercolours of the 16th to 20th century. The museum contains ceramics, Delft, Wedgwood, Whieldon, Worcester, Derby Ware etc, and an 18th-century glass collection. Temporary exhibitions.

∅ (0926) 26559.
Open: Mon-Sat 10-1 & 2-5; also Thu evenings 6-8. (Closed: Good Fri, Xmas & New Year's Day).
🔲 🐕 (ex guide dogs).

LEEDS
West Yorkshire   Map 8 SE23.
Kirkstall Abbey
Abbey Road
Extensive and impressive ruins of abbey founded in 12th century by Cistercian monks from Fountains Abbey. The chapter house, cloisters and abbot's lodgings are of interest.

∅ Leeds (0532) 755821.
Open: daily, dawn-dusk.
🔲

Leeds City Art Gallery
The Headrow
Permanent collection of Victorian and 20th-century paintings and sculpture, including work by Renoir, Courbet, Sisley, Bonnard, Vuillard and Derain, and En-

glish watercolours. Also here, the Henry Moore Centre for the Study of Sculpture shows how sculptors have lived and worked in different times and countries.

∅ (0532) 462495.
Open: Mon, Tue, Thu, Fri 10-6, Wed 10-9, Sat 10-4, Sun 2-5. (Closed: Xmas, Boxing Day & 1 Jan).
🔲 🖵

Roundhay Park (Canal Gardens)
Eighty-foot fountain, Coronation House and glasshouse, with Canal Gardens, rose gardens, a tropical plant house and an aquarium.

∅ (0532) 661850.
Open: daily, 9-dusk. Details not confirmed for 1988.
🖵 🔲

LEICESTER
Leicestershire   Map 4 SK50.
Belgrave Hall
Off Thurcaston Road (1m N) Not on plan
A fine early 18th-century house and gardens, now a museum with furnishings, stables with coaches and an agricultural collection.

∅ (0533) 666590.
Open: all year Mon-Sat 10-5.30, Sun 2-5.30. (Closed: Good Fri & Xmas).
🔲 (ground floor & gardens only) Shop 🐕 (ex guide dogs)

Guildhall
Guildhall Lane.   Plan: B3.
Medieval Guildhall and later the Town Hall of Leicester, Great Hall, Mayor's Parlour, Library and police cells.

∅ (0533) 554100.
Open: all year Mon-Fri & Sat 10-5.30, Sun 2-5.30. (Closed: Good Fri and 25 & 26 Dec).
Shop 🐕

Jewry Wall Museum & Site
St Nicholas Circle.   Plan: A4.
Museum of archaeology from prehistoric times to 1500. Remains of Roman baths and Jewry Wall.

∅ (0533) 544766.
Open: all year Mon-Sat 10-5.30, Sun 2-5.30. (Closed: Good Fri and 25 & 26 Dec)
Jewry Wall open: at any reasonable time.
🔲 (ground floor only) Shop
🐕 (ex guide dogs)

John Doran Museum
East Midland Gas, Leicester Service Centre, Aylestone Road (½m S on A426) Not on plan.
Housed in an historic building (a part of the Aylestone Road Gasworks) the collection shows all aspects of the history of the manufacture, distribution and use of gas, with documentary material as well as old appliances and equipment.

∅ (0533) 549414 Ext 2192.
Open: Tue-Fri 12.30-4.30. (Closed: BH's & Tue following BH Mon).
🔲 (ground floor only)

Leicestershire Museum & Art Gallery
New Walk.   Plan: D2.
Collections of 18th- to 20th-century English paintings and drawings, unique collection of 20th-century German Expressionist art, ceramics, silver, Egyptology. New geology and natural history environmental galleries in preparation. Extensive reference and study collections in Art and Natural Sciences with a very active educational programme.

∅ (0533) 554100.
Open: all year Mon-Sat 10-5.30, Sun 2-5.30. (Closed: Good Fri & Xmas).
🔲 Shop 🐕 (ex guide dogs)

Leicester Museum of Technology

Abbey Pumping Station. Corporation Road (1m N, off A5131) Not on plan.
Knitting gallery, power gallery, transport items, steam shovel. Original beam engines of 1891.

✆ (0533) 661330.
Open: all year Mon-Sat

10-5.30, Sun 2-5.30. (Closed: Good Fri & Xmas).
♿ (except beam engines)
Shop ✗ (ex guide dogs)

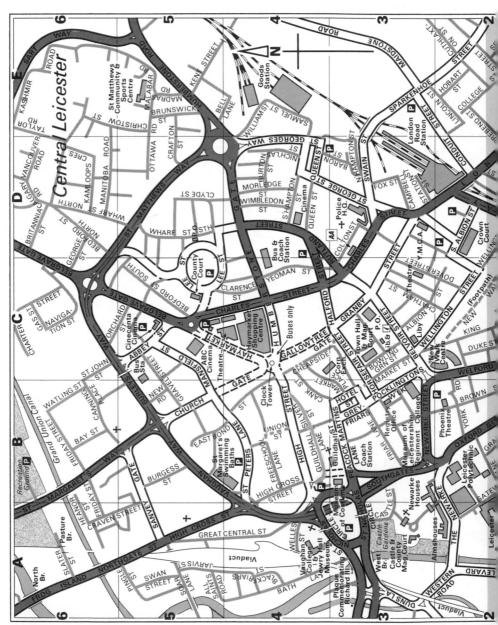

Leicestershire Record Office

57 New Walk.   Plan : **E1.**
Extensive collection of official and private archives, both rural and urban, relating

to the County of Leicestershire.

℘ (0533) 544566.
Open: Mon-Thu 9.15-5, Fri 9.15-4.45, Sat 9.15-12.15. (Closed: Sun & BH wknds Sat-Tue).
🅖 Shop ✗

Museum of Royal Leicestershire Regiment

Oxford Street.   Plan : **B3.**
Housed in Magazine Gateway the museum contains mementos, battle trophies and relics of the Leicestershire Regiment.

℘ (0533) 555889.
Open: Mon-Sat 10-5.30, Sun 2-5.30. (Closed: Good Fri & Xmas).
Shop ✗

Newarke Houses

The Newarke.   Plan : **B3.**
Social history of the city from 1500 to present day. 19th-century street scene. 17th-century room, local clocks, musical instruments.

℘ (0533) 554100.
Open: Mon-Sat 10-5.30, Sun 2-5.30. (Closed: Good Fri & Xmas).
🅖 (ground floor and gardens only) Shop ✗ (ex guide dogs)

University of Leicester Botanic Gardens

Beaumont Hall, Stoughton Drive South, Oadby (3½m SE, A6) Not on plan.
The gardens occupy an area of about 16 acres and include botanical greenhouses, rose, rock, water and sunken gardens, trees, herbaceous borders and a heather garden. They comprise the grounds of four houses; Beaumont, Southmeade, Hastings and The Knoll, which are used as student residences.

℘ (0533) 717725.
Open: Mon-Fri 10-4.30. (3.30 Fri).
🅖 plant sales ✗

Wygston's House Musuem of Costume

Applegate.   Plan : **B3.**
Displays of English costume from 1769 to 1924. Reconstruction of draper's, milliner's and shoe shops of 1920s.

℘ (0533) 554100.
Open: Mon-Thu 10-5.30, Sun 2-5.30. (Closed: Good Fri & Xmas).
🅖 (ground floor only) Shop ✗ (ex guide dogs)

LEIGH

Gt Manchester   Map 7 SJ69.
Pennington Flash Country Park

(1¼m SW on A572)
Once a derelict coalmining wasteland, now a 1000-acre country park including the Flash, a 170-acre lake, numerous footpaths, thousands of young trees and nature reserve, where a great variety of birds can be observed. The Information Centre has an exhibition on park wildlife.

℘ (0942) 828116
Open: Country Park accessible at all reasonable times.
Information Centre: All year, weekends at all reasonable times. (Closed Xmas)
🅖 ⌨ 🛋

LEISTON

Suffolk   Map 5 TM46.
Leiston Abbey

Remains of this 14th-century abbey include choir and transepts of church, and ranges of cloisters. Georgian house built into the fabric of the abbey.

Open: accessible at any reasonable time.
(AM)

LERWICK
see **Shetland**

LETCHWORTH
Hertfordshire   *Map 4 TL23.*
First Garden City Museum
296 Norton Way South
Thatched house with extension, containing the original offices of the architects of the Garden City, Barry Parker and Raymond Unwin. Displays explain the concept and development of Letchworth as the First Garden City.

⌀ (0462) 685647.
Open: Mon-Fri 2-4.30, Sat 10-1 & 2-4. Other times by arrangement.
⌷ (ground floor only) Shop
⌖

Museum & Art Gallery
Broadway
Museum contains displays of archaeological material of North Hertfordshire including important Iron Age and Roman finds from Baldock. Natural history gallery. Monthly art exhibitions.

⌀ (0462) 685647.
Open: Mon-Sat 10-5. (Closed BHs).
⌷ (ground floor only) Shop
⌖

Lewis (Isle of)
CALLANISH
          Map 13 NB23.
Callanish Standing Stones
Unique collection of megaliths comprising an avenue 27 ft in width, with 19 standing stones, terminating in a 37 ft-wide circle containing 13 additional stones. Other stones, burial cairns and circles may be seen in the near vicinity.

Open: accessible at all times.
(AM)

CARLOWAY
          Map 13 NB24.
Dun Carloway Broch
Well preserved broch of late prehistoric, about 30ft in height, one of the finest in the Western Isles.

Open: see page 4.
(AM)

LICHFIELD
Staffordshire   *Map 7 SK10.*
Lichfield Cathedral
Noted for its three graceful spires called the Ladies of the Vale. Begun in 1195, it was badly damaged during the Civil War, but three centuries of caring restoration have resulted in its present splendid condition. The Lady Chapel has lovely 16th-century stained glass windows.

Open: Mon-Sat 9-3.30, Sun 9-5.30. Details not confirmed for 1988.

Museum of the Staffordshire Regiment
(The Prince of Wales's) (3m SE)
Uniforms, badges and weapons, relics from the Sikh Wars, Crimea, Egypt, Sudan, South Africa and both World Wars. A medal display includes 8 of the 13 Victorian Crosses awarded to men of the Regiment, dating back to 1705.

⌀ Whittington (0543) 433333 Ext 240.
Open: Mon-Fri 8.30-4.30.
⌷

Solid Fuel Advisory Service Shire Horse Stables
Units 1 & 2, Birmingham Road
The shire horses of the Solid Fuel Advisory Service in their working environment, with the harness and vehicles they pull and a permanent display of solid fuel and appliances.

⌀ (05432) 52809.
Open: daily 9-4. (Closed Xmas Day).

LINCOLN
Lincolnshire   *Map 8 SK97.*
Lincoln Cathedral
The west front is Norman, the transept, nave, St Hugh's Choir and Angel Choir date mostly from the 13th century. Its three towers dominate the skyline for many miles.

⌀ (0522) 30320/44544.
Open: daily Apr-Sep 7.15am-8pm; Oct-Mar 7.15-6.
⌷ ⌷

LINDSEY
Suffolk   *Map 5 TL94.*
St James's Chapel
Rose Green
Small thatched flint and stone chapel, built in the 13th century.

Open: See page 4.
(AM)

LINLITHGOW
Lothian (West Lothian)   *Map 11 NT07.*
Beecraigs Country Park
(2m S on unclass road)
700-acre pine woodland country park, honeycombed with waymarked paths. Trout farm where visitors can feed the thousands of trout in the rearing ponds; red deer farm with walkway and viewing platform. Leisure-courses include archery, fishing, canoeing, sailing and orienteering. An AA viewpoint on Cockleroy Hill (913ft) gives far reaching views to the Bass Rock and to Great Fell on Arran.

⌀ (050684) 4516.
Open: Country Park accessible at all reasonable times; Park Centre Apr-Oct, Mon-Thu 9-5, Fri 9-4, Sat & Sun 10-6; Nov-Mar, Mon-Fri 9-5, Sat 11-4.
⌖

LITTLEHAMPTON

West Sussex   *Map 7 SJ39*

Littlehampton Museum

12A River Road

A Sea Captain's home overlooking the harbour offers local history with a maritime flavour. Fine ship paintings, early photos of town and river, historic maps, local archaeology of the Stone Age, Bronze Age and Roman times. Museum garden being restored. Temporary exhibitions every two months throughout year.

☎ (0903) 715149.
Open: Tue-Sat (also summer BH); 10.30-1 & 2-4.
♿ (ground floor only) Shop

LIVERPOOL

Merseyside   *Map 7 SJ39.*

Anglican Cathedral

The largest Anglican cathedral in the world: notable features include the Gothic arches (the highest ever built), the peals of bells (the highest and heaviest in the world), the cathedral organ (which has nearly 10,000 pipes), and the stained glass windows, one of which contains some 18,000 sq ft of glass. Architect Giles Gilbert Scott supervised the construction for more than half a century, and has a memorial in the cathedral. The foundation stone was laid in 1904 by King Edward VII, and the cathedral was finally completed and consecrated in October 1978, in the presence of HM Queen Elizabeth II.

☎ 051-709 6271.
Open: daily 9-6.
(Donations)
♿

Bluecoat Chambers

School Lane

A fine Queen Anne building in Liverpool's city centre with cobbled quadrangle and garden courtyard. Built as a charity school in 1717, it now houses a gallery, concert hall, artists' studio and craft shop.

☎ 051-709 5297.
Open: Mon-Sat 9-6.
Bluecoat gallery Tue-Sat 10.30-5. (Closed: Xmas, & BH's).
♿ (licensed) ♿

Liverpool City Libraries

William Brown Street

One of the oldest and largest public libraries in the country, with over two million books. Temporary Exhibitions.

☎ 051-207 2147.
Open: Mon-Fri 9-9.
Guided tours by prior arrangement.
♿ ♿ ✂

Metropolitan Cathedral (Roman Catholic)

Plans to build a cathedral here go back to the mid-19th century, but the existing structure was only consecrated in 1967 after five years of building. The most striking feature is the Lantern Tower, containing over 25,000 pieces of stained glass in a continuous progression of every colour of the spectrum.

Lichfield's shire horses

Liverpool: decoration in Anglican Cathedral

✆ 051-709 9222.
Open: daily 8-6.
(Donations)
🍴 🖈

Open Eye Gallery
90-92 Whitechapel
A constantly changing programme of photographic exhibitions.

✆ 051-709 9460.
Open: Mon-Sat 10-5.30.
(Closed Xmas).

Sudley Art Gallery
Mossley Hill Road
Contains the Emma Holt Bequest of fine 19th-century British paintings and sculpture.

✆ 051-724 3245.
Open: Mon-Sat 10-5, Sun 2-5.
(Closed: Good Fri, 24-26 Dec & New Year's day).
(Donation)

Walker Art Gallery
William Brown Street
Outstanding general collection of European paintings,
sculpture and drawings dating from 1300 to the present day, especially notable for Italian and Netherlandish paintings. Temporary exhibitions throughout year.

✆ 051-207 0001 Ext 264.
Open: Mon-Sat 10-5, Sun 2-5.
(Closed: Good Fri, 24-26 Dec & New Year's Day).
(Donation)
🖈 (Prior notice appreciated)
Shop ✄

LIVINGSTON
Lothian (West Lothian)   Map 11 NT06.
Almondell & Calderwood Country Park
(1m E on B7015 & B8046)
Consisting of two adjoining estates formally owned by the Earl of Buchan and Lord Torphichen, with a variety of wildlife, wild flowers and birds. Over four miles of paths have been constructed, with a nature trail. Spring and early summer are the best times to visit for fine displays of daffodils and rhododendrons. There is a visitors' centre at Stables Cottage.

✆ Mid Calder (0506) 882254.
Open: Country Park accessible at all reasonable times; Visitor Centre Apr-Sep Mon-Wed 9-12, 1-5, Thu 9-12, 1-4, Sun 10.30-12, 1-6. Oct-May Mon-Thu 9-12, 1-5, Sun 10-12, 1-4.30.
🖈 (Disabled visitors please ring ahead to ensure the gate will be opened.) 🍴 (✄ in visitor centre).

LLANALLGO
Gwynedd   Map 6 SH48.
Din Lligwy Ancient Village
(1m NW off A5205)
Remains of 4th-century village, with two circular and seven rectangular buildings encircled by pentagonal stone wall.
Open: accessible at all reasonable times.
(AM CADW)

LLANBERIS
Gwynedd   Map 6 SH56.
Dolbadarn Castle
Native Welsh stronghold with a three-storey, 13th-century round tower.

Open: accessible at all reasonable times.
(AM CADW)

Oriel Eyri
The aim of this purpose-built centre is to interpret the rich natural environment of Snowdonia and to illustrate the relationship between man and his surroundings. A variety of exhibitions is staged throughout the year.

✆ (0286) 870636
Open: Jun-Sep, Mon-Sat 10-5, Sun 1.30-5.
🖈 Shop ✄

LLANDRINDOD WELLS
Powys   Map 3 SO06.
Llandrindod Wells Museum
Temple Street
Archaeological exhibits, and objects excavated from Roman Camp at Castell Collen to north of town. Paterson doll collection is on show. Victorian Spa gallery with period costume and 19th-century chemist's equipment. Temporary exhibitions throughout the year.

✆ (0597) 4513.
Open: all year Mon-Fri 10-12.30 & 2-5, Sat 10-12.30 also 2-5 May-Sep.
🖈 (ground floor only) Shop ✄

Rock Park Spa
Norton Terrace
Situated in an 18-acre wooded park, the Pump Room has been restored to

its former glory and refurbished in Edwardian style, complete with pumps providing three spa waters for anyone to sample. In the Bath House there is an exhibition of the history of the spa and others in Wales (Craft markets on BHs only).

✆ (0597) 4307.
Open: daily Apr-Oct 10-6 (other times by arrangement).
♿ ☕

LLANELLI

Dyfed *Map 2 SN50.*

Parc Howard Art Gallery & Museum

Situated in a pleasant park, and containing paintings. Llanelli pottery and museum exhibits. From Mar-Oct a programme of exhibitions of paintings, porcelain, sculpture etc is in operation.

✆ (0554) 773538.
Open: daily Oct-Mar 10-4.30, Apr-Sep 10-6.
☕ Shop 🚫

LLANFIHANGEL-Y-PENNANT

Gwynedd *Map 6 SH60.*

Castell y Bere

(NW of Abergynolwyn on unclass road)

Built by Llywelyn the Great in 1221, Castell y Bere is a keep and bailey castle with two D-shape towers, a typical feature of Welsh castles. Although many of the walls are low there is some fine carved stonework still to be seen.

Open: accessible at all reasonable times.
(AM CADW)

LLANGYBI

Gwynedd *Map 6 SH44.*

St Cybi's Well

Rectangular structure, known also as Ffynnon Gybi, with dry-stone structure covering adjacent pool. Interior has wall niches and the corbelled beehive vaulting of a characteristically Irish type is unique in Wales.

Open: accessible at all reasonable times.
(AM CADW)

LLANIDLOES

Powys *Map 6 SN98.*

Old Market Hall

Hall-timbered building, standing in open arches, with museum on upper floor.

✆ Welshpool (0938) 4759.
Open: Etr, then Spring BH-Sep daily 11-1 & 2-5.
☕ 🚫

LLANSTEPHAN

Dyfed *Map 2 SN31.*

Llanstephan Castle

Remains of 11th- to 13th-century stronghold on west side of Towy estuary.

Open: accessible at all reasonable times.
(AM CADW)

LLANTHONY

Gwent *Map 3 SO22.*

Llanthony Priory

Augustinian foundation c. 1108 most of the present structure being 12th- or 13th-century and including west towers, north nave arcade and south transept. Former Priest's House is now a hotel. The Honddhu valley scenery in the Black Mountains is very picturesque but roads are narrow especially northwards towards lofty Gospel Pass leading to Hay-on-Wye.

Open: at all reasonable times.
(AM CADW)

LLANTILIO CROSSENNY

Gwent *Map 3 SO31.*

Hen Gwrt

(off B4233)

Rectangular enclosure of medieval house which is still surrounded by moat.

Open: at any reasonable time.
(AM CADW)

LLANTWIT MAJOR

South Glamorgan *Map 3 SS96.*

Town Hall

Originally 12th- and largely 17th-century medieval courthouse and market, known once as the 'Church Loft'. Retains original plan and comprises two storeys, curfew bell now in church.

✆ (04465) 37707.
Open: all year Mon-Fri 9-4, by appointment.
🚫

LLANWRTYD WELLS

Powys *Map 3 SN84.*

Cambrian Factory

A sheltered workshop employing disabled persons operated by Powys County Council and the Royal British Legion. Visitors can see an outstanding example of a working mill and all the manufacturing processes including wool sorting, dyeing, carding, spinning, warping, winding and weaving.

✆ (05913) 211.
Open: Mill, all year Mon-Thu, 8.15-4.30, Fri 8.15-2.45. (Closed: weekends & BH.) Shop Mon-Fri, 8.15-5.15; Sat May-Sep 9-4.30, Oct-Apr 9-noon (Closed: Sun & Xmas.)

LOCHCARRON

Highland (Ross and Cromarty) *Map 14 NG83.*

Strome Castle

(3m SE)

A fragmentary ruin of a stronghold of the Macdonalds of Glengarry, blown up by Kenneth Mackenzie of Kintail in 1602. There are wide views across the Inner Sound to

Scalpay, Raasay and the Coolins of Skye.

Open: accessible at all reasonable times.
(NTS)

LOCH GARTEN
Highland (Inverness-shire)
Map 14 NH91.
(2m E of Boat of Garten off B970)
The reserve became famous when ospreys returned here in the 1950's and they are still breeding on the north side of the loch. Access in that area is restricted to the sign-posted path and the observation hide where the birds can be viewed through tele-scopes. Other breeding birds include capercaillies, crested tits, red starts, siskins and Scottish crossbills. Red and roe deer are common, as are red squirrels.

⊘ Boat of Garten (047983) 694.
Open: Reserve, accessible at all reasonable times.

LOCHGILPHEAD
Strathclyde (Argyll)   Map 10 NR88.
Kilmory Castle Gardens
Thirty acres of grounds sur-rounding the castle. Many rare trees and shrubs have survived years of neglect, but the 18th-century gardens are being restored by the present owners. Woodland walks and nature trails.

⊘ (0546) 2127.
Open: all year, dawn to dusk.
🅰 (gardens only) ⊗

LOCHORE MEADOWS COUNTRY PARK
Fife (Fife)   Map 11 NT19.
(1½m N of Lochgelly on B920)
Developed on a mining wasteland, the country park covers nearly 1,000 acres and is dominated by Loch

Ore. There are numerous trails, paths and other re-creational facilities including sailing, canoeing, fishing and a nature reserve. The visitor centre has an interpretative display.

⊘ Ballingry (0592) 860086.
Open: Park Centre daily Apr-Sep 9-8, Oct-Mar 9-4.30.
🅰 ⊑ 𝔸 (⊗ in park centre)

LOCHWINNOCH
Strathclyde (Renfrewshire)
Map 10 NS35.
Lochwinnoch Community Museum
Main Street
A series of changing exhibi-tions reflecting the historic background of local agricul-ture, industry and village life.

⊘ (0505) 842615.
Open: Mon-Wed & Fri 10-1, 2-5 & 6-8, Sat 10-1 & 2-5.
🅰 ⊗

LOGGERHEADS
Clwyd   Map 7 SJ16.
Loggerheads Country Park
(on A494 between Ruthin and Mold)
A 67-acre country park in the valley of the River Alyn, which sometimes disappears down 'swallow holes' in the limestone country in dry weather. There is a 1½-mile nature trail and a restored corn mill near the information centre. A variety of wood-land birds may be seen.

⊘ Llanferres (035 285) 586.
Open: Country Park, accessible at all reasonable times; information centre most summer weekends; corn mill by prior arrangement.

LONDON *Greater London.*
Plans 1 & 2 pages 74 to 77.
Places within the London postal area are listed below in postal district order under East, North, South and West. Other places within Greater London or the surrounding area are listed under their respec-tive place names.

Plan 1 covers Central Lon-don. A grid reference is given for each place, eg: **Guildhall** Plan 1 : **F4.**

Plan 2 covers the surround-ing area. Each place has a number — marked on the map — followed by a grid re-ference eg. **Keats House** Plan 2 : **12 D4.**

═══════ EAST ═══════

E2
Bethnal Green Museum of Childhood
Cambridge Heath Road
Plan 2 : **2** E4.
A branch of the Victoria and Albert Museum. Its chief ex-hibits are toys, dolls and dolls' houses, model soldiers, puppets, games, model theatres, wedding dresses and children's costume.

⊘ 01-980 2415.
Open: Mon-Thu & Sat 10-6, Sun 2.30-6. (Closed: Fri, May Day, Spring BH Mon, 24-26 Dec & New Year's Day.)
🅰 (prior arrangement) Shop ⊗ (ex guide dogs)

Geffrye Museum
Kingsland Road   Plan 2 : **3** E4.
A collection of furniture and woodwork from the Eli-zabethan period to 1939, in-cluding a reconstruction of John Evelyn's 'closet of curiosities', contained in the former almhouses built c. 1713.

✆ 01-739 9893.
Open: Tue-Sat 10-5 Sun 2-5,
BH Mons 10-5. (Closed: Mon,
Good Fri, 24-26 Dec & New
Year's Day.)
⌨ 🖐 (ground floor only)
Shop ⚲

E6

Interpretative Centre, St Mary Magdalene Churchyard Nature Reserve

Norman Road   Plan 2 : **4 F4.**
Displays relating to natural
history and history of an interesting churchyard nature
reserve.

✆ 01-470 4525.
Interpretative Centre open:
Tue, Thu, Sat & Sun 2-5.
Nature Reserve open
summer
Mon-Fri 9-5, wknds 2-5,
winter Mon-Fri 9-4, wknds
2-4.
🖐 (ground floor only) Shop
⚲

E15

Passmore Edwards Museum

Romford Road   Plan 2 : **6 F4.**
Greater London and Essex
archaeology, biology, geology and history. Special exhibitions.

✆ 01-519 4296.
Open: Mon-Fri 10-5, Sat 10-1
& 2-5, Sun & BH 2-5.
🖐 (ground floor only) Shop
⚲

E16

North Woolwich Old Station Museum

Pier Road   Plan 2 : **7 F3.**
Imposing restored station
building with three galleries
of photographs, models, an
original turntable pit. From
Apr-Oct, on the first Sunday
in the month, a locomotive is
in steam.

✆ 01-474 7244.
Open: Mon-Sat, 10-5; Sun &
BH 2-5.
🖐 Shop ⚲

E17

Vestry House Museum of Local History

*Vestry Road, near
Hoe Street*   Plan 2 : **8 E5.**
A small museum located in a
former 18th-century work-
house standing in the conservation area 'Walthamstow
Village'. Historical items of
local interest from the Stone
Age onwards include a re-
constructed Victorian parlour. The Bremer Car, probably the first British internal
combustion engine car seen.
Local archives are available
for consultation by appointment.

✆ 01-527 5544 Ext 4391
or 01-509 1917.
Open: Mon-Fri 10-1, Sat 10-1
& 2-5.30. (Closed: BH) Details
not confirmed for 1988
🖐 (ground floor only) Shop
⚲

William Morris Gallery

*Water House, Lloyd Park,
Forest Road*   Plan 2 : **9 E5.**
William Morris lived in this
house, known as 'Water
House' from 1848-56. There
are exhibits of his fabrics,
wallpapers and furniture.
Also ceramics by William de
Morgan, furniture by Gimson
and Barnsley and work by
Mackmurdo and the Century
Guild. Pre-Raphaelite pic-
tures, sculpture by Rodin.
Events throughout the year.

✆ 01-527 5544 Ext 4390.
Open: Tue-Sat 10-1 & 2-5, and
1st Sun in each month 10-12 &
2-5. (Closed: Mon & BHs.)
🖐 (ground floor & gardens)
Shop ⚲

EC1

Museum of the Order of St John

*St John's Gate,
St John's Ln*   Plan 1 : **E5**
16th century Gatehouse, former entrance to the medieval Priory of the Order of St
John of Jerusalem. Now headquarters of the Modern
Order, whose charitable
foundations include St John
Ambulance and the Ophthal-
mic Hospital in Jerusalem.
Norman Crypt and 15th century Grand Priory Church.
The collections include
paintings, silver, furniture,
medals, insignia, and a collection relating to the St John
Ambulance, including medi-
cal instruments, photographs,
uniforms and personal
memorabilia of St John personalities and pioneers with
special features on the St
John Ambulance role in the
Boer War and World Wars.

✆ 01-2536 644 Ext 35.
Open Tue & Fri 10-6, Sat 10-4.
(Closed Etr, Xmas wk and
BH's). Guided tours 11 and
2.30.
Donations
🖐 (ground floor only) Shop

National Postal Museum

*King Edward Building, King
Edward St*   Plan 1 : **F4.**
Contains probably the finest
and most comprehensive
collection of postage stamps
in the world. Included are:
the RM Phillips collection of
19th-century Great Britain
(with special emphasis on the
One Penny Black and its
creation); the Post Office
Collection; a world-wide collection including practically
every stamp issued since
1878; and the philatelic cor-
respondence archives of
Thomas de la Rue and Co
who furnished stamps to over
150 countries between 1855
and 1965. Within these col-

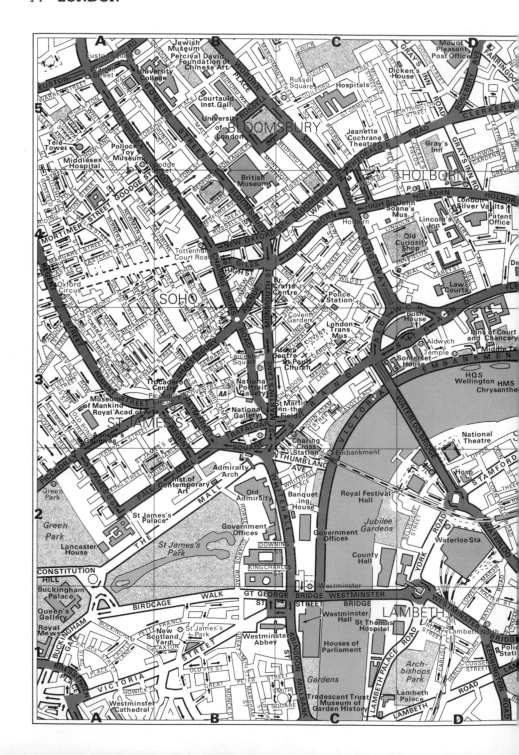

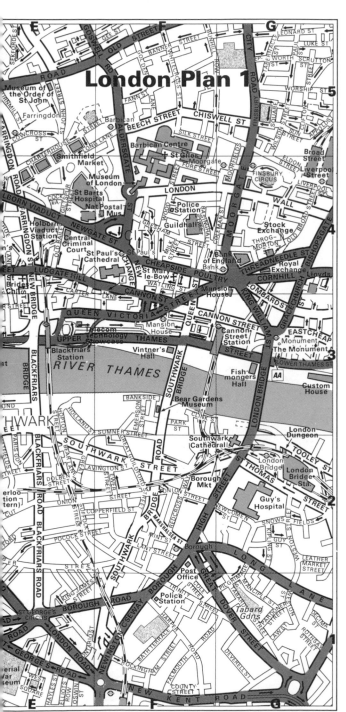

London Plan 1

lections are thousands of original drawings and unique proof sheets of every British stamp since 1840. Special exhibitions, and visits for up to 40 people may be arranged, with a guide and film show. Exhibition to mark 150th anniversary of the 'Travelling Post Office' system throughout 1988.

✆ 01-606 3769 & 01-432 3851. Open: Mon-Thu (ex BH) 9.30-4.30, Fri 9.30-4. ♿ (ground floor only) Shop 🚫

EC2

Guildhall

Plan 1 : **F4.**
Rebuilt in 1411 but only the walls of the great hall, porch and crypt survive from the medieval building. It was severely damaged in the Great Fire and the Blitz. Restoration work, completed in 1954 was carried out to designs by Sir Giles Scott. Here the Court of Common Council, which administers the city, meets and entertains. The **Guildhall Library** contains an unrivalled collection of books, manuscripts, and illustrations on all aspects of London. The **Guildhall Clock Museum** with 700 exhibits illustrates 500 years of time keeping.

✆ 01-606 3030
Open: daily May-Sep 10-5, Oct-Apr Mon-Sat 10-5. (Closed: Xmas, New Year, Good Fri, Etr Mon & infrequently for Civic occasions). ♿ (ground floor only) Shop 🚫 (ex guide dogs)

Museum of London

London Wall   *Plan 1 :* **F4.**
The museum was formed by amalgamating the former London Museum and the

London Plan 2

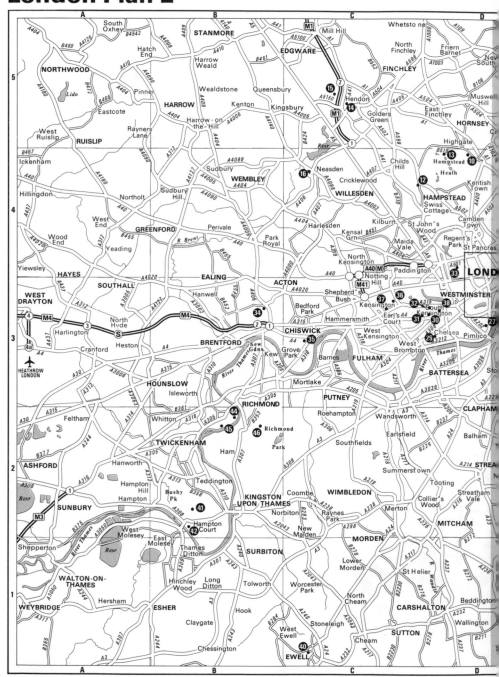

London Plan 2

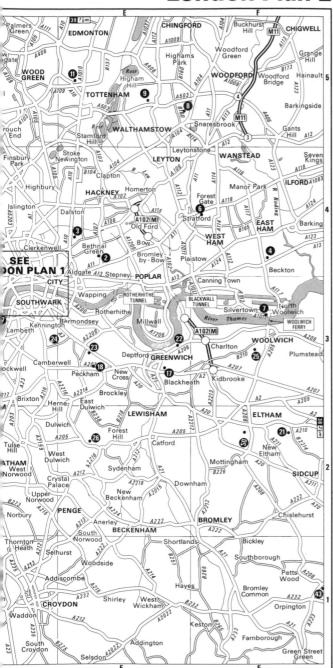

Guildhall Museum. The present purpose-built premises were opened in 1976 and the museum is devoted entirely to London and its people. Everything on show contributes to the story of London during the past 2,000 years. Included are Royal treasures from the City, a barber's shop from Islington, sculptures from the Temple of Mithras, a 1930 Ford, Selfridge's lift, a medieval hen's egg, a Roman bikini and the Great Fire experience.

✆ 01-600 3699 Ext 240.
Open: Tue-Sat 10-6, Sun 2-6.
(Closed: BH & Xmas.)
Parties by arrangement.
☕ (licensed) 🅰 Shop ✗ (ex guide dogs)

Stock Exchange
Plan 1 : G4.
The centre of industrial finance, where stocks and shares in individual companies are bought and sold. The trading floor may be viewed from the gallery and guides are present to explain the scene. A colour film may be seen by prior arrangement.

✆ 01-588 2355.
Open: Mon-Fri 9.45-3.15.
Last guided tour 2.30.
(Closed: PH's. Parties must book in advance.)
Shop ✗

EC3

Lloyd's of London
Plan 1 : G4.
The world's leading insurance market, moves into a new headquarters building of advanced design in Lime Street in May 1986. It incorporates a purpose-built exhibition encompassing Lloyd's 300 years in the City as well as a visitors viewing area.

The 'wedding cake' spire of St Bride's church, EC4

⌀ 01-623 7100
Open: Mon-Fri 10-4 (pre-booked groups), (10-2.30 general public).
♿ (by appointment) Shop ⌀

EC4

Central Criminal Courts
Old Bailey   Plan 1 : **E4.**
On the first day of each session the judges carry posies of flowers and the courts are strewn with herbs, a custom dating from the time when it was necessary to disguise the stench of Newgate Prison. Most of the major trials of this century have been heard here including those of Crippen, Christie, Haig, the Kray brothers and more recently Peter Sutcliffe, the Yorkshire Ripper. When the courts are in session visitors may sit in the public galleries. It is often necessary to queue.

⌀ 01-248 3277.
Open: Mon-Fri, 10.30-1 & 2-4.

Mansion House
Plan 1 : **G4.**
This Palladian building designed in 1739-53 by George Dance the Elder is the official residence of the Lord Mayor of London. The principal rooms are the Egyptian Hall, or dining room, and the Salon which contains 19th-century tapestries and an enormous Waterford glass chandelier.

⌀ 01-626 2500 Ext 324.
Open: Tours Tue, Wed & Thu 11 & 2. For tickets apply to: Diary Secretary to the Lord Mayor. Tours last 1 hour.
⌀

Middle Temple Hall
The Temple   Plan 1 : **D3.**
A fine example of Tudor architecture built during the reign of Queen Elizabeth I and completed about 1570. Hall features double hammer beam roof. Also stained glass showing shields of past readers. The most treasured possession is the 29 ft long high table, made from a single oak tree of Windsor Forest. Another table was made from timbers of the Golden Hind in which Sir Francis Drake, a member of the Middle Temple, sailed around the world. Portraits of George I, Elizabeth I, Anne, Charles I, Charles II, James, Duke of York and William III line the walls behind the high table.

⌀ 01-353 4355.
Open: Mon-Fri 10-12 & 3-4.30. (Closed: BH.)
⌀

St Brides Crypt Museum
Fleet Street   Plan 1 : **E4.**
Internationally known as the 'parish church of the press'. It has been the site of seven previous churches, the existing structure having been meticulously restored to Wren's original design. A wealth of history and relics can be seen on permanent display in the crypt museum.

⌀ 01-353 1301.
Open: Mon-Sat 9-5; Sun 9-8.

St Paul's Cathedral
Plan 1 : **F4.**
Wren's masterpiece, built in the late 17th and early 18th centuries is 515 ft long and 242 ft across at its widest point, crowned by a beautiful central dome rising to a height of 365 ft and 112 ft in diameter.

⌀ 01-248 2705.
Open: 8-6 all year round, except Sunday, which is open for worship only. Tourist office Mon-Fri 10.45-6pm Sat 11-4.15pm. (Donations)

Telecom Technology Showcase
135 Queen Victoria St
Plan 1 : **E3.**
Two display floors featuring the past, present and future of Britain's telecommunications. There are many working exhibits charting 200 years of progress from the earliest telegraphs, to satellites and optical fibres.

⌀ 01-248 7444.
Open: Mon-Fri 10-5. (Closed: BH.)
♿ Shop ⌀ (ex guide dogs)

───── NORTH ─────

N6

Highgate Cemetery
Swains Lane   Plan 2 : **10 D4.**
One of the private cemeteries which sprang up in the 1830's. The Eastern

part is well known for the grave of Karl Marx. The Western part is now a Managed Wildlife Nature Reserve. Other famous Victorians buried here include George Eliot, Faraday and Charles Dickens's family.

✆ 01-340 1834.
Open: daily, Apr-Sep 10-5, Oct-Mar 10-4 (Last admission ½ hour before closing); Western cemetery guided tours on the hour daily, Apr-Sep 10-4, Oct-Mar 10-3. (Donations)

N17

Bruce Castle Museum
Lordship Lane   Plan 2 : **11 E5.**
An E-shaped part Elizabethan, part Jacobean and Georgian building, with an adjacent circular 16th-century tower, which stands in a small park. The museum contains sections on local history, postal history and the Middlesex Regiment, also known as the 'diehards'.

✆ 01-808 8772.
Open: daily 1-5 Museum of Middlesex Regiment Tue-Sat 1-5 (Closed: Good Fri, Xmas & New Year's Day).
⊠ (ground floor & grounds only) Shop ⊗

NW3

Keats House
Keats Grove   Plan 2 : **12 D4.**
Regency house, former home of the poet Keats. *Ode to the Nightingale* was written in the garden. Manuscripts and relics.

✆ 01-435 2062.
Open: please telephone for opening times.
Guided tours by appointment.
⊠ (ground floor only) Shop ⊗

Kenwood, Iveagh Bequest
Hampstead Lane   Plan 2 : **13 D4.**
Mansion re-modelled c. 1765 by Robert Adam, with fine grounds, bequeathed to the nation in 1927 by Lord Iveagh. Notable library, furniture, and works of art including paintings by Rembrandt, Hals, Vermeer, Reynolds and Gainsborough. Collections of 18th-century shoebuckles and jewellery. Summer exhibitions. Concerts.

✆ 01-348 1286.
Open: daily; Apr-Sep 10-7; Feb, Mar & Oct 10-5; Nov-Jan 10-4. (Closed: Good Fri & 24-25 Dec).
(Charges for special exhibitions)
⌨ ⊠ (ground floor & garden only) Shop ⊗ (except in grounds)

NW4

Church Farm House Museum
Greyhound Hill   Plan 2 : **14 C5.**
Old gabled house, dating from 1660s, now museum of local interest. Period furnished kitchen and dining room. Changing exhibitions.

✆ 01-203 0130.
Open: all year, Mon-Sat 10-1 & 2-5.30 (Tue 10-1 only). Sun 2-5.30. (Closed: Good Fri, 25 & 26 Dec, 1 Jan.)
⊠ (garden only) Shop ⊗

Royal Air Force Museum
Plan 2 : **15 C5.**
Entrance via M1, A41 (Aerodrome Rd, off Watford Way) or A5 (Colindale Av, off Edgware Rd).
The museum, on the former Hendon airfield, covers all aspects of the history of the RAF and its predecessors. Over 40 aircraft are on display from the Bleriot XI to the 'Lightning'. Twelve galleries depict over 100 years of milit-

ary aviation history. The Battle of Britain Museum has been built on a site adjacent to the main Museum. It contains British, German and Italian aircraft which were engaged in the great air battle of 1940. Also in the same complex is the vast new Bomber Command Museum which contains a striking display of famous bomber aircraft including the Lancaster, Wellington and Vulcan.

✆ 01-205 2266 Ext 38.
Open: all year Mon-Sat 10-6, Sun 2-6. (Closed: Good Fri, May Day, 24-26 Dec & 1 Jan). *RAF Museum free. Battle of Britain Museum £1 (ch & pen 50p). Bomber Command Museum £1 (ch & pen 50p). Party 20+.
⌨ (licensed) ⊠ Shop ⊗

NW10

Grange Museum
Neasden Lane (centre of roundabout)
Plan 2 : **16 C4.**
Dating from around 1700, the building originally formed part of the outbuildings of a large farm and was later converted into a Gothic cottage. Permanent collections tell the story of the area that is now the London Borough of Brent. Changing temporary exhibitions, local history library, display on the British Empire Exhibition for which Wembley Stadium was built. Two period rooms of late 19th century and early 20th century, and reconstructed draper's shop.

✆ 01-908 7432.
Open: all year, Tue-Thu, 12-5 (8pm Wed), Sat 10-5. (Closed: BH.) Details not confirmed for 1988
Parties by advanced booking only.
⊠ (ground floor only) Shop ⊗

══ SOUTH ══

SE1

Imperial War Museum
Lambeth Road   Plan 1 : **E1.**
Founded 1917 and established 1920 by Act of Parliament, this museum illustrates and records all aspects of the two World Wars and other military operations involving Britain and the Commonwealth since 1914. Extensive renovation and redevelopment will entail gallery closures from 1986 and a major interim exhibition on the two World Wars is being mounted while the work is in progress. Various reference departments, open by appointment only.

☏ 01-735 8922.
Open: all year, daily Mon-Sat 10-5.50, Sun 2-5.50. (Closed: Good Fri, May Day, 24-26 Dec, & 1 Jan.)
♿ Shop ⚘ (ex guide dogs)

Tradescant Trust Museum of Garden History
St Mary-at-Lambeth, Lambeth Palace Road.
Plan 1 : **C1.**
Historic building and newly made period knot garden containing 17th-century plants. Nearby stand the tombs of the John Tradescants (father and son) and Captain Bligh of the 'Bounty'. Temporary exhibitions, concerts and lectures. Enquiries to: The Tradescant Trust, 74 Coleherne Court, London SW5 0EF.

☏ 01-261 189.
Open: (13 Mar-4 Dec) Mon-Fri, 11-3; Sun 10.30-5. (Closed: From 2nd Sun in Dec to 1st Sun in Mar.)
⚖ ♿ Shop

SE3

Rangers House
Chesterfield Walk
Plan 2 : **17 E3.**
Suffolk collection of Jacobean and Stuart portraits housed in 18th-century villa, former home of Philip Stanhope, 4th Earl of Chesterfield. Collection contains a set of portraits by William Larkin, among the finest to survive from the Jacobean period and a small collection of Old Masters. Three first floor rooms house the Dolmetsch collection of musical instruments, on loan from the Horniman Museum. The chintz bedroom contains walnut furniture of the early 18th century. Also chamber concerts and poetry readings. Educational programme, holiday projects and workshop.

☏ 01-853 0035.
Open: daily (4pm Nov-Feb) 10-5, (Closed: Good Fri. 24-25 Dec.)
♿ (ground floor only) Shop ⚘

SE5

South London Art Gallery
Peckham Road   Plan 2 : **18 E3.**
Presents ten exhibitions a year, mostly of contemporary art drawn from local sources. Collections include drawings, paintings and prints by British artists, 1700 onwards with topographical works of local subjects; these can be seen by pre-arrangement.

☏ 01-703 6120.
Open: only when exhibitions are in progress, Tue-Sat 10-6, Sun 3-6 (Closed: Mon.)
Shop ⚘

SE9

Eltham Palace
Plan 2 : **20 F2.**
Noted for great hall with remarkable 15th-century hammer-beam roof. An old bridge spans the moat.

☏ 01-859 2112 Ext 255.
Open: Nov-Mar, Thu & Sun 10.30-4; Apr-Oct, Thu & Sun 10.30-6. Opening arrangements subject to possible alteration.
(AM)

Winter Gardens
Avery Hill Park   Plan 2 : **21 F2.**
Approximately 750 species of tropical and temperate plants can be seen here in cold, temperate and tropical houses, a collection second only to the Royal Botanical Gardens at Kew. Nursery production unit open spring BH weekend. Tennis and putting available.

☏ 01-850 3217.
Open: all year Mon-Fri 1-4, Sat, Sun & BH 11-4.30 (6pm summer). (Closed: 1st Mon each month & 25 Dec.)
⚖ ♿

SE10

Royal Naval College
Plan 2 : **22 E3.**
Group of buildings designed by Webb (late 17th century) and Wren (early 18th century), with additions by Hawksmoor, Vanbrugh and Ripley. Formerly Naval Hospital, becoming College in 1873. Chapel rebuilt in 18th century, and Painted Hall ceiling by Sir James Thornhill.

☏ 01-858 2154.
Open: all year (Painted Hall & Chapel only) daily (ex Thu) 2.30-5 (last admission 4.30). (Closed 24 Dec-1 Jan.)
Shop ⚘

SE15

Livesey Museum
682 Old Kent Road
Plan 2 : **23 E3.**
Museum displays one major

exhibition every year, dealing mainly with Southwark's past and present, including permanent exhibition of Southwark Street furniture.

✆ 01-639 5604.
Open: when exhibition is in progress, Mon-Sat 10-5. ✗ ⅃ (ground floor only) Shop

SE17
Cuming Museum
155/ 157 Walworth Road
Plan 2 : 24 D3.
Contains Roman and medieval finds from the suburb of Southwark, south of London Bridge. Examples from the local 'Delft' pottery industry, items associated with Dickens and Michael Faraday (born locally in 1791), the equipment of a family dairy firm which served the neighbourhood for over 150 years. Also a collection relating to London superstitions.

✆ 01-703 3324 Ext 32.
Open: all year Mon-Fri 10-5.30 (7pm Thu), Sat 10-5. ✗ (ex guide dogs)

SE18
Museum of Artillery in the Rotunda
Repository Road   *Plan 2 : 25 F3.*
Circular structure designed by John Nash, which stood at one time in St James's Park. It contains a very interesting collection of artillery.

✆ 01-854 2242/3127.
Open: all year, Apr-Oct, Mon-Fri 12-5, Sat & Sun 1-5; Nov-Mar, Mon-Fri 12-4, Sat & Sun 1-4. (Closed: Good Fri, 24-26 Dec & 1 Jan.) ⊓ Shop

SE23
Horniman Museum
London Road   *Plan 2 : 26 E2.*
Ethnographical and large natural history collections including vivaria. Exhibition of musical instruments from all parts of the world. Extensive library and lectures and concerts in spring and autumn. Special exhibitions. Education Centre programmes.

✆ 01-699 2339.
Open: all year Mon-Sat 10.30-6, Sun 2-6. (Closed: 24-26 Dec). Details not confirmed for 1988. ⅃ ⊟ Shop ✗ (ex guide dogs)

SW1
Buckingham Palace — Changing the Guard
Plan 1 : A1.
The forecourt of Buckingham Palace is patrolled by troops from the Brigade of Guards, the Queens personal bodyguard. The Changing of the Guard, a ceremony lasting about half an hour, takes place most mornings and is a very popular and colourful ceremony.

✆ 01-730 3488 (London Tourist Board).
Takes place 11.30, subject to alteration (summer daily, winter alternate days).

Houses of Parliament
Plan 1 : C1.
A mid 19th-century building in Gothic style based on a design by Sir Charles Barry with additional detail by Augustin Pugin, the original building having been destroyed by fire in 1834. Two chambers are set either side of a central hall and corridor, the House of Lords to the south and the House of Commons to the north. The clock tower, 320 ft high, contains Big Ben, the hour bell weighing 13½ tons, and the Victoria tower stands 340 ft high. The House of Commons suffered bomb damage in 1941 and a new chamber was constructed to the design of Sir Giles Gilbert Scott and opened in 1950.

✆ 01-219 3090 & 3100.
To gain admission to the Strangers' Galleries join the queue at St Stephens entrance from approx 4.30pm Mon-Thu, approx 9.30am Fri (House of Commons) or from approx 2.30pm Tue & Wed, from 3pm Thu & occasionally 11am Fri (House of Lords) or by arrangement with MP (House of Commons) or Peer (House of Lords). Free although guides require payment if employed. ⅃ (by arrangement)
Bookstall ✗ (ex guide dogs)
also **Westminster Hall**
Built 1097-99 by William Rufus, it is the oldest remaining part of Westminster. The glory of the hall is the cantilever or hammerbeam roof, the earliest and largest roof of its kind in existence, built between 1394 and 1401.

✆ 01-219 3090.
Tours am by arrangement with an MP only. Free although guides require payment if employed. ⅃ (by arrangement) ✗ (ex guide dogs)

Tate Gallery
Millbank   *Plan 2 : 27 D3.*
Opened in 1897 the gallery comprises the national collections of British painting and 20th-century painting and sculpture. Hogarth, Blake, Turner, Constable and the Pre-Raphaelites are particularly well-represented in the British Collection and the Modern Collection traces the development of art from Impressionism through postwar European and American art including Abstract Impressionism and Pop, to the present day. The Clore Gallery,

for the Turner Collection, opened in Apr 1987.

✆ 01-821 7128 & Recorded information.
Open: all year (ex Good Fri, May Day, 24-26 Dec & 1 Jan) 10-5.50, Sun 2-5.50.
Free (ex for special exhibitions). Free lectures, films and guided tours most days.
⌑ (licensed) 12-3 (closed Sun) ⌑ (coffee shop) 10.30-5.30, Sun 2-5.15.
🅱 Shop 🐾 (ex guide dogs)

Westminster Cathedral
Ashley Place   Plan 1 : **A1.**
The largest and most important Roman Catholic church in England; a Byzantine structure completed in 1903 just seven years after the foundation stone was laid. Built entirely or red brick with contrasting bands of Portland stone, its interior is ornamented with marble and beautiful mosaics.

✆ 01-834 7452.
Open: daily, 7am-8pm.
(Donations)

SW3

National Army Museum
Royal Hospital Road
*Plan 2 : **29 D3.***
Contains a permanent chronological display of the history of the British, Indian and Colonial forces from 1485. Among the exhibits are uniforms, weapons, prints, photographs, manuscripts, letters, glass, china, silver and relics of British commanders and mementoes of Britain's soldiers. There is a special display of the orders and decorations of the Duke of Windsor and also those of five great field marshals — Lords Roberts, Gough, Kitchener and Wolseley and Sir George White VC. The pic-

ture gallery includes portraits by Beechy, Romney and Lawrence, battle scenes and pictures of Indian regiments. The reading room is open Tue-Sat 10-4.30 to holders of readers' tickets, obtainable by written application to the Director.

✆ 01-730 0717.
Open: all year Mon-Sat 10-5.30, Sun 2-5.30. (Closed: Good Fri, May Day, 24-26 Dec & 1 Jan).
Lectures etc for school parties.
🅱 ⌑ Shop 🐾

SW7

Geological Museum
Exhibition Road   Plan 2 : **30 D3.**
Established at present premises in 1935, the Geological Museum now forms part of the British Museum (Natural History). Exhibits include a piece of the Moon and the largest exhibition on basic earth science in the world — The Story of the Earth. This is split into four main sections: the Earth in Space, which includes an exhibit showing that an observer 150 million light years away, looking through an immensely powerful telescope, would see dinosaurs roaming around in a Jurassic landscape. The Earth's Interior and Crust; Geological Processes; and Geological Time. There is also a famous collection of fine gemstones, showing them in their parent rock, in natural crystal form and in their final cut state. The regional geology of Great Britain and ore deposits of the world are also displayed. Permanent exhibitions are British Fossils, Britain Before Man and an exciting new exhibition, Treasures of the Earth.

✆ 01-589 3444 (Due to change during currency of guide).
Open: all year Mon-Sat 10-5.30, Sun 2-5.30. (Closed: Good Fri, May Day, 24-26 Dec & 1 Jan.)
⌑ 🐾 Shop 🅱 (ex mezzanine floor)

Science Museum
Exhibition Road   Plan 2 : **32 D3.**
Extensive collections, including aero-engines; agriculture; astronomy; atomic and nuclear physics; rail; road; sea and air transport; civil, electrical, marine and mechanical engineering, telecommunications, domestic appliances, 'Gas Industry' gallery, etc. Two galleries with items from the Wellcome Collection of the History of Medicine, galleries on Printing, Paper making and Lighting. Also a children's gallery and 'Launch Pad', with many working demonstrations. Exhibition on space technology and new exhibitions on Plastics and Optics.

✆ 01-589 3456 Ext 632.
Open: daily, Mon-Sat, 10-6, Sun 2.30-6. (Closed: Good Fri, May Day, 24-26 Dec & 1 Jan.)
Donations.
⌑ 🅱 Shop 🐾

―――― WEST ――――

W1

Agnew's Galleries
43 Old Bond Street Plan 1 : **A3.**
London galleries established in 1860 as expansion of the Vittore Zanetti art business which originated in Manchester. Thomas Agnew, who entered the business in 1817, later became a partner. In 1932 a limited company, Thomas Agnew and Sons, was formed. Annual exhibitions include a watercolour exhibition devoted to English

watercolours and drawings of the 18th and 19th centuries. Jan & Feb, and an exhibition of Old Master paintings (for sale) from the 14th to 19th centuries. There are also exhibitions of French and English drawings from c. 1800 to the present day, work by English painters of this century and loan exhibitions in aid of charity. Many works pass through Agnew's on their way to famous art galleries and museums.

✆ 01-629 6176.
Open: all year Mon-Fri, 9.30-5.30 (6.30pm Thu, during major exhibitions). (Closed: BH.)
♿ Admission charge for some loan exhibitions.

Museum of Mankind
6 Burlington Gardens
Plan 1 : A3.
Houses the exhibitions, library and offices of the ethnography department of the British Museum. Its collections embrace the art and material culture of tribal, village and other pre-industrial societies, from most areas of the world excluding Western Europe. Also archaeological collections from the Americas and Africa. A few important pieces are on permanent exhibition, but the museum's policy is to mount a number of temporary exhibitions usually lasting for at least a year. A separate store in Shoreditch contains the reserve collection which can be made available for serious study by arrangement. Film shows and educational services also available.

✆ 01-437 2224 Ext 43.
Open: all year Mon-Sat 10-5, Sun 2.30-6. (Closed: Good Fri, May Day, 24-27 Dec & 1 Jan.)
♿ Shop ⊗ (ex guide dogs)

Wallace Collection
Hertford House,
Manchester Sq   *Plan 2 : 33 D4.*
An outstanding collection of works of art bequeathed to the nation by Lady Wallace in 1897, displayed in the house of its founders. Includes pictures by Titian, Rubens, Gainsborough and Delacroix together with an unrivalled representation of 18th-century French art including paintings, especially of Watteau, Boucher and Fragonard, sculpture, furniture, goldsmiths' work and Sèvres porcelain. Also valuable collections of majolica, European and oriental arms and armour.

✆ 01-935 0687.
Open: all year Mon-Sat 10-5, Sun 2-5. (Closed: Good Fri, May Day, 24-26 Dec & 1 Jan.)
♿ Shop ⊗

W3

Gunnersbury Park Museum
Popes Lane   *Plan 2 : 34 B3.*
Early 19th-century former Rothschild mansion, in fine park, now museum of local interest for the London Borough of Ealing and Hounslow with collections of archaeological discoveries, transport items, costume and topographical and social material. Rothschild coaches on display. Rothschild Victorian kitchens open to public on certain summer weekends. Changing exhibitions. Crafts shows.

✆ 01-992 1612.
Open: Mar-Oct (end of British Summer Time) Mon-Fri 1-5, Sat, Sun & BH 2-6; Nov-Feb, Mon-Fri 1-4, Sat, Sun & BH 2-4. (Closed: Good Fri & 24-26 Dec.)
♿ (ground floor only) Shop ⊗

W4

Hogarth's House
Hogarth Lane,
Great West Road
Plan 2 : 35 C3.
17th-century house where Hogarth lived for 15 years, with engravings, drawings and other relics.

✆ 01-994 6757.
Open: all year 11-6, Sun 2-6 (4pm Oct-Mar). (Closed: Tue & Good Fri, 1st two weeks Sep, last 3 weeks Dec & 1 Jan.)

W8

Commonwealth Institute
Kensington High Street
Plan 2 : 36 C3.
Contains over 40 exhibitions depicting life in the countries of the Commonwealth. Also Art galleries and Educational Research and information centre.

✆ 01-603 4535.
Open: Mon-Sat 10-5.30, Sun 2-5. (Closed: Good Fri, May Day, 24-26 Dec & 1 Jan.)
Special exhibitions admission charge.
⊡ (licensed) ♿ Shop ⊗ (ex guide dogs)

W14

Leighton House
12 Holland Park Road
Plan 2 : 37 C3.
Leighton House is a uniquely opulent and exotic example of High Victorian taste. Built for the President of the Royal Academy, Frederic, Lord Leighton, by George Aitchison, the main body of the house was completed in 1866. The fabulous Arab Hall, with its rare middle-eastern tiles, fountain and gilded decoration, is a 19th-century Arabian Nights' creation finished in 1879. Fine Victorian paintings by Lord Leighton and his contemporaries hang

in the rooms, and there are two galleries for exhibitions of modern and historic art. The quiet garden is ornamented with Lord Leighton's sculpture.

🖉 01-602 3316.
Open: all year, Mon-Sat 10-5 (6pm during temporary exhibitions). (Closed: Sun & BH). Garden open Apr-Sep 11-5.
🚫 (ground floor) ⊘

WC1

British Museum

Great Russell Street Plan 1 : **B4.**
Founded in 1753, one of the great museums, showing the works of man from all over the world from prehistoric to comparatively modern times. The galleries are the responsibility of the following departments: Egyptian; Greek and Roman; Western Asiatic, Prehistoric and Romano-British; Medieval and Later; Coins and Medals; Oriental; Prints and drawings. Each year, special exhibitions focus more detailed attention on certain aspects of the collections. Programmes on request. Gallery talks (Mon-Sat) Lectures (Tue-Sat) and Films (Tue-Fri). Children's trail at all times.

🖉 01-636 1555.
Open: all year, Mon-Sat 10-5, Sun 2.30-6. (Closed: Good Fri, May Day, 24-26 Dec & 1 Jan.) Occasional charge for special exhibitions.
🖨 (licensed) 🚫 Shop ⊘ (ex guide dogs)

Jewish Museum

Woburn House, Tavistock Sq
Plan 1 : **B5.**
A collection of ceremonial art, portraits and antiques illustrating Jewish life, history and religion. There are also two audio-visual programmes

explaining Jewish festivals and ceremonies.

🖉 01-388 4525
Open: Tue-Thu, 10-6 (& Fri during summer), Sun 10-12.45 (& Fri during winter) (Closed: Public & Jewish Hols). Details not confirmed for 1988.
🚫 Shop ⊘

Percival David Foundation of Chinese Art

53 Gordon Square Plan 1 : **B5.**
A unique collection of Chinese ceramics, dating from between the 10th and 18th centuries, the Sung, Yuan, Ming and Ch'ing dynasties. Presented to London University by Percival David in 1951.

🖉 01-387 3909.
Open: Mon 2-5, Tue-Fri 10.30-5, Sat 10.30-1.

WC2

Africa Centre

King Street Plan 1 : **C3.**
The centre is a charity and of particular interest to those who wish to learn more about African culture. For those who wish to browse there are displays of paintings, photographs and craftware by African artists.

🖉 01-836 1973.
Open: Mon-Fri 9.30-5.30, Sat 10-4.

Contemporary Applied Arts

43 Earlham Street Plan 1 : **C4.**
Programme of special exhibitions and retail display including wallhangings, furniture, studio ceramics, pottery, wood, jewellery etc; books and magazines for craft and design.

🖉 01-836 6993.
Open: all year, Mon-Fri

10-5.30, Sat 11-5. (Closed: Sun & BH.) Details not confirmed for 1988
🚫 (ground floor only) ⊘

London Silver Vaults

Chancery Lane Plan 1 : **D4.**
Fine collection of antiques and modern silverware in an underground location. Visitors can browse and traders are happy to talk about their wares, look up hallmarks and explain histories.

🖉 01-242 3844.
Open: Mon-Fri 9-5.30, Sat 9-12.30.

National Gallery

Trafalgar Square Plan 1 : **B3.**
Founded by vote of Parliament in 1824, but was first opened in the present building in 1838. The gallery houses the national collection of masterpieces of European paintings from the 13th to 19th century. Collection includes van Eyck's Arnolfini Marriage, Velazquez's The Toilet of Venus, Leonardo da Vinci's cartoon 'The Virgin and Child with SS Anne and John the Baptist', Rembrandt's Belshazzar's Feast, Titian's Bacchus and Ariadne, and many more. Lunchtime lectures and guided tours daily; quizzes and worksheets available for children. Constantly changing programme of exhibitions, usually highlighting certain aspects of the collection.

🖉 01-839 3321 & recorded information: 01-839 3526.
Open: daily Mon-Sat 10-6, Sun 2-6. (Closed: Good Fri, May Day, Xmas period & 1 Jan.)
🖨 (licensed) 🚫 Shop ⊘

National Portrait Gallery

2 St Martin's Place Plan 1 : **B3.**
Contains national collection

National Portrait Gallery

of portraits of the famous and infamous in British history, including paintings, sculpture, miniatures, engravings, photographs, and cartoons. Special exhibitions several times a year.

⌀ 01-930 1552.
Open: all year Mon-Fri 10-5, Sat 10-6, Sun 2-6. (Closed: Good Fri, May Day, 24-26 Dec & 1 Jan.)
(Charges for special exhibitions).

St Paul's Church
Covent Garden   Plan 1 : **C3**.
The first new Anglican church to be built in London after the Reformation, St Pauls was designed by Inigo Jones for the 4th Earl of Bedford, between 1631 and 1633. It has long associations with the theatre since both the Theatre Royal, Drury Lane and the Royal Opera House are in the parish. Amongst the famous buried here are Claude Duval the highwayman, Grinling Gibbons, Thomas Arne, composer of *Rule Brittania*, and the actress Vivien Leigh. J. M. W. Turner was baptised here.

⌀ 01-836 5221.
Open: Mon-Fri 9.30-4.30.

The Sir John Soane's Museum
13 Lincoln's Inn Fields
Plan 1 : **C4**.
The house of Sir John Soane (1753-1837), the architect, built in 1812 and containing his collections of antiquities, sculpture, paintings, drawings, and books, including the Sarcophagus of Seti I (1292 BC). The Rake's Progress and the Election series of paintings by William Hogarth. Architectural Drawings Collection open by appointment.

⌀ 01-405 2107.
Open: all year Tue-Sat 10-5.
Lecture tours Sat 2.30.
(Closed BH.)
⌀

LOTHERTON HALL
West Yorkshire   Map 8 SE43.
Lotherton Hall Bird Gardens
The Gardens, close to Leeds, are on a charming rural estate set in beautiful landscaped grounds with waterfalls and ornamental ponds. Two shire horses make trips around the estate. Here are to be found one of the finest, and developing, collections of species in the country — many of them rare and endangered. Other animals, such as deer, wallabies and chinchillas, also live here.

⌀ Leeds (0532) 813723.
Open: Etr-Oct, Tue-Fri 10-4.15; Sat, Sun & BH 11-6 (last admission 5.15).
Admission charged at Lotherton Hall.
⌀ ⌀ ⌀

LOWESTOFT
Suffolk   Map 5 TM59.
Royal Naval Patrol Service Association (Naval Museum)
Sparrows Nest Gardens
The museum includes collections of hundreds of photographs from World War II, models of minesweepers and naval ships, war relics, war medals, naval uniforms and the 'Victoria Cross' room.

⌀ (0502) 86250.
Open: daily Etr BH & May-Oct, 10-12 & 2-4.30. Coach parties by appointment.
⌀ (licensed) ⌀ (ground floor only) Shop

LUDGERSHALL
Wiltshire   Map 4 SU25.
Ludgershall Castle
(7m NW of Andover on A342)
Norman motte and bailey castle with large earthworks and flint walling of later royal castle.

Open: all reasonable times.
(AM) ⌀ (part of site only & village cross)

LUTON
Bedfordshire   Map 4 TL02.
Museum and Art Gallery
Wardown Park
Collections illustrate natural history, culture, and industries of Luton and Bedfordshire with particular reference to straw hat and pillow lace trade. 'Luton Life' gallery includes a reconstructed street display.

⌀ (0582) 36941.
Open: daily, Mon-Sat 10.30-5, Sun 1.30-6 (1.30-5 in winter).
(Closed: Xmas & New Year's day.)
⌀ (ground floor only) Shop
⌀

LYDFORD

Devon   *Map 2 SX58.*

Lydford Castle
*midway between
Okehampton & Tavistock off
A386*
Remains of mid 12th-century stone keep, altered a century later. The lower floor was once a prison and the upper floor became Stannary Court, established to administer local tin mines.

Open: at all reasonable times.
(AM)

LYDIARD PARK

Wiltshire   *Map 4 SU18.*

(1m N of M4 (junc 16) on unclass road)
Fine Georgian mansion set in pleasant park, together with the adjoining parish church of St Mary, which contains memorials to the St John family.

 Swindon (0793) 770401.
Open: daily, Mon-Fri 10-1 & 2-5.30, Sun 2-5.30. (Closed: Good Fri & Xmas.)
 Shop

LYTHAM ST ANNES

Lancashire   *Map 7 SD32.*

Premium Bonds Office, ERNIE
Moorland Road
Talk and film on ERNIE (Electronic Random Number Indicator Equipment).

 (0253) 721212.
Open: tours Mon-Thu 1.45.

MACCLESFIELD

Cheshire   *Map 7 SJ79.*

Macclesfield Museum and Art Gallery
West Park, Prestbury Road
Contains a notable collection of Egyptian antiquities, oil paintings and sketches including work by CF Tunnicliffe ARA and Landseer, and drawings and prints of a topographical nature. Also a small silk exhibition and a stuffed Giant Panda.

 (0625) 24067 or Northwich (0606) 4331.
Open: Etr Sat-Sep, Tue-Sun 2-4.30; Oct-Sat before Etr, Sat & Sun & BH 2-4.30.
 (except guide dogs)

MADRON

Cornwall   *Map 2 SW43.*

Lanyon Quiot
(2m NW on unclass Road)
One of the best examples of a megalithic tomb in Britain dating from between 2000-1600 BC: a large granite slab 18 inches thick, almost 9ft wide and 17ft long balanced on three upright stones.

Open: accessible at all reasonable times.
(NT)

MAESGWM

Gwynedd   *Map 6 SH72.*

Maesgwm Visitor Centre
The centre, located off the A470, eight miles north of Dolgellau, depicts the forest environment, the life and work of the forest and the history of the local gold mines. Leaflets are available for the nearby trail and there are many picnic places, 50 miles of waymarked walks and a wildlife observation hide which can be booked by telephone.

 Dolgellau (0341) 422289.
Open: Etr wk, then Whit-Sep daily 10-5.
 Shop

MAIDSTONE

Kent   *Map 5 TQ75.*

Museum and Art Gallery
Chillington Manor, St Faith's Street
Historic Elizabethan manor house, much extended over the years, housing outstanding collections of oil paintings and watercolours, furniture, ceramics, costume, natural history and local industry. Further important collections of ethnography, archaeology, and Japanese fine and applied art. Also on show is the museum of Queen's Own Royal West Kent Regiment.

 (0622) 54497.
Open: all year, Mon-Sat 10-5.30. (Closed BH) Details not confirmed for 1988.
Shop

MALHAM

North Yorkshire   *Map 7 SD86.*

Yorkshire Dales National Park Centre
Visitor Centre with interpretative display and audio-visual theatre for group use. Maps, walks, guides and local information available.

 Airton (07293) 363.
Open: daily Apr-Oct. Mid morning to late afternoon.

Man (Isle of)
DOUGLAS

Isle of Man   *Map 6 SC37.*

Manx Museum
Items illustrate island's archaeology, history, natural history, folk life and art. Also National Reference Library.

 (0624) 75522.
Open: all year, Mon-Sat 10-5. (Closed: 25 & 26 Dec, 1 Jan, Good Fri & the morning of 5 Jul.)
Shop (ex guide dogs)

MANCHESTER

Gt Manchester   *Map 7 SJ89.*

Athenaeum Gallery
Princess Street   *Plan : D4.*
The gallery has a constantly changing programme of temporary exhibitions. Please telephone for a current programme.

Opening doors to the World of books

Book Tokens can be bought and exchanged at most bookshops

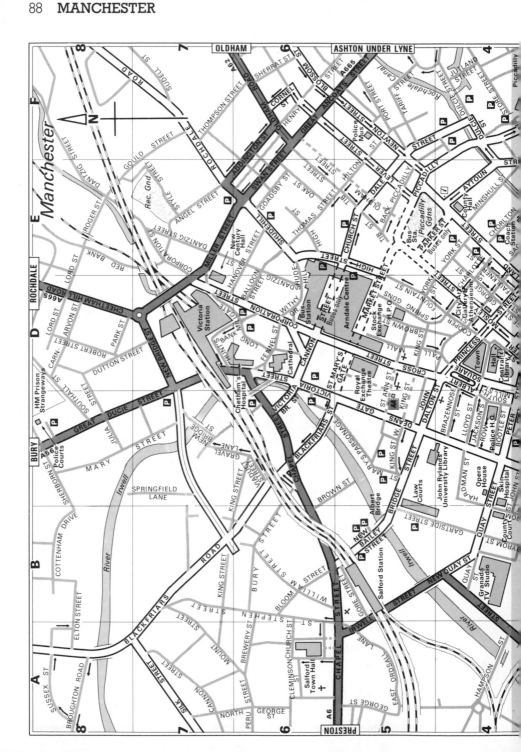

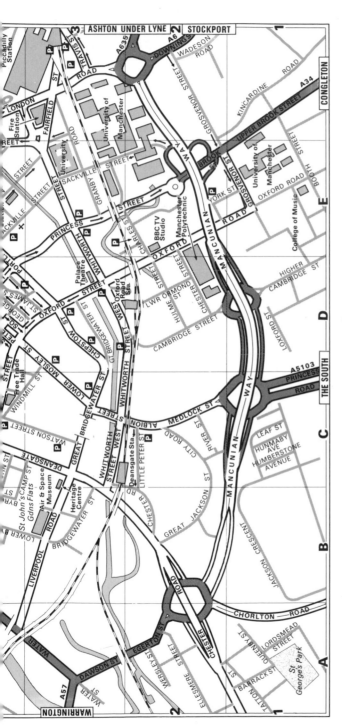

© 061-236 9422.
Open: daily Mon-Sat 10-6,
Sun 2-6.
Shop 🛆 (ground floor only)
⌀

City Art Gallery

Mosley Street   Plan : **D4.**
A sumptuous display of the
city's treasures in an
architectural masterpiece of
the Greek Revival. Paintings
by the Old Masters, Stubbs,
Gainsborough, Turner, and
the Pre-Raphaelites. Out-
standing collections of decorative arts, furniture, and
sculpture. Temporary exhibitions.

© 061-236 9422
Open: Mon-Sat 10-6, Sun 2-6.
Shop ⌀

Fletcher Moss Art Gallery

*Stenner Lane, off Wilmslow
Road, Didsbury (5½m S of
city off A5145) Not on plan*
Small gallery, set in the botanical gardens, and devoted
to the story of Manchester.
Old maps, paintings and
drawings illustrate the City's
meteoric rise. Also an important collection of paintings
now on show. Recently completed Arts and Craft room.

© 061-236 9422. Ext 223.
Open: Apr-Sept, Mon, Wed-
Sat 10-6, Sun 2-6.
⌀ 🛆 (ground floor only).

**Fletcher Moss Botanical
Gardens**

*Wilmslow Road, Didsbury,
(5½m S of city on A5145) Not
on plan.*
The park was presented to
the city early this century
and has been transformed
into beautiful botanical gardens. Because of its sheltered position the rock garden can grow Alpine, dwarf
and other unusual plants. In
addition there are conifers,
rhododendrons, many rare

shrubs and plants, an orchid house and wild garden.

𝍎 061-434 1877.
Open: daily, 7.45-dusk.
🖳 (closed Tue & Sat) 🖳

Gallery of English Costume
Platt Fields, Rusholme (2m SE of city) Not on plan
Famous costume collection displaying the changing styles of everyday clothes and accessories of the last 400 years. The exhibitions change at regular intervals and no one period is constantly on display.

𝍎 061-224 5217.
Open: daily (ex Tue) 10-6, Sun 2-6, Nov-Feb closes at 4pm.
🖳 (ground floor only) 🕉
Shop

Greater Manchester Police Museum
Newton Street   Plan : **F5.**
Occupying the old Newton Street police station, built in 1879. The ground floor displays a reconstructed 1920s charge room and cell corridor. The first floor has police uniforms and equipment, a forger's den and a photographic gallery.

𝍎 061-855 3290.
Open: daily Mon-Fri 9.30-3 (by appointment only).
🕉

John Rylands University Library of Manchester
Deansgate   Plan : **C4.**
Famous library, dating from 1851, containing over 3 million books, 17,000 manuscripts, extensive archival collections and c 600,000 titles in microform. Rare books division in the architecturally distinguished Rylands memorial building in Deansgate, holds regular exhibitions and lectures.

𝍎 061-834 5343.
Open: daily Mon-Fri 10-5.30, Sat 10-1. (Closed: BH & Xmas-New Year.)
🕉 Shop

Manchester Museum
The University, Oxford Road. (1m SE of city) Not on plan
Contains exhibits of archaeology and natural history including an extensive collection from Ancient Egypt, rocks, minerals, fossils, coins and native craftsmanship and huge study collections of over 8 million specimens. Frequent temporary exhibitions, and lectures.

𝍎 061-273 3333.
Open: daily Mon-Sat 10-5. (Closed: Good Fri, May Day & Xmas-New Year.)
🖳 Shop 🕉

Whitworth Art Gallery
University of Manchester, Whitworth Park (1½m SE of city) Not on plan
Founded in 1889 by Royal Charter. The principal collections are British watercolours including work by Blake, Turner, the Pre-Raphaelites and 1939-45 War Artists; Continental watercolours including works by Cézanne, Van Gogh and Picasso; Old Master drawings and prints, including examples by leading Renaissance masters such as Pollaiuolo, Mantegna and Dürer, and fine collection of Japanese prints; textiles, including the Whitworth Tapestry, designed by Paolozzi in 1968; historic wallpapers; and contemporary works of art. Frequent special exhibitions.

𝍎 061-273 4865.
Open: daily Mon-Sat 10-5 (Thu until 9pm).

(Closed: Good Fri & Xmas to New Year.)
🖳 (licensed) 🖳 Shop 🕉 (ex guide dogs).

Wythenshawe Horticultural Centre
Wythenshawe Park, Northendon (5½m S of city, off A5103) Not on plan
The 5½ acre centre provides a splendid all year round display of plants, much of which is used for the parks and gardens throughout the city. The extensive glasshouses contain the Tropical House with pineapples, the Cactus House contains the Charles Darrah collection.

𝍎 061-945 1768.
Open: daily 10-4 (no plants for sale).
🕉

MANSFIELD
Nottinghamshire   Map 8 SK56.
Museum & Art Gallery
Leeming Street
New display of William Billingsley porcelain, lustreware and Wedgwood. Watercolours of old Mansfield. Many temporary exhibitions. There is also a natural history gallery.

𝍎 (0623) 663088.
Open: daily Mon-Fri 10-5 & Sat 10-1 & 2-5. (Closed: Sun, BH & Local Authority holidays)
🖳 Shop 🕉

MARKET HARBOROUGH
Leicestershire   Map 4 SP79.
Harborough Museum
Council Offices, Adam & Eve Street
Museum illustrating the long history of the Harborough area, particularly the town's role as a marketing and social focus, hunting centre and medieval planned town.

✆ (0858) 32468 or Leicester (0533) 541333.
Open: daily Mon-Sat 10-4.30, Sun 2-5.
(Closed: Good Fri & Xmas.)
🚹 (Sat, Sun & BH by arrangement)
Shop ✖ (ex guide dogs)

MARSDEN
West Yorkshire   Map 7 SE01.
Tunnel End Canal & Countryside Centre
Reddisher Road
Displays on the history of canals, housed in the former tunnel keeper's cottage at the entrance to the Standedge Tunnel on the Huddersfield Narrow Canal. Also an interpretative centre devoted to this part of the Pennines.

✆ Huddersfield (0484) 846062.
Open: Tue-Sun 11-4; Etr-Oct 11-5. Restaurant Etr-Oct.
🍴 ♿ ✖ (ex guide dogs in museum).

MARYPARK
Grampian (Banffshire)   Map 15 NJ13.
Glenfarclas Distillery
(1m W)
One of the finest Highland Malt whiskies is produced here. There is an exhibition, museum, craft shop and visitor centre. Museum and exhibition now in French, German and Swedish.

✆ Ballindalloch (08072) 257.
Open: all year Mon-Fri 9-4.30; Jul-Sep also Sat 10-4. (Closed: 25 Dec & 1 & 2 Jan.)
🚹 (ground floor only) Shop

MARYPORT
Cumbria   Map 11 NY03.
Maritime Museum
Shipping Brow, 1 Senhouse Street.
Material of local and general maritime interest. Photographic display illustrating Maryport's history.

✆ (0900) 813738.
Open: Etr-Sep, Mon, Wed & Fri 10-5, Tue, Thu & Sat 10-1, 2-5, Oct-Etr daily ex Wed & Sun 10-12 & 2-4.
🚹 (ground floor only) Shop

MELROSE
Borders (Roxburghshire)
*   Map 12 NT53.*
Priorwood Garden
Special garden with flowers for drying. Visitor centre adjacent to Melrose Abbey and 'Apples through the Ages' orchard walk.

✆ (089682) 2965.
Open: daily Apr-Oct, 10-5.30, Sun 2-5; 7 Nov-24 Dec daily (ex Sun) 10-3.30.
Donations.
(NTS)

MELTON MOWBRAY
Leicestershire   Map 8 SK71.
Melton Carnegie Museum
Thorpe End
Museum illustrating past and present life of the area.

✆ (0664) 69946.
Open: Etr-Sep, Mon-Sat 10-5, Sun 2-5; Oct-Etr, Mon-Fri 10-4.30, Sat 10.30-4.
(Closed: Sun, Good Fri, 25-26 Dec & 1 Jan).
Details not confirmed for 1988.
Shop ✖ (ex guide dogs)

MENAI BRIDGE
Gwynedd   Map 6 SH57.
Tegfryn Art Gallery
Cadnant Road
A private gallery, standing in its own pleasant grounds near to shores of the Menai Straits. Exhibition of paintings by contemporary and prominent artists including many from North Wales. Pictures may be purchased.

✆ (0248) 712437.
Open: daily 10-1 & 2-5.
(Closed: Feb & Mon; 2 Oct-Etr).
🚹 (ground floor only)

MERTHYR TYDFIL
Mid Glamorgan   Map 3 SO00.
Garwnant Forest Centre
(5m N of Merthyr Tydfil off A470)
A focal point for the many forest facilities in the Brecon Beacons, with displays on the farming, water supply and forestry of the valleys. Trails and adventure play area.

✆ (0685) 3060.
Open: Etr-Sep, Mon-Fri, 10.30-4.45, BH 12-6.
Weekends Apr, Sat & Sun 2-4, May & Sep 2-5, Jun 2-6 & Jul & Aug 1-6.
Details not confirmed for 1988.
🍴 🚹 Shop

Joseph Parry's Cottage
4 Chapel Row
Birthplace of musician and composer Joseph Parry. Exhibition of his life and works and display of momentoes of Welsh male voice choirs. Open air museum with excavated section of Glamorganshire Canal and exhibits illustrating local industrial and social history.

✆ (0685) 83704.
Open: Mon-Fri 8.30-1 & 2-4.30.
✖ Shop 🚹 (ground floor & gardens)

MIDDLESBROUGH
Cleveland   Map 8 NZ42.
Dorman Museum
Linthorpe Road
Displays of local, social, industrial and natural history. A permanent display of regional and Linthorpe pottery together with a regular varied programme of temporary exhibitions.

✆ (0642) 813781.
Open: Mon-Fri 10-6, Sat 10-5.
(Closed: Xmas & New Year's Day.)
🚹 (ground floor only) Shop
✖

MILNATHORT
Tayside (Kinross-shire) Map 11 NO10.
Burleigh Castle
A 16th-century tower house, with a courtyard enclosure and roofed angle tower, dating from 1582.

Open: see page 4
Application to key keeper.
(AM).

MILNGAVIE
Strathclyde, (Dunbartonshire)
Map 11 NS57.
Lillie Art Gallery
Station Road
A permanent collection of 20th-century Scottish paintings are included in this modern purpose built art gallery. There are also displays of sculpture and ceramics, and temporary exhibitions of contemporary art.

⌀ Glasgow 041-956 2351 Ext 226.
Open: all year Tue-Fri 11-5 & 7-9, Sat, Sun 2-5.
🔲 🚫

MINSTER-IN-THANET
Kent   Map 5 TR36.
Minster Abbey
One of the oldest inhabited houses in Kent with some 11th-century work. Now home of a religious order.

⌀ Thanet (0843) 821254.
Open: all year, May-Oct, Mon-Fri, 11-12 & 2-4.30, Sat 11-12 & 3.30-5; Oct-Apr, Mon-Sat 11-12.
Donations (alms box)
Shop

MINTLAW
Grampian (Aberdeenshire)
Map 15 NK04.
Aden Country Park
(1m W Mintlaw off A950)
230 acres of beautiful woodland set in open farmland. The grounds of a former estate, the Park is the home of many varieties of plants and animals which can be explored by a network of footpaths including a specially developed nature trail.

⌀ (07712) 2857.
Park open: all year.
Buildings open: mid May-Sep, 12-6.

North-East Scotland Agricultural Heritage Centre
Set in the beautiful surroundings of Aden Country Park, the Centre brings alive the rich farming heritage of the North-east. There are two exciting permanent exhibitions: 'Weel Vrocht Grun' (well-worked ground) which shows the impact of innovations on farming life over the last 200 years. The 'Aden Estate Story' shows life in the 1920s on the estate, using an audio-visual programme, a reconstructed horseman's house and a costume guide. There are regularly changing temporary exhibitions too, also a nature trail (guided nature walks by prior arrangement) and craftworkers. Aden Farm and Field Day with vintage farm machinery, Clydesdale horse teams, and demonstrations, 12 June 1988.

⌀ (0771) 22807 or Banff (02612) 2521.
Open: May-Sep daily 11-5; Apr & Oct wknds only, 12-5.
🔲 (ground floor & grounds only).
🛒 Shop 🚫 (in Heritage Centre)

MISTLEY
Essex   Map 5 TM13.
Mistley Towers
Twin, square porticoed towers, remaining features of church erected originally by Robert Adam c 1776. A hall was built at about the same time of which only the Adam Lodges constructed in 1782 still stand.

Open: towers accessible at all reasonable times.
🔲 (exterior only) (AM)

MOEL FAMAU
Clwyd   Map 7 SJ16.
Moel Famau Country Park
(3½m NE of Ruthin. N of unclassified road between Loggerheads and Llanbedr-Dyffryn-Clwyd
The country park is situated on the Clwydian Range and includes the highest summit, Moel Famau 1817 ft. From here there are excellent views stretching from Snowdonia to Liverpool and beyond. A tower was planned for the summit to mark George III's golden jubilee but never reached its full intended height and collapsed during a storm in 1862. The eastern slope of Moel Famau has a forest rich in wood-loving birds. There is a forest trail.

Open: accessible at all reasonable times.
🛏

MOFFAT
Dumfries and Galloway
(Dumfriesshire)   Map 11 NT00.
Ladyknowe Mill
Small mill where visitors can see garments being made. Showroom for the sale of woollens, tweeds and tartans.

⌀ (0683) 20134.
Open: daily May-Oct 8.30-5.30; Nov-Apr 10-4.
🛒 (licensed) Shop 🚫

MONMOUTH
Gwent   Map 3 SO51.
The Kymin
(1¾m E off A4136)
This 800ft vantage point has views of nine counties. The hilltop is crowned by a Naval temple built in 1800 in com-

memoration of Britain's victories at sea and decorated with plaques commemorating fifteen admirals and their most famous battles.

Open: accessible at all reasonable times.
(NT)

MONTGOMERY
Powys   *Map 7 SO29.*
Montgomery Castle
Overlooking the small town of Montgomery, the castle was built by Henry III about 1223 on the site of an earlier Norman motte and bailey. For a time it was the home of the powerful Marcher family of Mortimer and the Herberts and it was here that the poet George Herbert was born in 1593. Assaults by Parliamentarians during the Civil War in 1644 left the castle in ruins.

Open: accessible at all reasonable times.
(AM)

MONTROSE
Tayside (Angus)   *Map 15 NO75.*
Montrose Museum and Art Gallery
Extensive collections covering local history from prehistoric times including the maritime history of the port, the Natural History of Angus and local arts.

⊘ (0674) 73232.
Open: Apr-Oct, Mon-Sat 10.30-1 & 2-5, Sun (Jul & Aug only) 2-5; Nov-Mar, Mon-Fri 2-5, Sat 10.30-1 & 2-5.
⬥ (ground floor only) Shop ⬥ (ex guide dogs).

MORECAMBE
Lancashire   *Map 7 SD46.*
Morecambe Bay Nature Reserve
Hest Bank (2½m NE on A5105)
Morecambe Bay contains the largest area of tidal sand in

the British Isles, a feeding ground for thousands of birds which can be seen at high tide on the 6000 acre RSPB reserve at Hest Bank. Waders, dunlins, oyster-catchers, curlews, ringed plovers, redshanks and bar tailed godwits are amongst the birds easily observed. Further north, there is a vast area of salt marsh backed by limestone cliffs. **Warning:** the advancing tide races across the sands and water channels are filled with deep water within minutes. There is an information centre at Leighton Moss, Silverdale (west side of level crossing).

⊘ (0524) 701601.
Open: Nature Reserve: accessible at all reasonable times. Information Centre & Shop: Apr-Sep Sat, Sun, Wed, Thu 10-5; Oct Sat, Sun, Wed 10-5.

MORCOMBELAKE
Dorset   *Map 3 SY49.*
S. Moores, Biscuit Factory
Biscuits have been made in Morcombelake since 1880 and daily output here now runs at about 60,000 biscuits. Baking takes place during the morning and this is the best viewing time.

⊘ Chideock (029 789) 253.
Open: all year Mon-Fri 9-5.
Shop and gallery.

MORETON CORBET
Shropshire   *Map 7 SJ52.*
Castle
Triangular group comprising keep of c 1200, gatehouse altered in 1579, and notable Elizabethan range of the same date, all damaged by Parliamentary forces in 1644.

Open: at all reasonable times.
(AM) ⬥

MOSTYN
Clwyd   *Map 6 SJ18.*
Art Gallery
12 Vaughn Street
This Art Gallery re-opened in 1979 and is housed in a building originally built as an art gallery by Lady Augusta Mostyn. Each year there is a series of temporary exhibitions together with talks, art films and workshop activities.

⊘ Colwyn Bay (0492) 79201.
Open: all year Tue-Thu, Sat 11-5, Fri 11-8.
⬥

MOTHERWELL
Strathclyde (Lanarkshire)   *Map 11 NS75.*
Strathclyde Country Park
(1m NW)
Covering an area which lay derelict and neglected for years, now vast country park. The artificial loch (nearly two miles long) has two beaches and various watersports, and a wide scope of other leisure activities are available, including nature trails and riverside walks. Overlooking the loch and the motorway which runs across the park stands the 120ft high Hamilton Mausoleum, also open to the public.

⊘ (0698) 66155.
Open: Country Park at all reasonable times. Visitor Centre Etr-Sep, daily 10-4; Oct-Etr, Sat-Sun 10-4 (Admission charge Hamilton Mausoleum tours) ⬥

MOUSA ISLAND
see under **Shetland**

MOW COP
Cheshire/ Staffordshire   *Map 7 SJ85.*
Mow Cop Folly
Perched on a gritstone ridge rising to 1100ft, this Gothic folly was built in 1754 by Ran-

dle Wilbraham, to create a focal point on the skyline.

Open: accessible at all reasonable times.
(NT)

MUIRSHIEL
Strathclyde
(Renfrewshire)   Map 10 NS36.
Muirshiel Country Park
(4m NW of Lochwinnoch on unclass road)
Set in wild upland country, with trails and walks. Windy Hill (1036ft) gives fine views. Many woodland and moorland birds can be seen as well as small mammals and in June there are fine displays of rhododendrons. The visitor centre has a display of natural history. Guided walks can be arranged.

✆ Lochwinnoch (0505) 842803.
Open: park daily, dawn-dusk; visitor centre daily Apr-Sep 9-8; Oct-Mar 9-4.30.

MUSSELBURGH
Lothian (Midlothian)   Map 11 NT37.
Pinkie House
A fine Jacobean building of 1613 and later, incorporating a tower of 1390. Fine painted ceiling in the long gallery. The house now forms part of the Loretto School.

✆ 031-665 2059.
Open: mid Apr-mid Jul & mid Sep-mid Dec, Tue 2-5. ✕

NEW ABBEY
Dumfries and Galloway
(Kirkcudbrightshire)   Map 11 NX96.
Shambellie House Museum of Costume
(¼m N on A710)
A costume collection, made by Charles Stewart of Shambellie, of European fashionable dress from the late 18th century to early 20th century. Mainly women's clothes and accessories although some

children's and men's clothes; also fancy dress costume.

✆ (038785) 375 or 031-225 7534.
(National Museums of Scotland)
Open: May-Sep, Thu-Mon 10-5.30, Sun 12-5.30.
Shop ✕

NEWARK-ON-TRENT
Nottinghamshire   Map 8 SK85.
Millgate Museum of Social & Folk Life
Collection reflecting the domestic, commercial and industrial life of the district from Victorian times onwards, including printing, with craft workshops, still being developed.

✆ (0636) 79403.
Open: all year Mon-Fri 10-12 & 1-5; Etr-Sep, 1.30-5.30.
Shop ✕ (ex guide dogs)

Newark Museum
(Newark & Sherwood DC.)
Local history, archaeology, natural history and art.

✆ (0636) 702358.
Open: all year Mon-Wed, Fri & Sat 10-1 & 2-5; Apr-Sep also Sun 2-5.
♿ (ground floor only) Shop ✕

Newark Town Hall
Market Place
Designed by the architect John Carr in 1773, the town hall is perhaps one of the finest of all Georgian town halls. On display is the town's collection of silver gilt and silver plate, generally of the

Mow Cop Folly, purpose-built as a ruin

17th and 18th centuries. Other items of interest are early historical records and various paintings including a collection by Joseph Paul.

✆ (0636) 700200 & 700233.
Open: daily Mon-Fri, 10-12 & 2-4. (Closed BH Mon.)
Other times by appointment.
♿ (ground floor only)

NEWBURN
Tyne and Wear   Map 12 NZ16.
Tyne Riverside Country Park
(between Newburn and Ovingham)
A long narrow country park based on footpaths along the banks of the River Tyne between Newburn and Ovingham. Sand martins and kingfishers may be seen on the river banks.

Open: accessible at all reasonable times.

NEWBURY
Berkshire   Map 4 SU46.
Newbury District Museum
The Wharf
In picturesque 17th- and 18th-century buildings. Displays include ballooning; Kennet and Avon Canal; traditional crafts; costume; Civil War battles of Newbury (with audio-visual); and local collections of archaeology, history, geology and birds. Also

cameras, pewter and pottery. Temporary exhibitions throughout the year.

✆ (0635) 30511.
Open: Apr-Sep, Mon-Sat (ex Wed) 10-6, Sun & BH 2-6; Oct-Mar, Mon-Sat 10-4. (Closed: Sun & Wed).
♿ (ground floor only) Shop ✗ (ex guide dogs)

NEWCASTLE-UPON-TYNE
Tyne and Wear   Map 12 NZ26.
Laing Art Gallery
Higham Place
British paintings and watercolours from the 18th century to the present day with works by Reynolds, Turner, Burne-Jones and others including the Northumberland artist, John Martin. Also a collection of silver, ceramics and glass including a fine display of 18th-century enamelled glass by William Bailby of Newcastle. Temporary exhibition programme.

✆ 091-232 7734.
Open: Tue-Fri 10-5.30, Sat 10-4.30, Sun 2-30-5.30.
♿ Shop ✗

Museum of Antiquities
University Quadrangle
The collection has been in the course of assembly since 1813, and was opened in its present form in 1960. Valuable collection of Roman and other antiquities, with models, reconstructions etc.

✆ 091-232 8511 Ext 3844/3849.
Open: Mon-Sat 10-5.
(Closed: Good Fri, 24-26 Dec & New Year's Day.)
♿ (prior arrangement) Shop ✗ (ex guide dogs)

Museum of Science & Engineering
Blandford House, West Blandford Street
Motive power (engine) gallery; pioneers of industry gal-

lery; maritime gallery; special exhibitions, educational activities, plus supporting displays.

✆ 091-232 6789.
Open: Tues-Fri 10-5.30, Sat 10-4.30. (Closed Xmas & 1 Jan.)
🚻 (10-3pm Tue & Fri) ✗ (ex guide dogs)

NEW GALLOWAY
Dumfries & Galloway
(Kirkcudbrightshire)   Map 11 NX67.
Galloway Deer Museum
(5m SW off A712)
In a converted farm this museum not only features the deer but also shows aspects of the history and wildlife of the area, including a display of live trout.

Open: daily Apr-Oct 10-5.

NEWPORT
Dyfed   Map 2 SN04.
Pentre Ifan Burial Chamber
(3m SE)
Remains of this chamber comprise capstone and three uprights with semi-circular forecourt at one end. Excavated 1936-37 when found to be part of vanished long barrow.

Open: at all reasonable times.
(AM)

NEWPORT
Gwent   Map 3 ST38.
Fourteen Locks Picnic Area
(NW, off B4591)
The picnic area takes its name from the flight of fourteen locks designed by Thomas Dadford on the Crumlin arm of the Monmouthshire and Brecon Canal. The 'staircase' enabled barges to climb 168 ft in less than 1,000 yards, and has a series of 'top', 'header' and 'side' ponds. The canal ceased in

1930. Waymarked walks start from the interpretative centre.

✆ (0633) 89402.
Open: Interpretative Centre Apr-Sep, Thu-Mon 10-5.30; Waymarked walks accessible at all reasonable times. Details not confirmed for 1988.
♿ ⛩

Museum & Art Gallery
John Frost Square
Archaeology and history of Gwent including Roman finds from Caerwent and Pontypool; Japanned ware; section on Chartist movement of 1838-40. Natural history and geology. Also collection of early English watercolours. The Newport Tourist Centre is housed here.

✆ (0633) 840064.
Open: Mon-Thu 9.30-5, Fri 9.30-4.30, Sat 9.30-4.
♿ Shop ✗ (ex guide dogs)

NEWTONMORE
Highland (Inverness-shire)
Map 14 NN79.
Clan Macpherson House & Museum
Relics and memorials of the Clan Chiefs and other Macpherson families. Prince Charles Edward Stuart relics, including letters to the Clan Chief (1745) and a letter to the Prince from his father (the Old Pretender). Royal Warrants, Green Banner of the Clan, swords, pictures, decorations and medals. Also James Macpherson's fiddle, and other interesting historical exhibits. Highland Games 1st Sat in August.

✆ (05403) 332.
Open: May-Sep, Mon-Sat 10-5.30, Sun 2.30-5.30. Other times by appointment.
(Donations)
♿ ✗ (ex guide dogs)

NEWTON STEWART

Dumfries and Galloway
(Wigtownshire)   *Map 10 NX46.*

Cree Weaving Mills

(½m N, on A714)
Producing high quality mohair products (from the fleece of the Angora goat). Visitors are shown weaving, brushing with natural teasles, and finishing processes for the outstandingly soft, light and warm wool.

⌀ 0938 2043.
Open: guided tours all year Mon-Fri 10-2.30; Shop Etr-Oct, Mon-Sat 9-5; Nov-Etr, Mon-Fri 9-5.
🅐 (ground floor only)

NEWTOWN

Powys   *Map 6 SO19.*

Robert Owen Memorial Museum

The Cross
Museum on the life and work of Robert Owen, born here in 1771. The pioneer of modern British socialism and father of the co-operative movement, Owen set up a very successful mill at New Lanark in the Industrial Revolution.

⌀ (0938) 2043.
Open: all year, Mon-Fri 9.45-11.45, 2-3.30; Sat 10-11.30.
🅐

Textile Museum

Commercial Street
Housed in the upper floor workshops of a woollen mill where handloom weavers once worked, the museum exhibits interesting relics from the days when Newtown had a thriving woollen industry. Exhibits include mill machinery, 19th century handlooms, cottage and mill shop fronts, and examples of wool and flannel.

Open: Apr-Oct, Tue-Sat 2-4.30.

W H Smith (1920s Replica Shop)

24 High Street
This branch of W H Smith is a unique combination of a shop and a museum. The shop has been completely restored to its original state at the time it was first opened in 1927, and on the first floor is the museum. Displays, photographs, models and memorabilia date back to 1792.

⌀ (0686) 26280.
Open: Mon-Sat 2-30-5.30 & BH Mons 9-12.
🅐 (Shop only)

NORTHAMPTON

Northamptonshire   *Map 4 SP76.*

Abington Park

Large landscaped town park with lakes, well planted with trees and noted for its colour in the autumn. Garden for the blind. Aviary with wide variety of birds.

⌀ (0604) 33193.
Open: at all reasonable times.
🅐

Carlsberg Brewery Limited

140 Bridge Street
Producing over 60 million gallons of lager annually, with the latest computer controlled equipment. Visitors can see the various brewing processes and at the end of the tour are invited to sample 'probably the best lager in the world'.

⌀ (0604) 234333.
Open: tours Mon-Fri 9.15 & 2.15 (always telephone Visitors Department in advance).
⌀

Delapre Abbey

(½m S off A508)
16th- to 19th-century house with fine porch, built on site of Cluniac nunnery. Contains

Northamptonshire Record Office and HQ of Northamptonshire Record Society.

⌀ (0604) 762129.
Abbey grounds, open: all year dawn-dusk. Walled garden open May to Sep only during daylight.
Certain parts of the interior shown Thu only, May-Sep 2.30-5; Oct-Apr 2.30-4.30.
🅐 (grounds only) ⌀ (in house)

Hunsbury Hill Country Park

(1¾m S off A45)
The Iron Age hill fort on the summit of Hunsbury Hill (370 ft) is the centrepiece of the 98-acre park, with a toposcope at the viewpoint overlooking Northampton. Surrounding attractions include an adventure playground, standard gauge railway and museum exploring the local ironstone industry.

⌀ (0604) 767216 (evenings only).
Open: accessible at all reasonable times.
Admission charge railway and museum.
⌀

NORTH BERWICK

Lothian (East Lothian)   *Map 12 NT58.*

North Berwick Law

(S off B1347)
A conical volcanic peak rising to 613 ft to the south of the town and an excellent viewpoint. The summit is crowned by a watch tower dating from Napoleonic times and an archway made from the jawbones of a whale.

Open: accessible at all reasonable times.

North Berwick Museum

Small museum in former Burgh school with sections on local and natural history, archaeology and domestic life. Exhibitions held throughout the summer.

✆ (0620) 3470.
Open: Jun-Sep, Mon-Sat 10-1 & 2-5, Sun 2-5.
Shop ✗

NORTH CREAKE
Norfolk   Map 9 TF83.
Creake Abbey
(1m N off B1355)
Church ruin with crossing and eastern arm belonging to a house of Augustinian canons founded in 1206.

Open: accessible at all reasonable times.
(AM)

NORTHENDEN
Greater Manchester   Map 7 SJ89.
Wythenshawe Hall
Wythenshawe Park
Inside this black and white half-timbered house are 17th-century panelled rooms with oak furniture, an early 19th-century library and a restored Georgian bedroom. Recently discovered behind the panelling is a rare example of Tudor wall painting. The house is surrounded by beautiful parkland with rare trees and shrubs, horticultural centre, an aviary and walled kitchen garden.

✆ 061-236 9422.
Open: Apr-Sep Mon & Wed-Sat 10-6.
♿ Shop ✗

NORTHINGTON
Hampshire   Map 4 SU53.
The Grange
(off B3046)
Built in the style of a Greek temple, this 17th-century mansion by William Samwell is one of the most important neo-classical country houses in Europe. Only viewable from the outside it features a massive Doric portico over-

looking a lake. Display boards show the history of The Grange.

Open: Mon-Sat 9.30-6.30, Sun 2-6.30. (Closes 4.30 in winter.)

NORTH WOOTTON
Somerset   Map 3 ST54.
Wootton Vineyard
North Town House
A vineyard set in the foothills of the Mendips, 3m from Wells, 9,000 vines specially imported from the Rhine and Alsace. The old farm buildings house a winery where fresh dry white wine is made. Visitors can walk in the vineyards and wines may be purchased direct from the cellar.

✆ Pilton (074989) 359.
Open: Mon-Sat 10-1 & 2-5.
Shop ✗

NORWICH
Norfolk   Map 5 TG20.
Cathedral
Herbert de Losinga, the first Bishop of Norwich, founded the cathedral in 1096. It is a superb building, and among its most notable features are the nave, with its huge round pillars, the bishop's throne (a Saxon survival unique in Europe), and the cloisters with their matchless collection of roof bosses.

✆ (0603) 626290.
Open: daily summer 7.30-7, winter 7.30-6.
(Donations)
♿ 🚻 ✗

City Hall
St Peter Street
Civic Plate and Insignia dating from 1549 on show; also to be seen is the Council Chamber. The Civic Regalia may be relocated to the Guildhall in 1988.

✆ (0603) 62223 Ext 2059.
Open: Mon-Fri 10-4, visits

by arrangement with the Director of Administration.
♿ (ground floor only) Shop. Details not confirmed for 1988.

Royal Norfolk Regimental Museum
Brittannia Barracks, Brittannia Road.
Contains a fine collection of medals, uniforms and weapons, paintings, silver and trophies amassed by the Regiment.

✆ (0603) 628455.
Open: Mon-Fri 9-12.30, 2-4. (Closed: BH.)
(Donations)
✗

St Peter Hungate Church Museum
Princes Street, near Elm Hill.
Fine church (1460), with hammer-beam roof and good Norwich painted glass, now museum of church art. Brass rubbing centre.

✆ (0603) 66723.
Open: Mon-Sat 10-5. (Closed: Good Fri, Xmas & New Year's day).
♿ Shop ✗

NOTTINGHAM
Nottinghamshire   Map 8 SK53.
Brewhouse Yard Museum
Castle Boulevard
Housed in 17th-century buildings on a two-acre site. The museum depicts daily life in the city in post-medieval times with period rooms and thematic displays. Unusual rock-cut cellars open showing their uses in the past. The museum contains material which can be handled or operated by the public. The cottage gardens contain unusual local plants.

✆ (0602) 411881 Ext 67 or 48.
Open: all year daily 10-12 & 1-5, last admission 11.45 & 4.45pm.

Costumes at Nottingham

(Closed Xmas.) Parties must book.
♿ (ground floor only) ✗ (ex guide dogs)

Canal Museum
Canal Street
On ground floor and wharfage of 19th-century warehouse, the museum tells the history of the River Trent from the Ice Age to the present day. Includes a local canal and river navigation, boats, bridges, archaeology, etc.

✆ (0602) 598835.
Open: Apr-Sep, Wed-Sat 10-12 & 1-5.45, Sun 1-5.45; Oct-Mar, Wed, Thu & Sat 10-12 & 1-5, Sun 1-5.
♿ Shop ✗

Green's Mill and Science Centre
Belvoir Hill, Sneinton
A partially reconstructed tower mill restored to working order with flour milling.

The adjacent Science Museum contains working models and exhibits illustrating the importance to science of George Green, one time miller and distinguished mathematician.

✆ (0602) 503635.
Open: Wed-Sun 10-12 & 1-5 also BH's. (Closed: Xmas day.)
♿ (ex mill) Shop ✗

Industrial Museum
Courtyard Buildings, Wollaton Park
Housed in 18th-century stable block are displays illustrating Nottingham's industrial history and in particular the lace and hosiery industries, together with exhibits on the pharmaceutical industry, engineering, tobacco industry and printing. New extensions house a mid-19th-century beam pumping engine, and heavy agricultural machinery. Outside yards display a horse gin from a local coalmine, Victorian street furniture etc.

✆ (0602) 284602.
Open: Apr-Sep, Mon-Sat 10-6, Sun 2-6; Oct-Mar, Thu & Sat 10-4.30; Sun 1.30-4.30, 19th-century beam pumping engine in steam last Sun in each month & BH.
Admission charge Sun & BH.
(Ticket valid for both this and Natural History Museum, Wollaton Hall.)
♿ Shop ✗

Museum of Costume and Textiles
43-51 Castlegate
Displays include costume from 1730 to 1960 in furnished room settings of c.1790, 1830, 1860, 1885, 1910 and 1935. Other rooms contain 17th-century costume and embroidery, the Lord Middleton collection, map tapestries of Nottinghamshire, dress accessories from 18th century to circa 1960. English, European and Asian embroidery, knitted, woven and printed textiles. Also hand- and machine-made lace.

✆ (0602) 411881.
Open: daily 10-5. (Closed: Xmas day.) ♿ (ground floor only)
Shop ✗

Natural History Museum
Wollaton Hall
Housed in imposing Elizabethan mansion by Robert Smythson, dating from 1580-1588, and situated in large park with deer. Wide range of displays including birds, mammal, mineral and fossil displays.

✆ (0602) 281333 & 281130.
Open: Apr-Sep, Mon-Sat
10-7, Sun 2-5; Oct, Mon-Sat
10-5.30, Sun 1.30-4.30;
Nov-Mar, Mon-Sat 10-4.30,
Sun 1.30-4.30.
Admission charge Sun & BH.
⌗ Etr-Sep ⚲ 🅿 (ground floor
& gardens) Shop ⊗

NUNEATON
Warwickshire   *Map 4 SP39.*
**Nuneaton Museum and Art
Gallery**
Riversley Park
A purpose-built structure,
situated in a pleasant public
park, it houses a permanent
collection of ethnography,
archaeology, the George
Eliot Collection and a display
of fine miniatures painted by
May B Lee (Lady Stott). From
March to May the Nuneaton
Festival of Art is held here.

✆ (0203) 326211.
Open: summer, Mon-Fri
12-7, Sat & Sun 10-7; winter
12-5 & 10-5.
🅿 (ground floor only) Shop
⊗

NUNEHAM
COURTENAY
Oxfordshire   *Map 4 SU59.*
**John Mattock Rose
Nurseries**
An internationally known
rose grower with display
gardens of hundreds of
thousands of roses grown
annually from leading rose
hybridists.

✆ (086738) 265 or 454.
Open: Mar-Oct 8.30-6; Oct-
Mar 8.30-5, Sun 11-6.
🅿

**Oxford University
Arboretum**
(on A423 just S of the village)
50 acres of conifers and
broad leaf trees.

✆ (0865) 242737.
Open: May-Oct Mon-Sat

8.30-5 & Sun 2-6.
🅿 ⊗

NUNNEY
Somerset   *Map 3 ST74.*
Nunney Castle
Moated structure modelled
on French 'Bastille', built by
Sir John de la Mere in 1373.
Surrounded by one of the
deepest moats in England.

Open: at all reasonable
times.
🅿 (exterior only) (AM)

OAKHAM
Leicestershire   *Map 4 SK80.*
Oakham Castle
off Market Place
Preserves a splendid Nor-
man hall, with unique collection of presentation horse-
shoes.

✆ (0572) 3654.
Open: all year; Grounds,
daily 10-5.30; Great Hall,
Tue-Sat & BH 10-1 & 2-5.30;
Sun 2-5.30; Nov-Mar closes
4pm. (Closed: Good Fri,
Xmas). Magistrates Court in
session on Mon.
🅿 Shop ⊗ (ex guide dogs)

Rutland County Museum
Catmos Street
Local archaeology, especially Roman and Anglo-Saxon,
craft tools and local history.
Courtyard containing various
farm wagons and agricultural
implements. Temporary ex-
hibitions. This is generally
agreed to be one of the best
collections of its kind.

✆ (0572) 3654.
Open: Apr-Oct, Tue-Sat &
BH 10-1 & 2-5, Sun 2-5; Nov-
Mar, Tue-Sat 10-1 & 2-5.
(Closed: Good Fri & Xmas).
🅿 (ground floor only) Shop
⊗ (ex guide dogs).

OAKWELL HALL
West Yorkshire   *Map 8 SE22.*
*In Nova Lane, near Birstall
Smithies (6m SE of Bradford)*

Elizabethan moated manor
house (1583), with Civil War
and Brontë connections. It
was 'Fieldhead', in Charlotte
Brontë's novel *Shirley*. There
is a recently opened Country
Park complex. Full programme of summer events.

✆ Batley (0924) 474926.
Open: all year Mon-Sat 10-5,
Sun 1-5.
⌗ ⚲ Shop ⊗

OBAN
Strathclyde (Argyll)   *Map 10 NM83.*
Caithness Glass
*Oban Glassworks,
Lochavullin Estate.*
Visitors can see the art of
paperweight making. Large
seconds shop.

✆ (0631) 63386.
Open: all year Mon-Fri 9-5.
May-Sep also Sat 9-1.
🅿 Shop ⊗

Macdonald's Mill
*(½m S of centre of Oban on
A816)*
Exhibition of the Story of
Spinning and Weaving, with
demonstrations of this
ancient Scottish industry.
Also showroom containing
modern products.

✆ (0631) 63081.
Open: Mar-May 8.30-5.30,
Jun-Sep 8.30-7.30, Oct 9-5.30.
⌗ 🅿 Shop ⊗ (ex guide dogs)

OGMORE
Mid Glamorgan   *Map 3 SS87.*
Ogmore Castle
On River Ogmore with inner
and outer wards and early
12th-century three-storeyed
keep preserving hooded
fireplace. West wall 40ft high,
and dry moat around inner
ward.

Open: see page 4.
(AM CADW).

OLD CLEEVE

Somerset   *Map 3 ST04.*
John Wood Sheepskins
Visitors can see sheepskins
being processed from their
natural state, including tan-
ning, dyeing and the crafting
of various sheepskin pro-
ducts.

✆ Washford (0984) 40291.
**Open: factory tours, Apr-
Oct Mon-Fri 10.45 & 11.30,
2.15 & 3.00 (parties by
appointment); showroom &
shop all year Mon-Fri 9-4.30;
also Sat & BH 10-4.**
🅰 ✗

OLD DAILLY

Strathclyde (Ayrshire)   Map 10 NX29.
Bargany Gardens
(4m NE of Girvan on B734)
Woodland walks; with fine
displays of snowdrops,
bluebells and daffodils in
spring. Fine display of
azaleas and rhododendrons
round lily pond in May and
June. Autumn colours. Many
ornamental trees. Plants for
sale.

✆ (046587) 227 or 274.
**Gardens open: Mar-Oct
daily until 7pm (or dusk).
(Donations)**
🅰

OLD WHITTINGTON

Derbyshire   *Map 8 SK37.*
Revolution House
Old house, once known as
Cock and Pynot (or Magpie)
Inn, with 17th-century fur-
nishings. Associated with the
1688 revolution.

✆ Chesterfield (0246) 32088.
**Open: 3 Apr-25 Sep, Wed-
Sun & BH Mon, 10-12 & 1-5.30.**
✗

Orkney (Isles of)
BIRSAY

Orkney   *Map 16 HY22.*
Earls Palace
*(14m N of Stromness on
A967)*

Located in a windy position
on the north-west corner of
the Orkney Mainland, this
large ruin was the residence
of the 16th-century Earls of
Orkney. The Palace was constructed around a courtyard
with projecting rectangular
towers at the corners, except
at the northwest.

**Open: accessible at all
reasonable times.**
🅰 **(AM)**

DOUNBY

Orkney   *Map 16 HY22.*
Click Mill
(NE of village, off B9057)
An example of one of the
rare old Orcadian horizontal
watermills, in working condition.

**Open: at all reasonable
times.**
(AM)

FINSTOWN

Orkney   *Map 16 HY31.*
Stenness Standing Stones
(3m SW on A965)
Remains of a stone circle,
second millennium BC. Nearby is the Ring of Brogar
(c.2000 BC) consisting of a
splendid circle of upright
stones with a surrounding
ditch.

**Open: at all reasonable
times.**
(AM)

HOY

Orkney   *Map 16 HY20.*
Dwarfie Stane
*(Off unclass road between
Moness Pier and Rackwick)*
Located in a remote glen
south of Ward Hill, the
Dwarfie Stane consists of a
great block of sandstone,
measuring 28ft long, 14ft
wide and 8ft tall, into which a
passage has been cut. No
other such rock-cut tomb is

***Cutting peat for Highland
Park Distillery, Kirkwall***

known in Britain and it is believed to be about 5000 years old.

Open: accessible at all reasonable times.

KIRKWALL

Orkney   Map 16 HY41.

Grain and Rennibister Earth Houses

Grain Earth House (½m W off A965); Rennibister Earth House (At Rennibister Farm, 4m W off A965)

Both excellently preserved earth houses date from the Iron Age and can be reached by descending a short ladder to an underground chamber from which there is an underground passage with supporting pillars.

Open: Grain Earth House — Apply to keykeeper at Ortak shop in nearby Industrial Estate Mon-Sat 9-5. Rennibister Earth House — accessible at all reasonable times.
(AM)

Highland Park Distillery

(1m S on A961)

Traditional methods are used with peat fires to dry the barley, hand-beaten copper pot stills for distilling and old sherry casks to mature the finished product. The correct maturing period of at least twelve years is strictly observed. Visitors are shown the complete process of whisky making from the barley store to the warehouses.

𝄢 (0856) 3107 (Visitors Centre - 4619).
Open: Mon-Fri. For guided tours' times, please telephone in advance.
𝄡

St Magnus Cathedral

Fine red and yellow sandstone Cathedral begun in 1137 by Earl Rognvald in memory of his uncle and predecessor Magnus, who was murdered by a rival about 1117. The polychrome stonework is considered to be the best of medieval age in Britain.

𝄢 (0856) 3535.
Open: daily Mon-Sat 9-1, 2-5.
𝄡

Tankerness House

Broad Street

Dating from the 16th century, this is one of the finest vernacular town houses in Scotland. It is now a museum of Orkney history introducing the island's fascinating archaeology.

𝄢 (0856) 3191.
Open: Mon-Sat 10.30-12.30 & 1.30-5; May-Sep, Sun 2-5.
♿ (ground floor only) Shop
𝄡

LAMB HOLM

Orkney   Map 16 HY40.

Italian Chapel

(8m S of Kirkwall on A961)

Converted in World War II from a couple of Nissen huts to an ornate chapel, by Italian prisoners of war. These prisoners also built the nearby Churchill Barriers linking the islands of Orkney Mainland, Lamb Holm, Glimps Holm, Burray and South Ronaldsay.

𝄢 Holm (085678) 278.
Open: at all reasonable times.
(Donations).
♿ 𝄡

ROUSAY

Orkney   Map 16 HY33.

Midhowe Broch and Tombs

(5½m W of Island's pier)

Standing on the cliff edge overlooking the small island of Eynhallow, this is a good example of an Iron Age broch with a walled enclosure cut off by a deep rock-cut ditch. Several secondary buildings, which have survived persistent coastal erosion, are dotted around the broch. Nearby is Midhowe Chambered Cairn, considered to be one of the best in Orkney. Its central chamber is almost 75ft long.

Open: accessible at all reasonable times.

STROMNESS

Orkney   Map 16 HY20.

Pier Arts Centre

Collection housed in warehouse building on its own stone pier. Also galleries for visiting exhibitions and children's work. Arts library and reading room in adjacent house.

𝄢 (0856) 850209.
Open: all year Tue-Sat 10.30-12.30 & 1.30-5; Sun. Jun-Aug only 2-5.
♿ (ground floor only) 𝄡

PAPA WESTRAY

Orkney   Map 16 HY45.

Knap of Howar

(W side of island near Holland House)

Recently confirmed as northwest Europe's oldest standing house. It was built over 5,000 years ago and visitors can see how large flagstones have been used for cupboards, hearths and seating. Other finds in the house have included whalebone mallets and unique stone borers and grinders. There are many other prehistoric monuments on the island.

Open: accessible at all reasonable times.
(AM)

WESTRAY

Orkney   Map 16 HY44.

Noltland Castle

Late 16th-century ruined castle which was never completed. It has a fine hall, vaulted kitchen and a notable winding staircase.

Open: at all reasonable times on application to Key Keeper. (AM)

ORPINGTON

Gtr London See page 00.

Priory Museum

The Priory, Church Hill,

London Plan 2 : 43F1.

13th- 14th-century clergy

house with addition of 15th-century manor house. Now small museum of local interest where special exhibitions are held during the year.

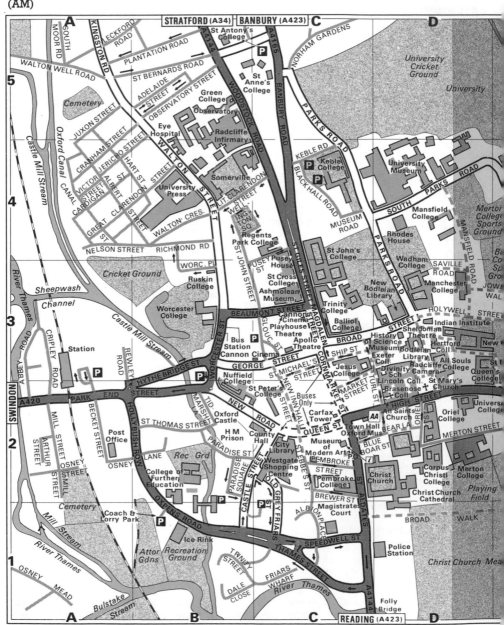

☎ (0689) 31551.
Open: all year Mon-Wed,
Fri, Sat 9-5 (5pm Sat)
(Closed PH).
♿ (ground floor only) ⚥

OSWESTRY

Shropshire   *Map 7 SJ23.*
Old Oswestry
(½m N)
Iron Age hill fort covering 68
acres, with five ramparts and
elaborate western portal.
Abutted by part of the
prehistoric Wat's Dyke.

Open: accessible at all
reasonable times.
Kissing Gate (AM)

OXFORD

Oxfordshire   *Map 7 SP50.*
Ancient and picturesque Uni-
versity city on rivers Cher-
well and Thames, dating
back to 8th century. The University, the oldest in Britain,
probably dates from c.1167
and consists of a large number of colleges built over a
period of several centuries,
many of which are among the
finest buildings of their age.
Access to some colleges is
restricted to certain times
and details may be obtained
from the Oxford Information
Centre, St Aldake's.

**Ashmolean Museum of Art
and Archaeology**
Beaumont Street   *Plan : C3.*
The oldest (1683) museum in
the country, housed in C R
Cockerell's building of 1845
(with later extensions). Its exhibits include archaeological
items of British, European,
Mediterranean, Egyptian
and Near Eastern origins.
Also exhibited are coins and
medals of all countries and
periods, in the Heberden
Coin Room; Italian, Dutch,
Flemish, French, and English
oil paintings, Old Master and
modern drawings, water-
colours, prints and miniatures; European ceramics;
English silver; Chinese and
Japanese porcelain; painting
and lacquer; Tibetan art; Indian sculpture and paintings;
Islamic pottery and metalwork; Chinese bronzes; casts
from the antique and objects
of applied art. Temporary exhibits throughout the year.

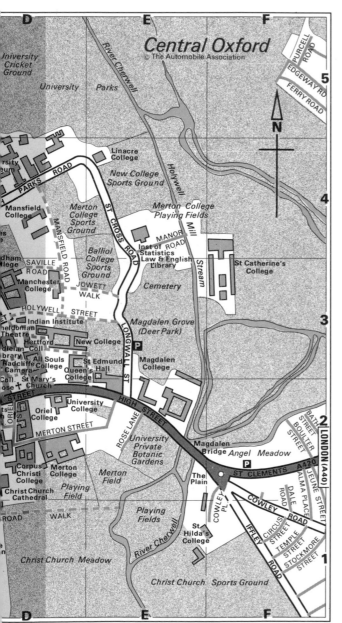

Central Oxford
© The Automobile Association

🕾 (0865) 278000.
Open: all year, Tue-Sat 10-4,
Sun 2-4. (Closed: Etr & during
St. Giles Fair in early Sep,
Xmas period & 1 Jan.)
(Donations)
Guided tours by
arrangement.
🛗 Shop ⌀

Museum of the History of Science
*Old Ashmolean Building,
Broad Street* *Plan : D3.*
Contains the finest collection
of early astronomical, mathe-
matical and optical instruments in the world. Housed
in the Old Ashmolean Building, a fine example of 17th-
century architecture which
was originally built to hold
the collection of Elias
Ashmole. One of the most
distinquished parts of the
present display is the series
of Islamic and European
astrolabes, once used for
astronomical calculations.
Also early microscopes and
other optical instruments,
photographic apparatus,
clocks and watches, air
pumps etc. Of special in-
terest are the penicillin material, H G J Moseley's X-ray
spectrometer, and a pro-
totype of Dr C R Burch's ultra
violet reflecting microscope
made in 1946.

🕾 (0865) 277280.
Open: Mon-Fri 10.30-1 &
2.30-4. (Closed: BH, Xmas
and Etr week).
Bookstall ⌀

Museum of Oxford
St Aldates *Plan : C2.*
Permanent displays of the
archaeology and history of
the university city from the
earliest times to the present
day. Temporary exhibitions.
Facilities for parties.

🕾 (0865) 815559.
Open: all year, Tue-Sat,

10-5. (Closed: Good Fri &
Xmas).
Bookshop ⌀

St Edmund Hall
College of Oxford University
Plan : E3.
This is the only surviving
medieval hall and has a Norman crypt, 17th-century din-
ning hall, chapel and quadrangle. Other buildings 18th-
and 20th-century.

🕾 (0865) 279006.
Open: all year, daily
7.30-dusk. (Closed: 23
Dec-1 Jan, 1-8 Apr & 27-30
Aug).
🛗 (ground floor & grounds
only) ⌀

University Private Botanic Garden
*High Street (by Magdalen
Bridge)* *Plan : E2.*
Gardens of great botanical
interest, founded in 1621, and
the oldest in the country.

🕾 (0865) 242737.
Open: all year Mon-Fri
8.30-5, (9-4.30 Oct-Mar), Sun
10-12 & 2-6 (2-4.30 Oct-Mar).
Greenhouses open daily
2-4. (Closed: Good Fri &
Xmas day.)
🛗 (grounds only) ⌀

PAIGNTON
Devon *Map 3 SX86.*
Oldway
19th-century house containing replicas of rooms at the
Palace of Versailles. Picturesque gardens. Tennis,
putting & bowling.

🕾 Torquay (0803) 550711.
House open: May-Sep,
Mon-Sat, 10-1 & 2.15-5.15,
Sun 2.30-5.30; winter Mon-
Fri 10-1 & 2.15-5.15
(Closed: Sat & Sun.) Closed
occasionally for Council
purposes.
🍴 summer only 🛗 (ground

floor & gardens only) ⌀ (ex
guide dogs)

PAISLEY
Strathclyde (Renfrewshire)
Map 11 NS46.
Coats Observatory
49 Oakshaw Street
Dating from 1883 but recently
renovated and installed with
modern technology, the
Observatory has resumed a
role of importance in the
realms of astronomy and
meteorology. There are displays relating to the history of
the building, astronomy,
meteorology and space
flight.

🕾 041-889 3151.
Open: Mon-Fri 2-5, Sat 10-1
& 2-5, Oct-Mar Thu 7-9pm
weather permitting.
(Closed Xmas & New Year).
Shop ⌀

Paisley Museum and Art Galleries
High Street
Collection illustrates local, industrial and natural history of
the town and district. Also a
world-famous collection of
Paisley shawls. The art collection concentrates on 19th-
century Scottish artists. In
1988 an exhibition will mark
Paisley's 500th anniversary
celebrations.

🕾 041-889 3151.
Open: Mon-Sat, 10-5.
(Closed PH).
🛗 (ground floor only) Shop
⌀

PALNACKIE
*Dumfries and Galloway
(Kircudbrightshire)* *Map 11 NX85.*
Orchardton Tower
A rare example of a circular
tower built originally in the
late 15th century.

Open: see page 4, on
application to the Key
Keeper.
(AM)

PENARTH
South Glamorgan   *Map 3 ST17.*
Turner House
A small gallery holding temporary and travelling exhibitions of pictures and objets d'art from the National Museum of Wales, and other sources.

✆ Cardiff (0222) 708870.
Open: Tue-Sat & BH Mons, 11-12.45 & 2-5, (Closed: 24-26 Dec & 1 Jan, Good Fri & May Day).
Shop ✗

PENARTH FAWR
Gwynedd   *Map 6 SH43.*
(3½m NE of Pwllheli, off A497)
Part of a house built probably in early 15th-century, preserving hall, buttery and screen.

Open: accessible at all reasonable times.
(AM CADW)

PENMACHNO
Gwynedd   *Map 6 SH75.*
Penmachno Woollen Mill
In the 17th century, cloth woven by cottage weavers was washed and finished in the Pandy (Fulling Mill) for making into flannel shirts for local quarrymen and farmers. Power looms introduced in the 19th century now weave lightweight tweed and rug cloth. Story of Wool exhibition and Mill Shop.

✆ Betws-y-Coed (06902) 545.
Open: daily pre Etr-mid Nov. Weaving, Mon-Fri. Audiovisual of Story of Wool. (Closed: Sun and early & late season.)
🍽 Shop ✗

PENMON
Gwynedd   *Map 6 SH68.*
Penmon Priory
There has been a religious settlement here since the 6th-century. The Priory church and adjacent ruins date from the 12th century, and have the best Romanesque detail in North Wales. To the north of the church is the holy well where St Seiriol is said to have baptized converts. On the opposite side of the road is a dovecote dating from about 1600 and crowned with an open hexagonal lantern. There are about one thousand nesting holes.

Open: ruins, well, dovecote accessible at all reasonable times.
(AM)

PENZANCE
Cornwall   *Map 2 SW43.*
Penlee House, Museum & Art Gallery
Penlee Park
The history and development of the district from earliest man to the 1980s. Exhibition of Newlyn School of Painting.

✆ (0736) 63625.
Open: all year, Mon-Fri 10.30-4.30 (Gallery closed 12.30-2.30) Sat 10.30-12.30. (Exhibition of paintings closed 12.30-2.30) (Closed: BH's). Admission charge paintings exhibition Jun-Sep.
🦽 (ground floor & grounds only) Shop ✗

PERTH
Tayside (Perthshire)   *Map 11 NO12.*
Black Watch Regimental Museum
Balhousie Castle, Hay Street
Treasures of the 42nd/73rd Highland Regiment from 1725 to the present day, including, paintings, silver, colours and uniforms.

✆ (0738) 21281 Ext 30.
Open: Mon-Fri 10-4.30 (Winter 3.30); Sun & PHs Etr-Sep 2-4.30. Other times & parties 20+ by appointment. (Donations)
Shop ✗

Caithness Glass
Inveralmond Industrial Est
All aspects of glass making can be seen from the viewing gallery at this purpose-built visitor centre. Collectors' Museum. Also a factory seconds shop.

✆ (0738) 37373.
Open: all year Mon-Sat 9-5, Sun 1-5. (11-5 Etr-Sep).
🍽 (licensed) 🦽 Shop

Dewar's Scotch Whisky
J Dewar's & Son Ltd, Inveralmond
Visitors are given a 1½-hour tour, showing blending, bottling, and despatch of whisky, and coopering of casks. Whisky sampling may be available.

✆ (0738) 21231.
Open: guided tours all year, Mon-Thurs 10.15 and 2.15, Fri 10.15. (Closed company holidays). Contact tour organiser in advance. Childen under 14 not admitted.
✗

Fair Maid's House
North Port
Situated near the historic North Inch where the battle of the Clans was fought in 1392. In the 14th-century it became the home of Simon Glover, a glovemaker whose daughter Catherine was the heroine of Sir Walter Scott's 'Fair Maid of Perth'. The house was a guildhall for over 150 years. It was renovated in the 19th-century and is now a centre for Scotttish crafts. A recently uncovered wall is said to be the oldest one visible in Perth. The up-

stairs gallery has changing exhibitions of paintings, sculptures, tapestries etc.

✆ (0738) 25976.
Open: all year, Mon-Sat 10-5. Gallery 11-4.
⚕ (ground floor only).

Perth Museum & Art Gallery
78 George Street
Purpose-built to house collections of fine and applied art, social and local history, natural history and archaeology. Special events monthly.

✆ (0738) 32488.
Open: Mon-Sat 10-1 & 2-5.
Shop ⚥

The Round House
Marshall Place
Built and designed by Dr Adam Anderson in 1832 the building was the first waterworks in the city. In 1974 it was restored by Perth Town Council and is now the Tourist Information Centre. There is a 360° slide programme showing Perth in sound and vision.

✆ (0738) 22900/27108.
Open: all year, Mon-Fri 9-7, Sat 9-6; Jun-Sep also Sun 12-5. Details not confirmed for 1988.

PETERBOROUGH
Cambridgeshire   Map 4 TL19.
City of Peterborough Museum and Art Gallery
Priestgate
Collections include local geology, archaeology, natural history and articles from former French prisoners' jail at Norman Cross. Also painting and a small collection of ceramics and glass as well as temporary exhibitions.

✆ (0733) 43329.
Open: May-Sep Tue-Sat 10-5; Oct-Apr Tue-Sat 12-5.

Fair Maid's House, Perth

(Closed: Good Fri & Xmas.)
Shop ⚥

PETERHEAD
Grampian (Aberdeenshire)
            Map 15 NK14.
Arbuthnot Museum and Art Gallery
St Peter Street
Specialises in local exhibits, particularly those relating to the fishing industry with Arctic and whaling specimens. Also a British coin collection.

✆ (0779) 77778.
Open: all year, Mon-Sat 10-12 & 2-5. (Closed: PH.)
Shop ⚥ (ex guide dogs)

PITLOCHRY
Tayside (Perthshire)   Map 14 NN95.
Faskally
(2m NW)
Incorporates woodland and lochside parking with picnic area and forest walk.

✆ Dunkeld (03502) 284.
Open: daily Apr-Sep, dawn-dusk.
⏸ ⚕

PLYMOUTH
Devon   Map 2 SX45.
City Museum & Art Gallery
Drake Circus
Collections of paintings and drawings, ceramics (espe-

cially Plymouth porcelain), silver; archaeology and local history. Cottonian collection of Old Master drawings, engravings and early printed books. Monthly exhibitions.

✆ (0752) 668000 Ext 4878.
Open: all year Mon-Fri 10-5.30, Sat 1-5. (Closed: Good Fri & 25, 26 Dec.)
⚕ Shop ⚥

Royal Citadel
Magnificent entrance gateway, dated 1670 and designed probably by Sir Thomas Fitz for stronghold, begun by Charles II in 1666. The remaining buildings from the fort include the Guard House, Governor's House and Chapel.

Open: May-Sep, guided tours daily 2-6. Winter access only by permission of the Ministry of Defence. Enquire at Guardroom.
(AM)

PONTEFRACT
West Yorkshire   Map 8 SE42.
Pontefract Museum
Salter Row
Displays on the history of Pontefract from prehistoric times to present. Wide range of temporary exhibitions.

✆ (0977) 797289.
Open: all year, Mon-Sat

10.30-5, Sun 2.30-5. (Open Spring & Summer BH). ⓓ ⚬

PONTERWYD
Dyfed   *Map 6 SN78.*
Bwlch Nant-Yr-Arian Forest Visitor Centre
(3m W)
Operated by the Forestry Commission in Rheidol to interpret the forest as part of the landscape, form of land use, traditional industry, part of local community, habitat for wild life and as a place for recreation and relaxation. Forest walks in the vicinity.

⊘ (097085) 694 or Cresswood (09743) 404.
Open: Etr-Sep, daily 10-5 (Sat & Sun) 12.30-5 (6pm in Jul & Aug).
⌒ ⓓ Shop

PONTYPRIDD
Mid Glamorgan   *Map 3 ST09.*
Welsh Characters
Models of miners, hill farmers, coracle men, as well as sculptured figures from Welsh folklore and amusing Welsh rugby characters and other pieces are made here in an individual slightly 'primitive' style. Visitors can watch John Hughes (the sculptor) and his team at work.

⊘ (0443) 405001.
Open: all year Mon-Fri 9-5, Sat 10-5, Sun 2-4, BH 11-4.30. (Closed Xmas.)

POOLE
Dorset   *Map 4 SZ09.*
Upton Park Country Park
Upton Road (off A35)
On the north shore of Poole Harbour, 55 acres of parkland meadow and garden, largely the grounds of historic Upton House. After years of neglect the area is being restored in the tradition of a small country estate. The attractive formal gardens are in the style of Humphrey Repton and the parkland's fine trees are a special feature. A combination of natural and man-made landscape provides a good habitat for many different plants and animals.

⊘ (0202) 673555.
Open: daily 9-dusk. House open Sun noon-6 only.
⌒ ⓓ (ornamental gardens only)

PORTHMADOG
Gwynedd   *Map 6 SH53.*
Ffestiniog Railway Museum
Located in Harbour Station and includes old four-wheeled hearse converted from quarryman's coach, one of the original steam locos (1863), historic slate wagon, model steam engine (1869), and maps and diagrams illustrating history of the well-known narrow-gauge railway.

⊘ (0766) 2340 or 2384.
Open: Feb-Dec every weekend & Mar-Nov when train services operating.
⊈ (licensed) ⓓ Shop

PORTSMOUTH
Hampshire   *Map 4 SZ69.*
Round Tower
Broad Street, Old Portsmouth
Dating from the early 15th century, this is the first permanent defensive work to be built in Portsmouth and commands the entrance to the Harbour. It now provides an excellent vantage point.

⊘ (0705) 827261.
Open: daily.
⚬ (ex guide dogs)

PRESCOT
Merseyside   *Map 7 SJ49.*
Prescot Museum of Clock & Watch-Making
34 Church Street
An attractive 18th-century town house containing exhibits about the clock, watch and tool making industry of the area. Display includes a reconstruction of part of a traditional watchmaker's workshop, examples of hand tools and machinery used to make the many intricate parts of watch and clock movements. Changing temporary exhibition programme.

⊘ 051-430 7787.
Open: all year Tue-Sat & BH Mon, 10-5, Sun 2-5. (Closed: 24-26 Dec, New Year's Day & Good Fri.)
ⓓ (ground floor only) Shop ⚬

PRESTON
Lancashire   *Map 7 SD52.*
Harris Museum & Art Gallery
Market Square
Impressive neo-classical building containing extensive collections of Fine and Decorative Arts. Includes paintings by the Devis family, the Newsham bequest of 19th-century paintings and sculpture and the Houghton bequest of ceramics. Also contemporary art. New Story of Preston gallery telling history of town and surrounding area. Temporary exhibitions.

⊘ (0772) 58248.
Open: Mon-Sat 10-5. (Closed: BH's.) Guided tours by prior appointment.
⊈ ⓓ ⚬ (ex guide dogs)

PRESTONPANS
Lothian (East Lothian)   *Map 11 NT37.*
Scottish Mining Museum
Prestongrange
Oldest documented coal mining site in Britain, with 800 years of history. Cornish Beam Engine, Visitor Centre (machine), Exhibition Hall,

16th-century Customs Port, Self-drive Coal Heritage Trail to Lady Victoria Colliery. This is a new independent twin-site museum of coal mining in Scotland.

⌀ 031-663 7519.
Visitor centre open: all year Mon-Fri 10-4 (3.30 in winter), Sat & Sun 12-5. Special steam days first Sun of month Apr-Sep.
⌖ (ground floor only) ⌀ (ex guide dogs)

PRESTWICH
Gt Manchester   *Map 7 SD80.*
Heaton Hall
Heaton Park (on A665)
The finest neo-classical house in the north, surrounded by extensive parkland. Designed by James Wyatt for the Earls of Wilton, the house has magnificent decorated interiors and commands panoramic views of Manchester. The unique Pompeiian room has recently been restored and changing exhibitions are displayed in the new Heaton Gallery. Sunday afternoon concerts. Flower Festival.

⌀ 061-773 1231.
Open: Apr-Sep Mon, Wed-Sat 10-6 also Sun 2-6. (Subject to alteration)
⌑ ⌖ (ground floor only) Shop ⌀

QUEEN'S VIEW
Tayside (Perthshire)   *Map 14 NN85.*
Tummel Forest Centre
Exhibits show changes in the Tummel Valley since Queen Victoria's visit in 1866. Audio-visual programmes, forest walks and information desk.

⌀ Pitlochry (0796) 3437.
Open: daily, Etr-mid Oct 9.30-5.30.
⌖ Shop ⌀

RADCLIFFE
Gt Manchester   *Map 7 SD70.*
Radcliffe Tower
Tower Street, off Church Street East
Remains of medieval tower once part of a larger hall occupied by the Radcliffe family. Adjacent to medieval parish church.

⌀ 061-705 5871.
Open: at all reasonable times.
⌖

RAMSEY
Cambridgeshire   *Map 4 TL28.*
Abbey Gatehouse
A 15th-century Benedictine ruin.

Open: daily, Apr-Oct 10-5 (or dusk) (NT)

Ramsey Abbey
House (now a comprehensive school) erected c. 1600 on the site of a Benedictine monastery, fragments of which still remain. An interesting mixture of architectural styles, reflecting its varied history, the house was extended and refurbished by architects, Sir John Soane and Edward Blore in the 19th century.

⌀ (0487) 813285.
Open: Apr-Oct (NT)
⌀

RAMSGATE
Kent   *Map 5 TR36.*
Ramsgate Museum
Ramsgate Library, Guildford Lawn
A display of objects, pictures and documents illustrating the history of Ramsgate.

⌀ Thanet (0843) 593532.
Open: all year Mon-Wed 9.30-6, Thu & Sat 9.30-5 Fri 9.30-8. (Closed: BH.) ⌖ ⌀

RAWTENSTALL
Lancashire   *Map 7 SD82.*
Rossendale Museum
Whitaker Park, Haslingden Road
Set in pleasant parkland with moorland views, the museum is housed in a former Victorian mill owner's mansion. Apart from special temporary exhibitions throughout the year, there is a varied collection of permanent exhibits of fine arts and furniture, and industrial and domestic artefacts.

⌀ Rossendale (0706) 217777.
Open: all year Mon-Fri, 1-5 (Wed also 6-8; Apr-Sep) Sat 10-12 & 1-5; (Sun, 2-4; Apr-Oct) BH 2-5. (Closed: Xmas & New Year.)

READING
Berkshire   *Map 4 SU77.*
Blake's Lock Museum
In an attractive Victorian building, the museum illustrates the history of industrial and commercial life in Reading, with a section on its waterways. There are reconstructions of a family baker, barbers and a printers workshop.

⌀ (0734) 55911 Ext 2242.
(Reading Museum & Art Gallery)
Open: Mon-Fri 10-5 Sat, Sun 2-5.
⌖ ⌂ Shop ⌀

Museum & Art Gallery
Blagrave Street
Noted especially for its exceptional collection of exhibits from Roman Silchester, the museum also features finds from the River Thames area, including a splendid Bronze Age torc from Moulsford, and displays of local natural history. Some exhibitions change monthly. See also: Silchester, Calleva Museum.

℗ (0734) 55911 Ext 2242.
Open: all year Mon-Fri 10-5.30 & Sat 10-5, Sun 2-5.
Shop ⌀

REAY
Highland (Caithness)   Map 14 NC96.
U.K.A.E.A. Dounreay Exhibition
(2m NE)
Information panels, models, participatory displays and charts relating to fast reactors and nuclear energy generally. Housed in a former airfield control tower overlooking the plant which is conspicuous for its 135 ft sphere and the prototype fast reactor.

℗ Thurso (0847) 62121 Ext 656.
Open: daily, Etr-Sep 9-4.30.
Exhibition, Public tours of the prototype fast reactor, starting at 12 noon.
Tickets available from Exhibition or Thurso Tourist Information Centre.
⊓ ⌷ (ground floor only) Shop

REIGATE
Surrey   Map 4 TQ24.
Priory Museum
Bell Street
Contained in house, originally founded in 1235, and converted into Tudor mansion, of which the hall fireplace is the finest surviving relic. Palladian stucco changed the face of the building in 1779, and the painted staircase by Verrio c 1710 is a notable example. House now used as a school and a part is a small museum with changing displays. Special exhibitions throughout the year.

℗ (0737) 245065.
Museum open: Weds only in term time 2-4.30 & some Sats 11-4 only in term time.
Conducted tour if requested.
⌷ (ground floor only) Shop ⌀

REIGATE HEATH
Surrey   Map 4 TQ25.
Old Windmill
220-year-old mill, converted into a church in 1882. Services (3pm on third Sun of each month between May and Oct.) Restored in 1964.

Open: accessible all year daily, 10-dusk. Key available from Club house. ⌷ ⌀

RICHMOND-UPON-THAMES
Gt London   see page 76
Richmond Park.
London Plan 2 : 46 B3.
Charles I enclosed the park area as part of a Royal Estate in 1637 and successive monarchs shaped the land to suit their hunting needs. Sometimes described as 'wild countryside' on London's doorstep, it nowadays has large numbers of red and fallow deer roaming unharmed. With other kinds of wildlife in evidence, the park is a favourite haunt for naturalists and tourists alike. The formal gardens at Pembroke Lodge and the various plantations show a wealth of exotic shrubs and wild flowers. A popular part is the Isabella Plantation, now a woodland garden with rhododendrons, azaleas, and a running brook. 18-acre Pen Ponds have been specially built for angling (a fishing permit is required). Adam's Pond, where the deer are seen to drink, is also used for model sail boats.

℗ 01-948 3209.
Open: (Summer) 7am till dusk; (Winter) 7.30-dusk.
⌺ ⌷

ROCHESTER
Kent   Map 5 TQ76.
Guildhall Museum
High Street
A major portion of the building dates from late 17th-century and has magnificent decorated plaster ceilings. The collections include local history, archaeology, arms and armour, dolls, toys and Victoriana, models of local sailing barges, fishing vessels. Shorts flying boats and Napoleonic prisoner-of-war work. The museum also houses the civic plate, regalia and archives of the city.

℗ Medway (0634) 48717.
Open: daily 10-12.30 & 2-5.30.
(Closed: 1 Jan, Good Fri & Xmas.)
⌷ (ground floor only) Shop ⌀ (ex guide dogs)

ROTHERHAM
South Yorkshire   Map 8 SK49.
Art Gallery
Brian O'Malley Library and Arts Centre, Walker Place
Continuous programme of temporary exhibitions including, at times 19th- and 20th-century paintings from the museum collections, and Rockingham pottery.

℗ (0709) 382121 Ext 3549.
Open: Tue-Fri 10-6, Sat 10-5.
(Closed: Sun, Tue, & BH.)
⌺ (licensed) ⌷ Shop ⌀

Museum
Clifton Park
Late 18th-century mansion reputed to be designed by John Carr of York. Contains 18th-century furnished rooms, family portraits, and period kitchen. Displays of Victoriana, local history, local Roman antiquities, numismatics, glass and glass-making, church silver, and 19th- and 20th-century paintings. Also British ceramics, including Rockingham, local geology and natural history. Temporary exhibitions.

℗ (0709) 382121 Ext 3519 or 3569.
Open: Apr-Sep, Mon-Thu &

which now stands in Ruthwell church was restored by him, and the museum also contains drawings and other documents relating to this cross.

✆ Clarencefield (038787) 640
Open: daily, summer 10-6, winter 10-4. (Closed for Custodian's holiday).
Evenings by arrangement; parties by appointment only. 🗐

Ruthwell Cross
(off B724)
One of Europe's most famous carved crosses resting in the parish church in an apse built specially for it. The date is probably late 7th-century and the 18ft-high cross is richly carved with Runic characters showing the earliest form of English in Northumbrian dialect.

Open: key of church obtainable from the Key Keeper, Kirkyett Cottage, Ruthwell.
(AM)

SAFFRON WALDEN
Essex   Map 5 TL53.
Saffron Walden Museum
Museum Street
Built in 1834, the museum houses collections of local archaeology, natural history, ceramics, glass, costume, furniture, toys, ethnography, geology and local history. Special events include Walden's 750th Anniversary celebrations with special exhibitions and events in grounds Apr-Sep. Reproductions of the Pepys' Mazer Bowl will be available.

✆ (0799) 22494.
Open: Apr-Sep, Mon-Sat 11-5, Sun & BH 2.30-5; Oct-

Sat 10-5, Sun 2.30-5; Oct-Mar Mon-Thu & Sat 10-5, Sun 2.30-4.30. (Closed: Fri.)
🗐 (ground floor only) Shop 🐕 (ex guide dogs)

ROTHES
Grampian (Moray)   Map 15 NJ24.
Glen Grant Distillery
Established in 1840. The whisky produced here is regarded as one of the best, and is used in many first-class blends as well as being sold as a single Glen Grant Malt in bottles. Traditional malt whisky methods of distillation are used together with the most modern equipment. Reception, shop and Hospitality Bar.

✆ (03403) 494.
Open: Apr-Oct, Mon-Fri 10-4.
Details not confirmed for 1988.
Shop 🐕 (ex guide dogs)

ROTHESAY
Isle of Bute, Strathclyde
Buteshire
See **Bute, Isle of**

ROTTINGDEAN
East Sussex   Map 5 TQ30.
Rottingdean Grange, Art Gallery & Museum
Early Georgian house, remodelled by Lutyens, now a library, art gallery and museum with Kipling exhibits. It includes part of the

---

National Toy Museum. Frequent temporary exhibitions.

✆ Brighton (0273) 31004.
Open: Mon, Thu & Sat 10-5; Tue & Fri 10-1 & 2-5. (Closed: Wed, Good Fri, Xmas and Jan 1.)
Shop 🐕

ROUSAY
See **Orkney**

ROYSTON
Hertfordshire   Map 5 TL34.
Royston Museum
Lower King Street
Former chapel schoolroom, which contains a local history museum with displays depicting the history of the town. Regular temporary exhibitions.

✆ (0763) 42587.
Open: Wed & Sat only 10-5.
🗐 (ground floor only) Shop 🐕

RUTHWELL
Dumfries & Galloway (Dumfriesshire)   Map 11 NY16.
Housed in the building where savings banks first began, the museum traces their growth from 1810 to the present day, with original letters, books and papers. The display also traces the life of Dr Henry Duncan, the founder of savings banks. The 7th-century preaching cross

Mar, Mon-Sat 11-4, Sun & BH
2.30-5. (Closed: Good Fri
and 24 & 25 Dec.)
&. (ground floor & gardens
only) Shop %

ST ABBS
Borders (Berwickshire) Map 12 NT96.
**St Abbs Head (Nature
Reserve)**
(N from B6438)
This exposed headland north
of Eyemouth has fine cliffs
rising to 300 ft. It is an important site for cliff nesting seabirds in south east Scotland.
Kittiwakes and guillemots are
the most numerous with
smaller numbers of fulmars,
shags, razorbills, herring
gulls and puffins. The headland is a good landfall site for
autumn migrants and a number of rarities have been recorded. In 1983 St Abbs
Head was declared a National Nature Reserve.

Open: accessible at all
reasonable times. (NTS)

ST ALBANS
Hertfordshire   Map 4 TL10.
City Museum
Hatfield Road
Displays collections relating
to natural history and geology of south-west Hertfordshire. Salaman collection of
craft tools with reconstructed
workshops.

℘ (0727) 56679.
Open: Mon-Sat 10-5.
(Closed: Sun & BH.)
Shop &. (ground floor only)
% (ex guide dogs)

ST ANDREWS
Fife (Fife)   Map 12 NO51.
**Crawford Centre for the
Arts**
93 North Street
Established by the University
and named after the late Earl
of Crawford and Balcarres
(former University Rector).

The centre has a programme
of changing art exhibitions
and theatre which takes
place in the galleries and studio.

℘ (0334) 76161.
Open: Mon-Sat 10-5; Sun
2-5
(Admission charge for
theatre performances.)
⌨

ST BEES
Cumbria   Map 11 NX91.
**St Bees Head (Nature
Reserve)**
*(on public footpath north of
car park on seafront)*
Sandstone cliffs rising to
almost 300 ft with wide views
to the Isle of Man and Dumfries and Galloway. On the
headland there is a large
seabird colony with guillemots, razorbills and puffins. A
cliff path runs between St
Bees and Whitehaven.

Open: accessible at all
reasonable times.

ST CATHERINE'S POINT
Isle of Wight
See **Wight, Isle of**

ST DAVID'S
Dyfed   Map 2 SM72.
Cathedral
Centrepiece of the smallest
city in Britain is the cathedral
which lies in a hollow for protection from invasion. Dating
from 12th-14th centuries, it is
built of purple sandstone
quarried locally. The nave
slopes three feet from one
end to the other and is noted
for its Irish oak roof. The tower rises to 116 ft.

℘ (0437) 720392.
Open: daily 8-6. Details not
confirmed for 1988.
(Donations)
&.

ST DOGMAELS
Dyfed   Map 2 SN14.
St Dogmaels Abbey
Standing near the centre of
the village, the ruinous
Abbey was founded in the
12th century by monks of the
French order of Tiron. The
north and west walls of the
nave still rise to almost their
original height.

℘ Cardigan (0239) 613230.
Open: accessible at all
reasonable times.
&. (AM)

ST HELENS
Merseyside   Map 7 SJ59.
Pilkington Glass Museum
*(on Prescot Road, A58 1m
from town centre)*
History of glassmaking from
Egyptians to present day,
with some of the finest examples of glass in the world.
Various temporary exhibi-
tions throughout the year.

℘ (0744) 692499 or 692014.
Open: all year Mon-Fri 10-5,
Sat, Sun & BH 2-4.30; (also
open until 9 on Weds, Mar-
Oct). (Closed: Xmas-New
Year.)
&. Shop %

ST HILARY
South Glamorgan   Map 3 ST07.
Old Beaupré Castle
(1m SW)
Ruined manor house, rebuilt
in 16th century, with notable
Italianate gatehouse and
porch. Porch is three-storey
and displays Basset arms.

Open: at any reasonable
time. (Closed Sun.)
(AM CADW)

ST IVES
Cambridgeshire   Map 4 TL37.
Norris Museum
The Broadway
A comprehensive collection
of Huntingdonshire local his-
tory, including fossils,

archaeology and bygones, water-colours of local features, work in bone and straw by French prisoners at Norman Cross. Also Huntingdonshire lacemaking.

✆ (0480) 65101.
Open: May-Sep, Tue-Fri 10-1 & 2-5, Sat 10-12 & 2-5, Sun 2-5; Oct-Apr Tue-Fri 10-1 & 2-4, Sat 10-12. (Closed: BH weekends.)
Shop

ST NICHOLAS
Dyfed   Map 2 SM83.
Tregwynt Woollen Mill
(1½m SW)
Woollen mill in 18th century building where yarns have been made for 200 years. Visitors can see the mill in operation and some of the processes like twisting, cone winding, warping and weaving. Products include tapestry bed covers woven in various designs.

✆ St Nicholas (03485) 225.
Open: Mill, Mon-Sat 9-5 (Sat open but not in operation); mill shop Mon-Sat, 9-5.

ST OLAVES
Norfolk   Map 5 TM49.
St Olaves Priory
near Fritton Decoy
Remains of small Augustinian priory. Exceptional early example of brickwork dating from late 13th century or early 14th century.

Open: any reasonable time.
⌖ (ground floor & gardens only) (AM)

SALCEY FOREST
Northamptonshire/Buckinghamshire
Map 4 SP85.
(W of B526 on Harlwell road about 8 miles S of Northampton)
Managed by the Forestry Commission, Salcey Forest contains both deciduous and coniferous trees. Planting began in 1847 and now there are a variety of trees growing separated by rides. The forest contains a rich variety of wildlife including pheasants, woodcocks, owls and deer. Part of the forest has been leased as a nature reserve.

Open: accessible at all reasonable times.
⌖

SALFORD
Gt Manchester   Map 7 SJ89.
Museum of Mining
Buile Hill Park, Eccles Old Road
In an attractive Georgian building, the museum has two reproduction coal mines, a large gallery dealing with all aspects of coalmining and its history and a gallery of mining art. A large mining reference library and archives centre are available for research purposes. Tape commentary points are installed in reproduction coal-mines.

✆ 061-736 1832.
Open: Mon-Fri 10-12.30 & 1.30-5, Sun 2-5. (Closed: Sat 24-26 Dec, 1 Jan & Good Fri.)
⌖ (ground floor only) Shop ⌀ (ex guide dogs)

Ordsall Hall Museum
Taylorson Street
Half-timbered manor house, with later brick-built wing (1639), includes Tudor Great Hall, Star Chamber with 14th-century features and Victorian farmhouse kitchen. On upper floor are local and social history displays.

✆ 061-872 0251.
Open: Mon-Fri 10-5, Sun 2-5. (Closed: Good Fri, 25-26 Dec & New Years Day.)
⌖ (ground floor only) ⌀

Salford Museum & Art Gallery
The Crescent, Peel Park
The ground floor displays a period street scene typical of a northern industrial town at the turn of the century. The first floor art galleries house a large collection of works by LS Lowry, as well as a regular series of temporary art exhibitions and displays of decorative arts.

✆ 061-736 2649.
Open: Mon-Fri 10-1 & 2-5, Sun 2-5. (Closed: 25-26 Dec, New Years Day & Good Fri.)
⌖ Shop ⌀

SALTCOATS
Strathclyde (Ayrshire)   Map 10 NS24.
North Ayrshire Museum
A museum in the ancient former parish church, with interesting old churchyard gravestones. Exhibits portray local historical items, and early 19th-century interiors.

✆ (0294) 64174.
Open: summer Mon-Sat 10-4; winter Thu, Fri & Sat 10-4.
⌖ (ground floor only) ⌀

SANCREED
Cornwall   Map 2 SW42.
Carn Euny Ancient Village
(1m SW)
Iron-Age village site with characteristic Cornish 'fogon' (subterranean hiding hole), 66ft long with circular chamber.

Open: any reasonable time.
(AM)

SANDOWN
Isle of Wight
See **Wight, Isle of**

SAUNDERSFOOT
Dyfed   Map 2 SN10.
Saundersfoot Pottery & Craft Shop
Wogan Street

Hand thrown ceramicware made by Carol Brinton who opened the pottery in 1970. A range of decorative and small colourful pottery is on display and frequent demonstrations of all processes can be seen. The shop also has one of the best selections of craft goods in the area.

℘ (0834) 812406.
Open: daily, Apr-Sep, 10-5.30; demonstrations on most summer evenings between 8 & 10. Winter months by appointment only. Details not confirmed for 1988.

SCALLOWAY
See **Shetland**

SCUNTHORPE
Humberside   *Map 8 SE81.*
Borough Museum & Art Gallery
Displays of local history, archaeology and natural science. New video room features, film on iron and steel making in Scunthorpe. Programme of temporary exhibitions.

℘ (0724) 843533
Open: Mon-Sat & BH 10-5, Sun 2-5. (Closed: Xmas).
⬚ (ground floor & grounds only) Shop ⌀ (ex guide dogs)

SEAFORD
East Sussex   *Map 5 TV59.*
Seven Sisters Country Park
Exceat (1½m E)
The country park occupies 692 acres of attractive Sussex downlands, chalk cliffs, shingle beach and wet lands beside the Cuckmere River. Wide variety of birds and salt loving plants; the downland is noted for its orchids and is grazed in the summer by Southdown sheep. At Exceat there is an Information Centre and a nature trail.

℘ Eastbourne (0323) 870280.
Open: country park accessible at all reasonable times, car park — dawn to dusk; Information Centre daily Etr-Oct 11-5.30; Nov-Etr weekends only 11-4.
⬚ ⼞ ⌀ (unless on lead)

SEDBERGH
Cumbria   *Map 7 SD69.*
National Park Centre
72 Main Street
Visitor centre with interpretative display. Maps, walks, guides and local information available.

℘ (0587) 20125.
Open: daily, Apr-Oct, mid morning-late afternoon. Details not confirmed for 1988.

SEDLESCOMBE
East Sussex   *Map 5 TQ71.*
Nortons Farm Museum & Farm Trail
(4½m NW of Hastings on A21)
Depicts the carthorse era with a fine display of carts, ploughs and handtools. The Farm Trail takes visitors round the fruit and arable farm, where cart horses are still used.

℘ (042487) 471.
Open: daily Apr-Sep, 9-5.
⬚ ⼞ ⌀

SELBORNE
Hampshire   *Map 4 SU73.*
Selborne Hill
(from car park signed in Selborne village.)
The wooded slopes of Selborne Hill rise steeply to 700 ft to the west of Selborne, home of Gilbert White, the 18th-century naturalist. There are many fine walks through the beech woods, although care should be taken in wet weather as paths become very slippery and muddy.

Open: accessible at all reasonable times.
(NT)

SEVERN BORE
River Severn   *Map 3 SO71.*
The Severn Bore is a tidal wave that occurs when the moon and the sun exert their maximum influence, causing a difference of 30 to 34 ft between high and low tide in the estuary. This occurs on at least 35 days a year. The tide enters the narrowing estuary at Sharpness and forces its way in a series of waves, until it levels out in the Gloucester area.

The best places to see the Bore are at Stonebench on the east bank, 3 miles SW of Gloucester, off B4008, and at Minsterworth on the west bank, 5 miles W of Gloucester, on the A48. Full details of times can be obtained from most AA Centres.

SHAP
Cumbria   *Map 12 NY51.*
Shap Abbey
An abbey of the Premonstratensian order, dedicated to St Mary Magdalene, with buildings dating from 1201-1540, when abbey was dissolved.

Open: at all reasonable times.
⬚ (AM)

SHEFFIELD
South Yorkshire   *Map 8 SK38.*
City Museum
Weston Park
A regional museum of geology, natural sciences, archaeology, and Sheffield area trades, including cutlery, plate and ceramics. Educational facilities for schools and colleges.

℘ (0742) 768588.
Open: all year, Mon-Sat

10-5, Sun 11-5; Jun, Jul &
Aug 10-8; Sun 11-8. Museum
may close earlier during Jun-
Aug; visitors should check
first. (Closed: 24-26 Dec.)
[symbol] (ground floor only) Shop
[symbol] (ex guide dogs)

Sheffield Manor
Manor Lane
A ruined manor house which
began as a medieval hunting
lodge enlarged in the 16th
century and between 1406
and 1616 principal seat of the
Earls of Shrewsbury. The
house fell into disrepair in
the 17th century and in the
early 1900s the site was
cleared of all except the surviving 16th-century struc-
tures. Now undergoing restoration and archaeological
excavation to recover in-
formation about the house
and earlier hunting lodge.

[symbol] (0742) 768588.
Open: May-Oct, Wed-Sun
10-6.30.
Opening times subject to
availability of staff. For
visitors safety, access to
some parts of the site may be
restricted.
[symbol] (ground floor & gardens
only) [symbol] (ex guide dogs)

Shepherd Wheel
Whiteley Woods
An early water-powered cut-
ler's grinding establishment.

[symbol] (0742) 367731.
Open: all year, Wed-Sat
10-12.30 & 1.30-5, Sun
11-12.30 & 1.30-5. (Nov-Feb
4pm closing.)
[symbol]

SHERE
Surrey   *Map 4 TQ04.*
Silent Pool
(½m W on A25)
Shaded by trees with footpath around, this crystal clear
water is formed by a strong
spring. Legend states King

John watched a local girl
bathing here. She drowned
herself in a fit of shame. Any-
body visiting this quiet water
might easily imagine that her
spirit lingers here still.

Open: at all reasonable
times.

Shetland Isles

LERWICK
Shetland   *Map 16 HU44.*
Clickheinen
(½m S of Lerwick)
A   prehistoric   settlement
which was occupied for over
1,000 years. Remains include
a partially demolished broch.

Open: see page 4.
(AM)

Fort Charlotte
(Overlooking harbour)
Artillery fort begun in 1665 to
protect Sound of Bressay in
Anglo-Dutch War, renovated
in 1781 during American War
of Independence.

Open: see page 4.
(AM)

Shetland Museum
Lower Hillhead
A   comprehensive   local
museum of the Shetland Islands from pre-history to the
present day. Displays of folk
life, shipping, archaeology,
art and textiles.

[symbol] (0595) 5057.
Open: all year Mon-Wed,
10-7. Thur & Sat 10-5.
Fri 10-7. (Closed: Sun).
Exhibitions all year round.
Shop

Shetland Workshop Gallery
4-6 Burns Lane
The gallery is located in two
old dwelling houses in one of
Lerwick's oldest lanes. Visitors can see local artists and
craftsmen at work.

[symbol] (0595) 3343.
Open: all year Mon, Tue,
Thu-Sat 9.30-1, 2-5.

MOUSA ISLAND
Shetland   *Map 16 HU42.*
Mousa Broch
The best preserved late pre-
historic drystone tower in
Scotland. It rises to a height
of 40ft and, uniquely, is
almost fully intact. Reached
by boat from Leebottom on
Mousa Sound.

Open: see page 4. Apply
keeper.
(AM)

SCALLOWAY
Shetland   *Map 16 HU33.*
Scalloway Castle
Erected by Patrick Stewart,
Earl of Orkney c.1600, de-
signed on the two-stepped
plan.

Open: see page 4, on
application to the key
keeper. Closed: Tue & Wed
afternoons in Winter.
(AM)

SHOREHAM-BY-SEA
West Sussex   *Map 4 TQ20.*
Marlipins
(Sussex Archaeological
Society)
A Norman and later flint
building, possibly a ware-
house, now a maritime and
local history museum.

[symbol] (07917) 62994.
Open: May-Sep, Mon-Sat
10-1 & 2-5, Sun 2-5.
(Donations)
Shop [symbol]

SHREWSBURY
Shropshire   *Map 7 SJ41.*
Bear Steps
St Alkmund's Square
Recently restored, timber
framed, 14th-century cottage
with shops and meeting hall.
Art exhibitions all year
round.

℘ (0743) 56511.
Open: all year Mon-Sat 10-5.
Shop ⌀

Quarry Park
On the banks of the River
Severn and overlooked by
Shrewsbury School. Centre-
piece of the park is the Ding-
le a sunken one-acre garden
with lake, woodland garden,
rock garden and an annual
bedding display of thousands
of plants.

Open: daily 8-dusk.
⌂ ⌖

SIDMOUTH
Devon   *Map 3 SY18.*
The Donkey Sanctuary
(3m E off A3052)
Visitors can see the many
animals taken into care, from
geriatrics to the very young.
Many donkeys have suffered
neglect and ill treatment and
the sanctuary's aim is to love
and care for them for the rest
of their lives.

℘ (03955) 6391.
Open: all year round 8 till
dusk
⌖ ⌗ ⌂ ⌀ (unless on lead)

SILCHESTER
Hampshire   *Map 4 SU66.*
Calleva Museum
Dealing with the Roman town
of Calleva Atrebatum, this
small museum includes
panels of photographs, maps
and other illustrative materials as well as actual objects
excavated here, in order to
present a brief account of life
in the nearby walled Roman
town (see Reading Museum).

℘ (0734) 700362 (mid-day,
evenings & weekends).
Open: accessible daily
9-sunset. Details not
confirmed for 1988. ⌖ ⌀

SKENFRITH
Gwent   *Map 3 SO42.*
Skenfrith Castle
*(7m NW of Monmouth on
B4521)*
13th-century Marcher keep
within a towered curtain wall,
the work of Hubert de Burgh.
One of the three 'trilateral'
castles at Gwent.

Open: at all reasonable
times. (AM CADW & NT)

SKIPTON
North Yorkshire   *Map 7 SD95.*
Craven Museum
Town Hall, High Street
Contains collection dealing
especially with the Craven
district. There are important
exhibits of folk life, lead mining and prehistoric and Roman remains.

℘ (0756) 4079.
Open: Apr-Sep, Mon, Wed-
Fri 11-5, Sat 10-12 & 1-5, Sun
2-5; Oct-Mar, Mon, Wed-Fri
2-5, Sat 10-12 & 1.30-4.30.
Open some BH & PH, phone
to check.

SOUTHAMPTON
Hampshire   *Map 4 SU41.*
Art Gallery
*Civic Centre, Commercial
Road*
18th- to 20th-century English
paintings. Continental Old
Masters of 14th to 18th century. Modern French paintings. Collection of sculpture
and ceramics. Of special interest are paintings and
drawings of the 'Camden
Town Group'. Particularly
good collection of contemporary British painting and
sculpture. Temporary exhibitions.

℘ (0703) 832769.
Open: all year Tue-Fri 10-5,
Sat 10-4, Sun 2-5. Late
opening Thu 8. (Closed:
25-27 & 31 Dec.)
⌖ Shop ⌀

Bargate Guildhall Museum
Above Bar
The medieval North gate of
the city. The upper floor,
once a guildhall, is used to
house displays on special
themes.

℘ (0703) 224216.
Open: all year Tue-Fri 10-12
& 1-5, Sat 10-12 & 1-4, Sun
2-5. (Closed: 25-27 & 31 Dec
& BH.) Shop ⌀

God's House Tower
Winkle Street
Early fortified, sea-defensive,
building dating from 1300s.
Now a museum of South-
ampton's archaeology from
Bronze Age to medieval
times.

℘ (0703) 220007.
Open: all year Tue-Fri 10-12
& 1-5, Sat 10-12 & 1-4,
Sun 2-5. Shop ⌀

Tudor House Museum
*Bugle Street, St Michael's
Square*
A restored, half-timbered
16th-century house, containing a museum of antiquarian
and historical interest, social
and domestic history, some
costume and jewellery.
Tudor garden reached
through the museum.

℘ (0703) 332513.
Open: all year Tue-Fri 10-5,
Sat 10-4; Sun 2-5. (Closed:
25-27 & 31 Dec & BH Mon.)
⌖ (ground floor & garden
with help) Shop ⌀

**Wool House Maritime
Museum**
Town Quay
This 600-year-old building,
once a wool house, has but-
tressed stone walls and old
roof timbering. Houses an interesting maritime museum.

℘ (0703) 223941 & 224216.
Open: all year Tue-Fri 10-1

& 2-5, Sat 10-1 & 2-4, Sun 2-5. (Closed: 25-27 & 31 Dec.) ⬚ (ground floor only) Shop ✕

SOUTH MOLTON
Devon   *Map 3 SE72.*
South Molton Museum
Town Hall, Market Street
Part of the Guildhall, a stone-fronted building of c.1743 entered through open arcaded frontage. Local history, old charters, weights and measures, pewter, old fire engines, giant cider press. Monthly art, craft and educational exhibitions.

✆ (07695) 2951.
Open: Feb-Nov Mon (ex Mar, Oct & Nov) Tue, Thu & Fri 10.30-12.30 & 2-4, Wed & Sat 10-12. (Closed BH.) ⬚ (ground floor only) Shop ✕

SOUTHPORT
Merseyside   *Map 7 SD31.*
Atkinson Art Gallery
Lord Street
19th- and 20th-century oil paintings, watercolours, drawings and prints, 20th-century sculpture. Also visiting exhibition programme.

✆ (0704) 33133 Ext 129.
Open: all year, Mon, Tue, Wed & Fri 10-5, Thu & Sat 10-1.
Shop ✕

Botanic Gardens Museum
Church Town (situated in public park)
Collections of local history, natural history, 18th- and 19th-century china, a display of the local shrimping industry; and a rare example of an early dug-out canoe from the nearby Martin Mere. Also Ainsdale National Nature Reserve display reconstructed. Victorian parlour and Cecily Bate collection of dolls. Life-

boat display. A watch and clock exhibition Sep-Oct.

✆ (0704) 27547.
Open: all year, Tue-Sat & BH Mon 10-6 (5pm Oct-Apr), & Sun 2-5. (Closed: Mon & Good Fri, also Fri following BH, 25 Dec & 1 Jan.) ⬚ ⬚ (ground floor only) Shop ✕

SOUTH SHIELDS
Tyne & Wear   *Map 12 NZ36.*
Arbeia Roman Fort & Museum
Baring Street
Roman fort at the easternmost end of the Hadrianic frontier, displaying fort defences, stone granaries, gateways, headquarters building, tile kilns and latrine. Museum contains site finds and interpretation. Full-scale simulation of a Roman gateway with interior scenes of life at the fort in Roman times.

✆ (0632) 561369.
Open: May-Sep, Tue-Fri 10-5.30, Sat 10-4.30 & Sun 2-5; Oct-Apr, Tue-Fri 10-4 & Sat 10-noon. (Closed: Sun.) ⬚ Shop ✕

South Shields Museum & Art Gallery
Ocean Road
The museum shows the archaeology, history and natural history of South Shields. A maritime display includes a section on the evolvement of the lifeboat and local shipbuilding. The Catherine Cookson Gallery reflects the life and environment of the famous authoress.

✆ 091-456870.
Open: all year Tue-Fri 10-5.30, Sat 10-4.30, Sun 2-5. (Closed: Good Fri, 25 & 26 Dec.) ⬚ Shop ✕

SOUTHWOLD
Suffolk   *Map 5 TM57.*
Southwold Museum
Bartholomew Green
Formerly known as Dutch Cottage Museum, it contains relics of Southwold light railway and also illustrations of local history.

Open: daily Spring BH-30 Sep. Also Etr Mon & May Day BH, 2.30-4.30. Details not confirmed for 1988.

SPEY BAY
Grampian (Morayshire) Map 15 NJ36.
Tugnet Ice House
The largest ice house in Scotland, built in 1830. It contains exhibitions on the history and techniques of commercial salmon fishing on the River Spey; the geography, wildlife and industries of the Lower Spey area including shipbuilding at nearby Kingston. There is also an audio-visual on the 'Spey from source to mouth'.

✆ Forres (0309) 73701
Open: Jun-Sep 10-4.
⬚ Shop ✕

STAFFORD
Staffordshire   *Map 7 SJ92.*
Art Gallery
Lichfield Road
Art gallery showing temporary exhibitions of contemporary art, craft and photography. Craft shop selling a wide range of high quality work from British craftsmen; selected for quality by the Crafts Council.

✆ (0785) 57303.
Open: all year, Tue-Fri 10-5, Sat 10-4.
Shop ✕ (ex guide dogs)

Stafford Castle
Ruined castle dating from 12th century with inner and outer bailey, demolished by Parliamentary forces in 1643.

Partly rebuilt c.1800 in Gothic style.

Open: at all reasonable times.

STAPLEHURST
Kent　　　　　　　*Map 5 TQ74.*
Iden Croft Herbs
Frittenden Road
In quiet country in the heart of Kent, the farm has hundreds of varieties of herbs and plants. Several herb demonstration gardens, an aromatic garden and other growing areas.

✆ (0580) 891432.
Open: daily Apr-Oct 9-5; Nov-Mar, Mon-Sat 9-5. Sun 11-5 summer months only.
⌨ ♿

STEVENAGE
Hertfordshire　　　　*Map 4 TL22.*
Stevenage Museum
St George's Way
This museum, in the undercroft of the parish church of St George, tells the story of Stevenage from the earliest times to the present day. Temporary exhibitions.

✆ (0438) 354292.
Open: all year, Mon-Sat 10-5. (Closed BH.)
⌨ ♿ Shop ⌀

STINCHCOMBE
Gloucestershire　　　*Map 3 ST79.*
Cider Mill Gallery
(1m E of A38) Blanchworth Farm
Traditional farmhouse cider making, seasonally made (around October) using old horse-drawn mill and press. Pictures around the mill show the processes. Art gallery, craft shop and Victorian dolls house.

✆ Dursley (0453) 46746.
Open: Jun-Aug, Tue-Sun, 11-5; Apr, May, Sep-Dec,

Tue-Sat 11-5. Other times by appointment.
♿ Shop

STIRLING
Central (Stirlingshire)　　Map 11 NS79.
Mar's Wark
Broad Street
A partly ruined Renaissance mansion with a gatehouse enriched by sculptures. Built by the Regent Mar in 1570.

Open: at all reasonable times.
(AM)

Stirling Smith Art Gallery & Museum
40 Albert Place, Dumbarton Road
Stirling's story — a permanent display of the history of Stirling from William Wallace to the present day. Lively programme of exhibitions throughout the year, featuring contemporary and historical art, local and social history.

✆ (0786) 71917.
Open: Apr-Oct, Tue-Sat 10.30-12.30 & 1-5; Sun 2-5 Nov-Mar, Wed-Sun 2-5 (10.30-5 Sat)
♿ Shop ⌀

STOCKTON-ON-TEES
Cleveland　　　　　*Map 8 NZ41.*
Preston Hall Museum
Yarm Road (2m S on A19)
Museum illustrates Victorian social history, and collections include costume, arms, armour and period rooms. Also 19th-century reconstructed street with working blacksmiths and farrier.

✆ (0642) 602474 (weekends: 781184).
Open: all year, Mon-Sat 9.30-5.30, Sun 2-5.30. Last admission 5pm.
⌨ ⚲ ♿ (ground floor & gardens only) Shop ⌀ (ex guide dogs)

Stoke-on-Trent: decorating a Coalport China figure

STOKE-ON-TRENT
Staffordshire　　　　*Map 7 SJ84.*
City Museum & Art Gallery
Bethesda, Hanley
Exhibits include one of the largest and finest collections of ceramics, with the emphasis on Staffordshire pottery and porcelain. There is also a programme of temporary exhibitions.

✆ (0782) 202173.
Open: all year Mon-Sat 10.30-5, Sun 2-5. (Closed: Xmas week & Good Fri.)
⌨ (licensed) ♿ Shop ⌀

Coalport Craft Centre
Park Street, Fenton
World famous for its fine bone china tableware, figurines, floral studies, cottages and hand painted collector's pieces. The company was established in 1750 in Shropshire and moved to Stoke-on-Trent in 1926, becoming a member of the Wedgewood Group in 1967. The craft centre provides an opportunity to see the making and hand painting of fine bone china.

℘ (0782) 45274 or 204141 or 45274.
Open: Mon-Thu 9.30-4.30, Fri 9.30-12.30 & BH except Xmas. Factory tours are chargeable & by appointment only.

Ford Green Hall
Ford Green Road, Smallthorne.
A timber-framed farmhouse built in about 1580 for the Ford family. Brick wings were added in the early 1700s. Furnished with items and utensils used by a farming family from the 16th to the 19th century. Guided tours only (45 mins). Phone prior to visit as the hall closes without notice to accommodate school groups.

℘ (0782) 534771.
Open: all year Mon, Wed, Thu & Sat 10-12.30 & 2-5, Sun 2-5. (Closed: Xmas & New Year.) Tours at 10.45, 11.45, 2.15, 3.15 & 4.15. Last admission 45 mins before closing.
⌗ ♿ (ground floor only) Shop ✗

Minton Museum
London Road
Founded in 1793 by Thomas Minton who gave his name to the business, makers of the 'worlds most beautiful china'. The museum displays examples of Minton ware from 1800 to the present day.

℘ (0728) 49171.
Open: Mon-Fri, 9-12.30 & 2-4.30. (Closed: factory holidays). Admission charge for factory tour.
⌑ Shop ✗

Sir Henry Doulton Gallery
A tribute to Sir Henry Doulton, the gallery contains pottery treasures and artistry representing over 150 years. Nearly 300 figures, some rare

and some very early pieces. Displays by outstanding artists, experimental ceramics and exhibits demonstrate the variety of the Royal Doulton tradition, accompanied by archive material, sketches and pattern books.

℘ (0782) 85747.
Open: all year Mon-Fri 9-4.30. Charges for factory tours. (Closed factory holidays.)
Shop ✗

STOKE-SUB-HAMDON
Somerset   Map 3 ST41.
Stoke-sub-Hamdon Priory
A 15th-century Ham-Hill stone house, once a chantry and retaining original screens and part of great hall.

Open: daily 10-6.
(NT)

STONEHAVEN
Grampian (Kincardineshire)   Map 15 NO88.
Stonehaven Tolbooth
Old Pier, The Harbour
Once a 16th-century storehouse of the Earls Marischal, later used as a prison. Now a fishing and local history museum.

℘ Peterhead (0779) 77778.
Open: Jun-Sep, Mon, Thu, Fri & Sat 10-12 & 2-5, Wed & Sun 2-5.
♿ (ground floor only) Shop ✗ (ex guide dogs)

STOURBRIDGE
West Midlands   Map 7 SO98.
Thomas Webb Crystal
Dennis Hall, King William Street, Amblecote
The museum is housed in one of the largest rooms of 18th-century Dennis Hall and contains a fascinating variety of glassware, including superb examples of the work of artists and craftsmen such as

George and Thomas Woodall, William Fritsche, Jules Barbe, John Thomas Fereday and many others. There are also numerous interesting documents which are reminders of the long and illustrious history of Thomas Webb Crystal. During the conducted factory tour visitors will see many of the traditional glassmaking and hand cutting techniques used for almost 150 years.

℘ (0384) 392521.
Open: all year Mon-Fri 10-4 (last factory tour 3pm). (Closed BH.)
⌑ (licensed) ⌗ Shop ✗

STRANRAER
Dumfries & Galloway (Wigtownshire)   Map 10 NX06.
Wigtown District Museum
London Road
Permanent displays on geology, natural history, archaeology and social history of the district with special exhibits on dairy farming and material relating to Sir John Ross, the Arctic explorer.

℘ (0776) 5088.
Open: Mon-Fri 10-5, Sat 10-1 & 2-5.

STREET
Somerset   Map 3 ST43.
The Shoe Museum (C & J Clark Ltd)
High Street
The museum is housed in the oldest part of the factory and contains shoes from Roman times to the present, Georgian shoe buckles, caricatures and engravings of shoemakers, costume illustrations and fashion plates, shoe machinery, hand tools, advertising material, and 19th-century documents and photographs illustrating the early history of the firm from the founding in 1825 by Cyrus Clark.

✆ (0458) 43131.
Open: Etr Mon-Oct, Mon-Sat 10-4.45. Winter months by appointment only.
♿ (main floor only) Shop ⊗

STROMNESS
See **Orkney**

STROUD
Gloucestershire   Map 3 SO80.
Stroud District (Cowle) Museum
Lansdown
The exhibits cover geology, archaeology, local crafts, industrial archaeology (including local mills and houses), and farmhouse household equipment. A full-length model of the dinasaur Megalosaurus is on display.

✆ (04536) 3394.
Open: all year Mon-Sat 10.30-1 & 2-5. (Closed: BH's)
Shop

SUNDERLAND
Tyne and Wear   Map 12 NZ35.
Grindon Close Museum
Grindon Lane
Edwardian period rooms, including chemist's shop and dentist's surgery.

✆ 091-51284042.
Open: all year Mon-Wed & Fri 9.30-12.30 & 1.30-6 (5pm Tue), Sat 9.30-12.15 & 1.15-4; Jun-Sep also Sun 2-5.
(Closed: 1 Jan, 5-8 Apr, 4 & 6 May, 24 & 26 Aug, 25 & 26 Dec.)
Shop ⊗

Museum & Art Gallery
Borough Road
The wildlife and geology of the North East. The history of Sunderland and its industries, particularly glass, pottery and shipbuilding. Period rooms, silver, paintings and a wide range of temporary exhibitions.

✆ 091-5141235.
Open: all year Tue-Fri 10-5.30, Sat 10-4, Sun 2-5, BH Mon 10-5. (Closed: Mon & BH's.)
🍴 (10-4.45 Mon-Fri, 10-12 Sat) ♿ Shop ⊗

Monkwearmouth Station Museum
North Bridge Street
Land transport museum in station built in 1848. The booking office, platform areas and footbridge have all been restored and there is also rolling stock. Displays inside the museum deal with transport in north-east England with a display showing the evolution of steam locomotives.

✆ 091-5677075.
Open: all year Tues-Fri & BH 10-5.30, Sat 10-4.30, Sun 2-5. (Closed: Good Fri, 25 & 26 Dec & 1 Jan.)
♿ Shop ⊗

SWANSEA
West Glamorgan   Map 3 SS69.
Glynn Vivian Art Gallery & Museum
Alexandra Road
Works by British and French masters and contemporary British artists. Collections of Continental and Swansea porcelain and pottery. Major contemporary exhibitions and Summer Festival Exhibition 17 Sep-12 Nov, also education service and craft outlet.

✆ (0792) 55006.
Open: daily 10.30-5.30 (Closed 25, 26 Dec & 1 Jan).
♿ (ground floor & sculpture court) Shop ⊗

Maritime & Industrial Museum
South Dock
Contains complete working woollen mill in continuous production. Displays relating to the industry and the Port of Swansea and its environment. Transport exhibits, maritime and agriculture sections.

✆ (0792) 50351.
Open: daily 10.30-5.30.
(Closed: 25, 26 Dec & 1 Jan.)
♿ Shop ⊗

SWARTHMOOR
Cumbria   Map 7 SD27.
Swarthmoor Hall
Elizabethan and later, the former home of George Fox, founder of the Quakers. The house is now administered by the Society of Friends.

✆ Ulverston (0229) 53204.
Open: mid Mar-mid Oct, Mon-Wed & Sat 10-12 & 2-5, Thu & Sun by arrangement only; mid Oct-mid Mar by appointment only.
♿ (ground floor only) ⊗

SWINDON
Wiltshire   Map 4 SU18.
Museum & Art Gallery
Bath Road
Contains a small collection of items of local interest and an art gallery. Visiting exhibitions alternate with pictures by 20th-century artists.

✆ (0793) 24161 Ext 3129.
Open: all year Mon-Sat 10-6, Sun 2-5. (Closed: Good Fri, 25 & 26 Dec.)
Shop ⊗

Richard Jefferies Museum
Coate Farm (off A345)
Birthplace in 1848 of Richard Jefferies, the nature writer, and now a museum exhibiting literature relating to local wildlife written by Jefferies and Alfred Owen Williams.

✆ (0793) 26161 Ext 3130.
Open: all year, Wed, Sat & Sun 2-5 (Closed: Xmas.)
Shop ⊗

TARDEBIGGE
*Hereford &
Worcester*　　　　*Map 7 SO96.*
Tardebigge Locks
*(Between Tardebigge and
Stoke Pound)*
Tardebigge Locks on the
Worcester and Birmingham
Canal were built by John
Woodhouse between 1812
and 1815 and are the largest
flight of locks in the country.
In a little over two miles the
canal is raised 217ft. The top
lock is much deeper than the
rest because in 1808 an experimental boat lift was installed, however it was soon
decided that it would not
stand up to constant rough
treatment. A deep lock was
constructed in its place. A
towpath runs along the eastern bank of the canal.

Open: accessible at all
reasonable times on towpath.

TAUNTON
Somerset　　　　*Map 3 ST22.*
Sheppy's
*Three Bridges (3½m SW,
A38)*
A traditional farm cider makers which has been commer-
cially producing cider since
1925. Today the farm has 20
acres of standard and 22
acres of bush orchards; there
is a farm and cider museum.

✆ (082346) 233.
Open: all year Mon-Sat 8.30-
dusk; (Etr-Xmas 12-2).
⬧ (ground floor only) Shop

TENBY
Dyfed　　　　*Map 2 SN10.*
Tenby Pottery
Upper Frog Street
All processes of pottery making can be seen from the
showroom; throwing, firing,
decorating, glazing and kiln-
packing. Everything is hand
thrown and individually decorated, ranging from thim-
bles to large plant pots.

*Making farmhouse cider
at Sheppy's, near Taunton*

✆ (0834) 2890.
Open: Mon-Fri 10.15-1 & 2.15-
5.30, Sat 10.15-1.

TEWKESBURY
Gloucestershire　　　*Map 3 SO83.*
Tewkesbury Abbey
The impressive Abbey
Church dates from Norman
times and in the 12th century
formed part of a Benedictine
Monastery. The tower is 132ft
high and dates from about
1150. The interior has some
fine Romanesque and Gothic
architecture; monuments to
historic families. During the
Dissolution of the Monasteries, the Abbey was saved
from destruction when the
towns people bought it for
£453.

✆ (0684) 292896.
Open: daily Apr-Sep 8.30-6;
Oct-Mar 8.30-5.
Donations.
⬧ ⚞ Shop

THETFORD
Norfolk　　　　*Map 5 TL88.*
Thetford Castle
One of the original motte and
bailey castles, at 80ft,
perhaps the largest still in
existence. This represents

the earliest form of castle,
before masonry was added.

Open: accessible at all
reasonable times.

Thetford Priory
Extensive remains of Cluniac
monastery founded at beginning of 12th century. The
14th-century gatehouse of
priory stands to its full height.

Open: at all reasonable
times.
⬧ (AM)

Warren Lodge
(2m NW of town, on B1107)
Remains of a two-storey hunting lodge in 15th-century flint
with stone dressings.

Open: at all reasonable
times.
⬧ (exterior only) (AM)

THETFORD FOREST
Norfolk　　　　*Map 5 TL88.*
Covering a vast area extending both sides of the Norfolk
and Suffolk border, Thetford
Forest's varied landscape
and wildlife can be explored

along the many rides, tracks and waymarked walks.

⌀ Thetford (0842) 810271.
Open: forest all year;
Information Centre at Santon Downham 2m E of Brandon Mon-Fri.
⌐

THORNHAM MAGNA
Suffolk   *Map 5 TM17.*
Thornham Magna Herb Garden
An 18th-century walled herb garden with herb knot garden and wild flowers and herbs. Woodland walks and comprehensive nursery.

⌀ Mellis (037983) 779.
Open: daily, 9.30-6.
⌐ ⌐

TILBURY
Essex   *Map 5 TQ67.*
Thurrock Riverside Museum
Civic Square
Illustrates the history of the River Thames and the people of its riverside. Ship and barge models, photographs, etc.

⌀ (03752) 79216.
Open: all year Tue-Fri 10-1 & 2-5.30, Sat 10-1 & 2-5. (Closed: Sun & BHs.) Advisable to telephone beforehand.
⌖ ⋇

TILLICOULTRY
Central (Clackmannanshire)   Map 11 NS99.
Clock Mill Heritage Centre
Upper Mill Street
The Clock Mill has been converted into a heritage centre and also includes a Tourist Information Centre. There are displays from the past and several craft workshops.

⌀ Stirling (0786) 75019.
Open: Apr & May wkdys 10-

12 & 2-4; wknds 10-5; Jun-Sep daily 10-6.
⌖ (ground floor only) Shop

TITCHWELL MARSH
Norfolk   *Map 9 TF74.*
(6m E of Hunstanton off A149)
An area where not only is the birdlife protected but new habitat is created. Nesting-ground to the ringed plover, oystercatcher, common and little tern; wading birds forage on the exposed muds between autumn and spring. Hides on the reserve provide the opportunity to view the birds at close range.

⌀ Brancaster (0485) 210432.
Open: public footpath all year. Visitor centre and hides Apr-Oct, 10-5.
Shop ⌐

TIVERTON
Devon   *Map 3 SS91.*
Tiverton Museum
St Andrew Street, near Town Hall. (Entrance from public car park)
Comprehensive museum housed in a restored 19th-century school containing numerous local exhibits; a Victorian laundry, two water-wheels, costume gallery, industrial gallery covering the Grand Western Canal and local trades, natural history and wartime rooms. Heathcoat Lace gallery featuring 19th-century lace making machine and other relics of Heathcoat Lace Making Factory. Agricultural section includes a collection of farm wagons and a complete smithy. A large railway gallery houses the GWR locomotive No 1442, and other railway relics.

⌀ (0884) 256295.
Open: Mon-Sat 10.30-4.30. (Closed: 19 Dec-1 Feb.)
⌖ (ground floor only) Shop ⋇ (ex guide dogs)

TOMATIN
Highland (Inverness-shire)   Map 14 NH82.
Tomatin Distillery
Visitors can see the process of whisky making, which relies on traditional skills and techniques, at the largest malt whisky distillery in Scotland.

⌀ (08082) 234.
Open: 9-4; tours by arrangement Mon-Fri.

TOMINTOUL
Grampian (Banffshire)   Map 15 NJ11.
Tomintoul Museum
The Square
Reconstructed farm kitchen and blacksmith's shop, Harness displays, local landscape and wildlife displays. Exhibition 'Scotland's Disappearing Wildlife' for one month in summer.

⌀ Forres (0309) 73701.
Open: 13 Apr-May & Oct, Mon-Sat 9-5.30; Sun 2-5.30; Jun & Sep, Mon-Sat 9.30-6, Sun 2-6; Jul & Aug, Mon-Sat 9-7, Sun 2-7. Details not confirmed for 1988.
⌖ Shop ⋇

TOMNAVOULIN
Grampian (Banffshire)   Map 15 NJ22.
Tamnavoulin-Glenlivet Distillery
(on B9008 6½m N of Tomintoul)
A video presentation is followed by a tour where visitors will see the process of whisky making, followed by whisky sampling in the hospitality lounge. Picnic area by the River Livet.

⌀ Glenlivet (08073) 442.
Open: Etr-Oct, tours 9.30-4. Details not yet confirmed for 1988.
⌐

TONDU
Mid Glamorgan   *Map 3 SS88.*
Glamorgan Wildlife Centre
(1m W)
A small nature reserve in open countryside, headquarters of Glamorgan Wildlife Centre. Exhibition area in centre building, giving an introduction to the wildlife of the county and the work of the Trust. Waymarked trail.

✆ Aberkenfig (0656) 724100. Open: most weekends Etr-Sep only. ⌂

TONGLAND
Dumfries and Galloway (Kirkcudbrightshire)   Map 11 NX65.
Tongland Tour
Tour of SSEB Galloway hydro-electricity scheme. It includes video presentation and a visit to the dam and power station at Tongland. A fish ladder is an added attraction.

✆ Kirkcudbright (0557) 30114. Open: May-Sep, Mon-Sat Tours 10, 11.30, 2, 3.30, by telephone appointment. Visitors taken to power station from Kirkcudbright by minibus. ⌀ (ex at discretion of guides)

TORQUAY
Devon   *Map 3 SX96.*
Pepe & Son
Kingskerswell Road, off Newton Road
Production of English and Italian type wines, matured in wooden casks giving them their characteristic flavour. A selection of wine making implements and various manufacturing processes is explained in the winery here. A vineyard, planted in 1981, can also be seen.

✆ (0803) 62166. Open: daily, 11-6. Free tasting.

TREFRIW
Gwynedd   *Map 6 SH76.*
Trefriw Woollen Mill
Woollen mill dating from 1859. All stages of woollen manufacture can be seen, including blending, carding, spinning, dyeing, warping, weaving and tailoring, also hydro-electric turbines. Large shop selling own products of pure new wool.

✆ Llanrwst (0492) 640462. Open: Mon-Fri 9-5.30 (Winter 5pm). (Closed: BH & 2 weeks Xmas, also 3rd Mon in Oct). ⌀ (Jun-Sep) ♿ (shop only) Shop ⌀ (in mill)

TREWINT
Cornwall   *Map 2 SX28.*
Wesley's Cottage
(near Altarnun)
Small 18th-century Methodist shrine, well-restored in 1950. John Wesley came here six times between 1744 and 1762. Annual Wesley Day service is held. Also Sun services in summer. Interesting testaments and period furnishings are on display. Wesley Day celebrations 24 May.

✆ Pipers Pool (0566) 86572. Open: all year, daily, 9-dusk. ♿ (ground floor only) Shop ⌀

TUNBRIDGE WELLS
Kent   *Map 5 TQ53.*
Tunbridge Wells Museum & Art Gallery
Civic Centre
Local and natural history, and Tunbridge ware. Collections of toys, dolls and domestic bygones. Exhibition 'This Gorgeous Mouchoir' (an exhibition of handkerchiefs) 17 Sep-13 Oct.

✆ (0892) 26121 Ext 171. Open: Mon-Fri 10-5.30 & Sat 9.30-5. (Closed: Sun, BH & Tue after spring & summer BH's, and Etr Sat). ⌀

TWICKENHAM
Gt London   *see page 76.*
Marble Hill House
An example of English Palladian school of architecture standing in a wooded park near the River Thames. Built 1724-9 for Henrietta Howard, mistress of George II and later Countess of Suffolk. Georgian paintings and furniture; Italian paintings in the Great Room by G. P. Panini. Richmond Shakespeare Society perform plays on the terrace in summer. 'Picnic Promenade' concerts in the grounds in Jul & Aug.

✆ 01-892 5115. Open: all year Mon-Thu, Sat & Sun 10-5 (4pm Nov-Jan). (Closed 24 & 25 Dec.) ⌀ (licensed) (Apr-Sep) ♿ (ground floor & gardens only) Shop ⌀ (ex in grounds)

Orleans House Gallery
Riverside   *London Plan 2 : 45 B2.*
Survivor of Orleans House, in which Louis Phillippe, Duc d'Orléans, King of the French 1830-48, lived in exile in the early 19th century. It was demolished in 1927. Surviving octagonal room, designed by James Gibbs in c. 1720, has exquisite plasterwork.

✆ 01-892 0221. Open: all year Tue-Sat 1-5.30 (4.30pm Oct-Mar) Sun & BH 2-5.30 (Oct-Mar 2-4.30). (Closed: 25 & 26 Dec and Good Fri.) Woodland gardens open all year, daily 9-dusk. ♿ (ground floor only) Shop ⌀

UFFINGTON
Oxfordshire   *Map 4 SU28.*
Castle & White Horse
Iron Age hill fort situated on the ancient Ridgeway at a height of more than 700ft on the Berkshire Downs. Below it, cut in the chalk, is the famous White Horse.

Both accessible any reasonable time.
(AM)

ULEY

Gloucestershire *Map 3 ST79.*

Uley Tumulus

Known as Hetty Pegler's Tump, this long barrow, 120ft by 85ft, has a chamber approached by means of a deep forecourt. The chamber forms part of a gallery grave.

Open: any reasonable time.
(AM)

UPMINSTER

Gt London *Map 5 TQ58.*

Tithe Barn Agricultural & Folk Museum

Hall Lane

15th-century thatched timber building contains large selection of old agricultural implements, craft and farm tools, domestic bygones and items of local interest, over 2,000 exhibits in all.

✆ (04024) 47535.
Open: 2 & 3 Apr, 7 & 8 May, 4 & 5 Jun & 2-3 Jul, 6 & 7 Aug, 3 & 4 Sep & 1 & 2 Oct, 1.30-6.
♿ Shop 🚫🐕

VENTNOR

Isle of Wight
See **Wight, Isle of**

WAKEFIELD

West Yorkshire *Map 8 SE32.*

Wakefield Art Gallery

Important collection of 20th-century paintings and sculpture. Special rooms devoted to locally born Barbara Hepworth and Henry Moore. Also temporary exhibitions.

✆ (0924) 370211 Ext 8031 (after 5 & Sat (0924) 375402).
Open: all year, Mon-Sat 10.30-5, Sun 2.30-5 & all BH's during Spring & Summer mths.
P (150 yds) ♿ (ground floor only) 🚫🐕

Wakefield Museum

Wood Street

Archaeology and history of Wakefield from prehistoric times to recent past. Waterton Collection of exotic birds and animals. Temporary exhibitions.

✆ (0924) 370211 Ext 7190 (after 5 & Sat (0924) 361767).
Open: all year Mon-Sat 10.30-5; Sun & all BH's spring and summer months 2.30-5.
♿ (ground floor only)

WALSALL

W Midlands *Map 7 SP09.*

Jerome K Jerome Birthplace Museum

Belsize House, Bradford Street

Birthplace of Jerome K Jerome, now restored as a museum, housing documents and memorabilia of the author. One room is a reconstruction of an 1850's parlour.

✆ (0922) 21244 Ext 3124.
Open: all year Tue-Sat 10-5. (Closed: Sun, Mon & BH.)
Shop

Museum & Art Gallery

Garman Ryan collection including important works by Blake, Degas, Van Gogh and Epstein. Regular loan exhibitions. Local history museum. Exhibition of Urban Landscape 1-30 Apr.

✆ (0922) 21244 Ext 3124 or 3115.
Open: Mon-Fri 10-6 & Sat 10-4.45. (Closed: Sun, Xmas & BH's).
♿ Shop 🚫🐕

WALTHAM ABBEY

Essex *Map 5 TL30.*

Waltham Abbey Gatehouse, Bridge & entrance to Cloisters

14th-century gatehouse with separate carriage and pedestrian entrances. Harold's Bridge is also 14th-century. Cloister entrance dates from 12th-century. In the historic Norman and later Abbey Church nearby is an undercroft museum.

Open: at any reasonable time.
(AM)

WANDLEBURY RING

Cambridgeshire *Map 5 TL45.*

(4m SE of Cambridge off A1307)

On the summit of the low Gog Magog Hills, the remains of an Iron-Age hill fort which once comprised a double rampart and ditch, 1,000 ft in diameter; about 110 acres of the hills have been protected by the Cambridge Preservation Society.

Open: daily.
(Donations welcome)
Run for dogs Shop

WANTAGE

Oxfordshire *Map 4 SU48.*

Vale & Downland Museum Centre

The Old Surgery, Church Street

A lively museum centre with displays on the geology, archaeology and local history of the Vale of the White Horse and the town of Wantage. Temporary exhibitions and local craft demonstrations occasionally.

✆ (02357) 66838.
Open: all year Tue-Sat 10.30-4.30 & Sun 2.30-5. (BH Mon check in advance).
☕ 🧺 ♿ (ground floor only)
Shop

WARRINGTON

Cheshire *Map 7 SJ68.*

South Lancashire Regiment (PWV) Regimental Museum

Peninsula Barracks, Orford

Military museum of South Lancashire Regiment from 1717 onwards.

⌀ (0925) 33563.
Open: all year, Mon-Fri 9-2.30 (ex PH), also for parties evenings & weekends by arrangement.
⚹

WARWICK
Warwickshire   *Map 4 SP26.*
St John's House
Coten End (Junction of A429 & A445 E of town)
Fine 17th-century house re-built by the Stoughton family on the site of an old hospital. It is now a branch of the County Museum (domestic scenes, costume, and music-al instruments), Victorian schoolroom. Includes the museum of the Royal War-wickshire Regiment on the first floor.

⌀ Leamington Spa (0926) 493431 Ext 2021. For Regimental Museum (0926) 491653.
Open: all year Tue-Sat & BH 10-12.30 & 1.30-5.30; May-Sep also Sun 2.30-5.
& (ground floor only) Shop

Warwickshire Museum
Market Place
17th-century Market Hall now a museum displaying the geology, history and natural history of Warwick-shire. Notable for the Shel-don tapestry map of War-wickshire, habitat displays and giant fossil plesiosaur. Temporary exhibitions throughout the year and chil-dren's holiday activities dur-ing the summer and Christ-mas.

⌀ (0926) 410410 Ext 2500.
Open: all year Mon-Sat 10-5.30; Sun (May-Sep only 2.30-5).
& (grounds only) Shop

Warwickshire Yeomanry Museum
The Court House, Jury Street
Display of military exhibits, includes uniforms, medals, militaria and weapons dating from 1794 to 1945. Also selected items of silver from the Regimental collection. There is a very fine display of paintings and pictures cover-ing the same period.

⌀ (0926) 492212.
Open: Good Fri-end Oct, Fri, Sat, Sun & BH 10-1 & 2-4. &
(gardens only) Shop ⚹

WASHINGTON
West Sussex   *Map 4 TQ11.*
Chanctonbury Ring
(1½m SE) Reached by footpath (South Downs Way)
Situated on the crest of the South Downs, Chanctonbury Ring consists of a clump of beech trees standing within the remains of an Iron Age fort. The trees were planted in 1760 by Charles Goring. Excavations at the fort have revealed remains of two Ro-man buildings and prehistor-ic barrows. There are good views from the summit.

Open: accessible at all reasonable times.

WATFORD
Hertfordshire   *Map 4 TQ19.*
Watford Museum
194 High Street
Museum describing the his-tory of the Watford area from earliest times to the present day. There are special fea-tures on brewing and print-ing together with a display of wartime Watford based on the 'Dad's Army' series writ-ten by Jimmy Perry from his Watford experience. A good art gallery and a constantly changing programme of ex-hibits.

⌀ (0923) 32297.
Open: all year Mon-Sat 10-5. (Closed: 25-26 Dec & New Year's Day.)
& Shop ⚹ (ex guide dogs)

WAYLAND'S SMITHY
Oxfordshire   *Map 4 SU28.*
(1m S off the B4507 Compton Beauchamp turning near end of unclass road)
A well preserved megalithic long barrow in a copse close to the Ridgeway path. The long barrow was excavated in 1919-1920 and revealed eight stone-age skeletons. Wayland the Smith figures in Scandinavian mythology as a maker of invincible weapons.

Open: accessible at all reasonable times.
(AM)

WEETING
Norfolk   *Map 5 TL78.*
Weeting Castle
A ruined 11th-century for-tified manor house, situated in a rectangular enclosure and preserving slight re-mains of a three storeyed cross-wing.

Open: at all reasonable times.
(AM)

WELSHPOOL
Powys   *Map 7 SJ20.*
Cockpit
New Street
During the 18th century cockfighting was a keenly followed sport and this grade II listed cockpit has been re-cently restored to original state.

Open: Apr-Sep, Mon-Fri 10-4.
&

Oriel Gallery
High Street
The largest collection of ori-ginal prints in mid-Wales are contained in this gallery

which also shows all the print processes of lithography, woodcraft and screen printing. Every month there are changing exhibitions with a wide range of subjects from sculpture and photography to textiles and painting.

Open: all year Mon-Sat 11-5.

Powysland Museum
Salop Road
Museum of archaeology and local history.

✆ (0938) 4759.
Open: all year Mon-Fri 11-1 & 2-5, Sat 2-4.30. (Closed: Wed in winter.) Shop ✗

WEST BRETTON
West Yorkshire   Map 8 SE21.
Yorkshire Sculpture Park
Bretton Hall College
Set in beautiful grounds, this park is the country's leading outdoor exhibition centre of contemporary sculpture, including works by Henry Moore and Barbara Hepworth. There is a programme of changing exhibitions, educational activities and events.

✆ (092485) 302.
Open: daily, summer 10-6; winter 10-4. ⬧ ⌂. Details not confirmed for 1988.

WEST BROMWICH
West Midlands   Map 7 SP09.
Oak House
Oak Road
Half-timbered 16th-century house, the result of three separate building phases. The rooms display superb period furnishings and furniture. An Elizabethan garden is at the front of the house.

✆ 021-553 0759.
Open: Apr-Sep, Mon-Sat 10-8 (ex Thu 10-1 & Sun 2.30-8); Oct-Mar, Mon-Sat 10-4 (ex Thu 10-1). ⬧ (ground floor & gardens only) ✗

West Bretton: 'Knife Edge' Sculpture by Henry Moore

WEST MALLING
Kent   Map 5 TQ65.
St Leonard's Tower
The surviving part of the former castle or fortified manor house belonging to Bishop Gundulph.

Open: at all reasonable times.
⬧ (grounds only) (AM)

WESTON-SUPER-MARE
Avon   Map 3 ST36.
Woodspring Museum
Burlington Street
The museum is housed in the old workshops of the Edwardian Gaslight Company. Around a central courtyard are displays of the Victorian

Seaside Holiday, an old chemist's shop, a dairy, a lion fountain with Victorian pavement mosaic and a gallery of wildlife in the district. Other exhibits include Mendip minerals and mining, local archaeology, costume rooms, transport from penny farthing to Weston Autogyro, cameras and the Dentist in 1900. Display featuring 'The Weston-super-Mare Story'. Changing exhibitions held in the Art Gallery. Adjoining is Clare's Cottage, a Westonian's home of the 1890s with period rooms, kitchen, parlour, bedroom and back yard. Also a room for the display of Peggy Nesbet dolls.

✆ (0934) 21028.
Open: all year Mon-Sat, 10-5 (ex Nov-Feb closed 1-2). (Closed: Good Fri, Xmas & New Year.)
⌨ ⬧ (ground floor only) Shop ✗

WEYMOUTH
Dorset   Map 3 SY67.
Radipole Lake and Lodmoor
(Radipole W of Weymouth, Lodmoor on A353 1m NE)
Two RSPB nature reserves close to the centre of large seaside town. Despite their proximity to this hubbub both have retained a natural feeling and a wealth of wildlife is attracted. At Radipole a large reserve overlooks the lake.

✆ (0305) 773519.
Open: reserve daily, dawn-dusk; information centre daily 10-5.
⌨ ⌂ ⬧ ✗

WHITEHAVEN
Cumbria   Map 11 NX91.
Whitehaven Museum & Art Gallery
Civic Hall
Lower gallery devoted to approximately 20 exhibitions

per year. The upper gallery features local history and Whitehaven-made pottery. Slide/tape shows usually featured in upper gallery.

✆ (0946) 3111 Ext 307.
Open: all year Mon, Tue & Fri 9-5, Sat 9-2. (Closed: BH.)
⟁ Shop ✗ (ex guide dogs)

WHITTINGTON
Staffordshire   Map 7 SK10.
Whittington Barracks, Staffordshire Regiment Museum
An interesting museum dispaying details of the Regiment's battle honours; captured trophies, weapons old and new, uniforms past and present, and a special display of medals.

✆ (0543) 433333 Ext 3240/3229.
Open: all year Mon-Fri 9-4.30; Sat, Sun & BH by appointment only. (Closed: Xmas & New Year).
⟁ Shop ✗

WICK
Highland (Caithness)   Map 15 ND35.
Caithness Glass
Harrow Hill
All aspects of glass blowing on view. There is also a factory seconds shop.

✆ (0955) 2286.
Open: all year Mon-Fri 9-5, Sat 9-1 (4.30 May-Sep).
⌂ ⟁ (ground floor & grounds only) Shop ✗ (in factory)

Castle of Old Wick
A four storeyed ruined square tower, known also as Castle Oliphant, probably of 12th century.

Open: accessible except when adjoining rifle range is in use.
(AM)

Castle Sinclair and Castle Girnigoe
(½m W of Noss Head Lighthouse)
Perched on the cliff edge on this bleak coastline the castles are reached along the coast from Noss Head Lighthouse. Little remains of Castle Girnigoe, built late in the 15th century but there are impressive remains of Castle Sinclair (1606-7). Both castles were strongholds of the Sinclairs but clan battles in the latter part of the 17th century left them in ruins.

Open: accessible at all reasonable times.

Wight (Isle of)
COWES
Isle of Wight   Map 4 SZ49.
Maritime Museum and Public Library
Beckford Road
Ship models, photographs, paintings, books and other items showing the island's maritime past.

✆ (0983) 293341.
Open: Mon-Fri 9.30-5.30, Sat 9.30-4.30. (Closed: BHs.)
Shop ✗

ST CATHERINE'S POINT
Isle of Wight   Map 4 SZ47.
St Catherine's Lighthouse
Situated at St Catherine's Point, 136 ft above the sea.

✆ Niton (0983) 730284.
Open: Mon-Sat only from 1pm-one hour before dusk, weather and other conditions permitting, at visitors own risk. Visitors are strongly recommended to telephone the keeper in advance. Cars not allowed within ¼m except on business.
✗

SANDOWN
Isle of Wight   Map 4 SZ58.
Museum of Isle of Wight Geology
Sandown Library, High Street
This museum, situated in the local library, houses a collection of fossils and exhibits of the island's geology.

✆ (0983) 404344.
Open: Mon-Fri 10-5.30, Sat & Sun 10-4.30. (Closed: Sun BH's.)
Shop ✗

VENTNOR
Isle of Wight   Map 4 SZ57.
Botanic Gardens
One of Britain's younger botanic gardens, but already acclaimed by horticulturalists for fine range of plants, palms, trees and exotic shrubs.

✆ Shanklin (098 386) 2942 855111.
Open: all year daily 10-5.
⌂ ⟁

YARMOUTH
Isle of Wight   Map 4 SZ38.
Fort Victoria Country Park
Remains of fort built in 1852-3 to protect the western approach to Portsmouth. Now being developed as a Country Park with free guided walks, exhibition, picnic and barbecue facilities. Spectacular views of the Solent. The Marine Aquarium shows a cross section of local marine life.

✆ (0983) 760860.
Open: Park daily. Aquarium open end Mar-Nov 10-6.
⌂ ⋒ ⟁ (ground floor & grounds only) Shop

WILLENHALL
West Midlands   Map 7 SO99.
Willenhall Lock Museum
A new museum about the people of Willenhall and

their town, the capital of the British lock industry.

✆ Walsall (0922) 21244 Ext 3115.
Open: all year Mon, Tue, Thu & Fri 9.30-6, Sat 9.30-12.30 & 2-4.30. (Closed: BH.)
Shop ✗

WILMINGTON
East Sussex   *Map 5 TQ50.*
The Long Man
(½m S on footpath)
The exact date of this 231 ft chalk cut figure on Windover Hill is unknown. It is thought that it may date from the 6th century. The figure holds an upright staff in each hand. During the 19th century the figure was renovated, having been almost lost from sight.

Open: accessible at all reasonable times.

WINCHESTER
Hampshire   *Map 4 SU42.*
See plan on pp. 128-9
Cathedral   *Plan : D2.*
Norman and all the later Gothic styles feature in this magnificent building which contains, among many other treasures, the tomb chests of many Saxon kings and queens. Memorials to Jane Austen and Izaak Walton will also be found here.

Open: daily. Donations welcomed.

Guildhall Gallery
Broadway   *Plan : D2.*
On show are local topographical views. Temporary exhibitions.

✆ (0962) 68166 Ext 2296.
Open: during exhibitions, Tue-Sat 10-5, Sun & Mon 2-5. (Closed Mon in winter.)
Subject to alteration.
♨ ⬕ Shop ✗

Pilgrims' Hall (School)
The Close   *Plan : D2.*
Its name is derived from the pilgrims who came to the shrine of St Swithun of Winchester (Bishop 852-862). Its most notable feature is the 14th-century hammerbeam roof. Today the hall is used by the Cathedral choir school.

✆ (0962) 54189.
Open: daily 9-6 (except when in use by the school for concerts, examinations etc.)

Serle's House
Southgate Street   *Plan : C2.*
A fine Baroque-style 18th century house, now incorporating the Royal Hampshire Regiment museum and memorial garden.

✆ (0962) 63658.
Open: all year Mon-Fri 10-12.30 & 2-4. (Closed BH.)
⬕ (ground floor & gardens only) Shop ✗

Botanic Gardens, Ventnor

The Great Hall of Winchester Castle
Castle Avenue, off High Street   *Plan : B2.*
The only surviving portion of the castle is the notable great hall of 1235 with Purbeck marble columns. At the west end is the legendary Round Table of King Arthur.

✆ (0962) 84184.
Open: Mar-Oct daily 10-5. Nov-Feb, Mon-Fri 10-5, Sat-Sun 10-4. (Closed: Good Fri & 25-26 Dec.)
(Donations)
⬕ Shop ✗ (ex guide dogs)

WINDSOR
Berkshire   *Map 4 SU97.*
Household Cavalry Museum
Combermere Barracks, St Leonards Road
One of the finest military museums in Britain. Uniforms, weapons, horse furniture and armour of the Household

Cavalry from 1660 to the present.

☏ (07535) 868222 Ext 203.
Open: all year Mon-Fri (ex BH) 10-1 & 2-5; 2nd weekend in May-1st weekend Sep also Suns 10-1 & 2-5 (ex BH Suns).
🔲 Shop ⌀

Windsor Castle
A restored Norman royal castle with 19th century additions for George IV by Wyattville.

☏ (07535) 68286.
Castle precinct open: daily 10-4.15; 30 Mar-30 Apr.

(Closed am 21 Apr) 10-5.15; May-Aug 10-7.15. (Closed 16 Jun); Sep-25 Oct 10-5.15; 26 Oct-Dec 10-4.15.
Always subject to closure, sometimes at very short notice.
🔲 Shop ⌀

WINSTER
Derbyshire   *Map 8 SK26.*
Market House
Stone-built 17th- or 18th-century market house in main street of village.

Open: most summer weekends.
Shop ⌀ (NT)

WIRRAL COUNTRY PARK
Cheshire/Merseyside   Map 7 SJ28/37.
The park follows a former railway line and includes the 'Wirral Way', a 12-mile footpath from West Kirby to Neston, the line runs along the Dee Estuary with access to the beach at various points; the haunt of vast congregations of ducks and wading birds outside the breeding season. Beyond Neston the track turns inland to Hadlow Road Station, at Willaston, where the booking hall is laid out as in the 1950's.

☏ 051-648 4371 (Visitor Centre, Thurstaston).

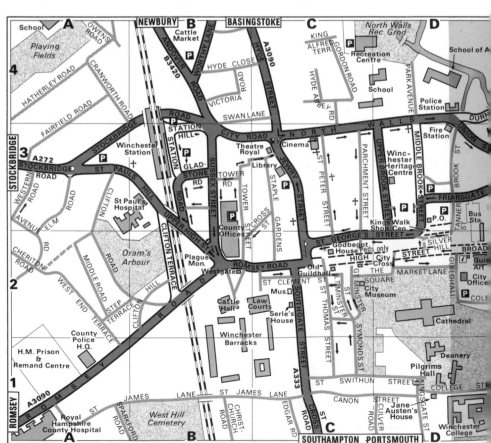

Open: park at all reasonable times; Visitor Centre and Hadlow Road Station, daily Nov-Mar, 10.30-3.30 (Station 10.30-4); Apr-May, Sep-Oct, 10.30-5; Jun-Aug 10.30-8. (Station 10.30-5). (Closed Xmas.)
🦽 (Visitor Centre)
🚉 Thurstaston, Caldy, Heswall, Parkgate, Neston, Willaston

WISBECH

Cambridgeshire   *Map 5 TF40.*
Wisbech and Fenland Museum

Contains fine collection of ceramics, objets d'art, archaeology, natural history and articles which illustrate Fenland life.

✆ (0945) 583817.
Open: all year Tue-Sat 10-5 (4pm Oct-Mar). (Closed: BH.) Museum library and archives available by appointment only.
Shop ✗

WITCOMBE, GREAT

Gloucestershire   *Map 3 SO91.*
Witcombe Roman Villa

A large courtyard Roman Villa in which a hypocaust and several mosaic pavements are presented.

Open: at all reasonable times. (Keys at farmhouse adjoining.)
(AM)

WOLVERHAMPTON

West Midlands   *Map 7 SO99.*
Bantock House Museum

Bantock Park, Bradmore Road
This 18th & 19th-century house contains important collections of English enamels, japanned tin and paper-maché products of the Midlands. Also shown are early Worcester porcelain, pottery, English and foreign dolls and toys and the Thomas Balston collection of Staffordshire portrait figures.

✆ (0902) 24548.
Open: Mon-Fri 10-7, Sat 10-6 & Sun 2-5. BH Mon & Tue 2-5 (Closed Good Fri, Etr Sun, Xmas & New Year's Day).
🦽 (ground floor & grounds only) ✗

Bilston Museum & Art Gallery

Mount Pleasant, Bilston
Houses a large collection of fine English painted and transfer printed enamels from 18th and 19th centuries. Also iron and steel artefacts relating to the industrial history of the area. Staffordshire pottery is on display and there are frequently held exhibitions of contemporary interest.

✆ (0902) 49143.
Open: all year Mon-Sat 10-5. (Closed: BH.)
✗

Central Art Gallery

Lichfield Street
18th- and 19th-century English water colours and oil paintings. Modern paintings, sculpture and prints. Fine Oriental collections and full programme of temporary exhibitions including 'New Spirit in Craft' 23 Apr-18 Jul &

Central Winchester
© The Automobile Association

'Japanese Decorative Art' 15 Oct-26 Nov.

✆ 0902-312032.
Open: Mon-Sat 10-6. (Closed BH).
🚐 🦽 Shop ⚹ (in house)

WOODHENGE
Wiltshire   *Map 4 SU14.*
(1m N of Amesbury)
Consisted formerly of six concentric rings of timber posts within a ditch. Positions of the posts are marked by concrete pillars. Discovered accidentally by aerial reconnaissance in 1925.

Open: accessible at all reasonable times.
🦽 (AM)

WORCESTER
Hereford and Worcester Map 3 SO85.
City Museum & Art Gallery
Foregate Street
Temorary art exhibitions from local and national sources. Natural history and geology displays. 19th-century chemists shop. Also collections of Worcestershire Regiment and Worcestershire Yeomanry Cavalry.

✆ (0905) 25371.
Open: all year Mon, Tue, Wed & Fri 9.30-6, Sat 9.30-5. Shop ⚹

Dyson Perrins Museum of Worcester Porcelain
Severn Street
The finest collection of Worcester china in the world, with an unrivalled display of pieces dating from 1751 to the present day.

✆ (0905) 23221.
Open: all year Mon-Fri 9.30-5 & Sat 10-5.
(Tours of works Mon-Fri by prior arrangement.)
🚐 (licensed) 🦽 Shop ⚹

Guildhall
High Street
The Guildhall has a fine early Georgian frontage and during the summer months Heritage displays portray Worcester's history and personalities, in sight and sound, with a very varied display featuring such people and places as Edward Elgar, Woodbine Willie, Vesta Tilley and the Music Halls. Also shown are the seven ages of Worcester.

✆ (0905) 723471.
Open: all year Mon-Fri 9.30-5 & occasional Sat in summer. (Closed BH.)
🦽 (ground floor only) ⚹

Tudor House
Friar Street
500-year-old timber-framed house, with a squint and an ornate plaster ceiling. Now a museum of local life featuring social and domestic history, including children's room, Edwardian bathroom and World War II Home Front Displays. Large agricultural exhibits are displayed in yard at rear.

✆ (0905) 25371.
Open: all year Mon-Wed & Fri-Sat 10.30-5.
🦽 (ground floor only) Shop ⚹

WORDSLEY
West Midlands   Map 7 SO88.
Stuart Crystal
Red House Glassworks
The Redhouse Cone and Museum opened Easter 1984 representing 200 years of glassmaking history. The factory tour enables the visitor to see at close hand the glassmaking process from raw materials to finished items.

✆ Brierly Hill (0384) 71161 Ext 274.

Redhouse Cone & Museum
Open: daily 9-5; Factory Tours Mon-Fri 10-11.15 & 1.30-3.15; (Fri closed 2.30pm). (Closed for tours 30 May-3 Jun & 25 Jul-5 Aug; all facilities closed 23-27 Dec & 1 Jan.) 🚐 🦽 Shop ⚹

WORKINGTON
Cumbria   Map 11 NY02.
Helena Thompson Museum
Park End Road
Costume, furniture and other decorative art in 18th-century house. Temporary exhibitions in former stable block.

✆ (0900) 62598.
Open: all year Mon-Fri 10-4, Sat 11-3. Parties by prior arrangement
🦽 (ground floor & garden only) Shop ⚹

WORKSOP
Nottinghamshire   Map 8 SK57.
Worksop Priory Church & Gatehouse
Church has unique Norman west front with twin towers and 12th-century Transitional nave, with 20th-century additions, 14th-century scroll ironwork on doors in south porch. Remarkable 14th-century double archway with large upper room which from 1623 housed the earliest elementary school in county. Elaborate façade with statues, and 15th-century wayside shrine and chapel.

Church open: daily 7.30-12 & 1.30-4.30; gatehouse Mon-Wed 9.30-1 & 2-4.
🦽 (ground floor only) Shop ⚹

WORTHING
West Sussex   Map 4 TQ10.
Worthing Museum & Art Gallery
Archaeology, Downland display, history of Worthing, pictures, pottery, toys and

dolls. Large costume collection. Frequent exhibitions.

✆ (0903) 39999 Ext 121, Sat only (0903) 204229. Open: Mon-Sat 10-6 (summer), 10-5 (winter).

WRAXALL

Somerset   *Map 3 ST63.*
Wraxall Vineyards
Set on the foothills of the Mendips, this 10-acre vineyard was founded in 1973 by the Holmes family. The two main vines are the German Müller Thurgau and the French hybrid Seyval. Visitors are welcome to look round unaccompanied and wines may be purchased from the shop.

✆ Ditcheat (074 986) 486 or 331.
Open: daily at all reasonable times.
Sales at the door

WREXHAM

Clywd   *Map 7 SJ35.*
Bersham Industrial Heritage
Bersham (2m SW)
An interpretative centre housed in a Victorian school building which is situated along an eight-mile industrial history trail. Exhibitions on John Wilkinson, the Bersham iron-works, the Davies Brothers, gatesmiths of Croes Foel and a reconstructed forge. Open day 7.

✆ (0978) 261529.
Open: Etr-Oct, Tue-Sat & BH 10-12.30 & 1.30-4, Sun 2-4; Nov-Etr, Tue-Fri 10-12.30 & 1.30-4, Sat 12.30-3.30.
🖼 Shop ⌀

WYRE FOREST

Herefs & Worcs/Shropshire
    Map 7 SO77.
Ranking alongside the New Forest and the Forest of Dean nearly 1,000 acres of the forest is now a National Nature Reserve. Special features are the numerous old meadows and orchards around the fringes, and Dowles Brook and its tributaries. These various habitats

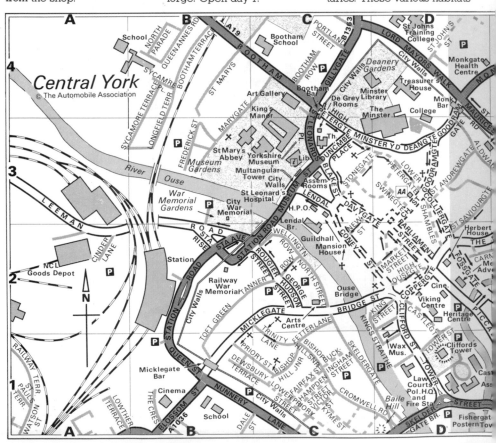

make it a good place for the naturalist.

Open: accessible at all reasonable times. Car park closes at dusk. Location W of Bewdley, Information centre on A456.

YARMOUTH, GREAT
Norfolk   *Map 5 TG50.*
Museum Exhibition Galleries
Central Library, Tolhouse Street
Travelling and local art exhibitions.

℘ (0493) 858900.
Open: all year Mon-Fri 9.30-5.30; Sat 9.30-1, 2-5.30.

(Closed: late May & Aug BH wknds, Xmas & New Year). ✗

Tolhouse Museum
Tolhouse Street
Late 13th-century building with old dungeons and exhibits on local history. Brass rubbing centre with wide range of replica brasses.

℘ (0493) 858900.
Open: all year (ex Good Fri, Xmas & New Year) Mon-Fri 10-1 & 2-5.30; (Sun Jun-Sep only).
Charge for brass rubbing Shop ✗

YARMOUTH
Isle of Wight
See **Wight, Isle of**

YELVERTON
Devon   *Map 2 SX56.*
Paperweight Centre
4 Buckland Terrace, Leg O'Mutton
Exhibition of over 800 beautiful antique and modern glass. Millefiori, faceted, diamond-cut dated and signed 'investment' paperweights, many for sale (from £3-£400).

℘ (0822) 854250.
Open: week before Etr-Oct, Mon-Sat 10-5; Nov-Etr Wed 1-5, also Sat 10-6 Nov-Xmas.
⌂ Shop

YEOVIL
Somerset   *Map 3 ST51.*
Yeovil Museum
Hendford Manor Hall
Local history and archaeology and specialised collections of costumes and firearms.

℘ Mon-Sat (0935) 24774.
Open: Mon-Sat 12 noon-5, Closed Sun & BH all year Mon-Wed, Fri & Sat 9.30-1 & 2-5.
Shop

YORK
North Yorkshire   *Map 8 SE65.*
Borthwick Institute of Historical Research
St Anthony's Hall, Peasholm Green   **Plan : E3.**
Originally a late 15th-century Guildhall, it has served in turn as poor-house, hospital, armoury, and Blue-Coat school. Now the Borthwick Institute of Historical Research, part of York University, with a collection of ecclesiastical archives. Exhibition of documents.

℘ (0904) 642315.
Hall open: all year Mon-Fri 9.30-1 & 2-5. (Closed: Xmas,

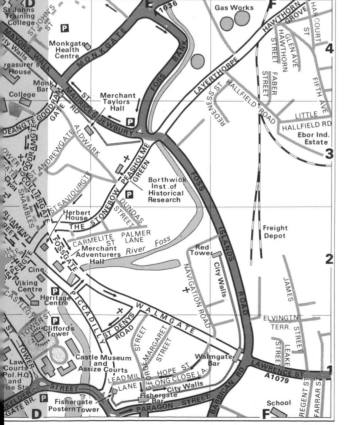

Etr. Search rooms closed week of Aug BH & preceding week.)
✗

Guildhall
off Coney Street Plan : *C2.*
A 15th-century building, restored after severe war damage. Hall with notable timbered roof. Underground passage leading to the river.

✆ (0904) 613161.
Open: May-Oct, Mon-Thu 9-5, Fri 9-4.30; Sat 10-5, Sun 2.30-4.30; Nov-Apr, Mon-

Thu 9-5, Fri 9-4.30. (Closed: Good Fri, 25 & 26 Dec & 1 Jan.)
♿ (ground floor only) ✗ (ex guide dogs)

King's Manor
Exhibition Square Plan : *C4.*
Former home of Abbot of St Mary's Abbey, later stopping place of James VI of Scotland on way to become James I of England, and of Charles I at time of Civil War. Much altered in early 17th century, and fully restored to become part of university in 1964.

✆ (0904) 430000.
Courtyards open; daily 9-5 (ex 25 Dec). Principal rooms open on certain days only during spring & summer. Check with porter.
♨ (ex PH) ♿ (gardens only) ✗

Museum Gardens Plan : *B3.*
Botanical gardens in which stand the ruins of St Marys Abbey with multangular tower nearby.

Open: daylight hours.

AA Viewpoints

A full list of AA Viewpoints, which provide excellent panoramas of the surrounding countryside, is given below. They can be located by using the map references given with each name.

ENGLAND
Avon, **Portishead** 1 m W of Portishead Map 3 ST47.
Cornwall, **Pendennis Head** 1 m SE of Falmouth Map 2 SW83.
Derbyshire, **Highoredish** 3 m E of Matlock Map 8 SK35.
Dorset, **Bulbarrow** 5 m S of Sturminster Newton Map 3 ST70.
Essex, **One Tree Hill** ¼ m NW of A13/B1420 junction 1½ m S of Basildon Map 5 TL68.
Gloucestershire, **Leckhampton Hill** 1 m S of Cheltenham on B4070 Map 3 SO92. **Robinswood Hill** 2 m S of City Centre in Robinswood Hill Country Park Map 3 SO81. **Symonds Yat** 3 m N of Coleford off B4432 Map 3 SO51.
Hampshire, **Portsdown Hill** 1 m N of Cosham Map 4 SU60.
Hereford & Worcester, **Clent Hills** S of A456, 2 m SW of Halesowen Map 7 SO98. **Windmill Hill** Waseley County Park 3½ m S of Halesowen Map 7 SO97.
Isle of Wight, **Bembridge Down** 2 m ENE of Sandown Map 4 SZ68.
Kent, **Farthing Corner** on Farthing Corner service area M2 Map 5 TQ86.
Leicestershire, **Beacon Hill** 2 m SW of Loughborough Map 8 SK51.
Oxfordshire, **Wittenham Clumps** 1½ m off A4130 Nr Brightwell Map 4 SU59.
Shropshire, **Clee Hills** 6 m E of Ludlow Map 7 SO67.
Somerset, **Dunkery Beacon** between Luccombe and Wheddon Cross Map 3 SS84. **Wellington Monument** 2½ m S of Wellington Map 3 ST11.
Staffordshire, **Central Forest Park** Stoke-on-Trent. Map 7 SJ84.
W Sussex, **Duncton Hill** 5 m SW of Petworth Map 4 SU91.

Warwickshire, **Magpie Hill** in Burton Dassett Hills Country Park Map 4 SP35.
Wiltshire, **Barbury Castle** in country park 5 m S of Swindon Map 4 SU17.
N Yorkshire, **Sutton Bank** 5 m E of Thirsk Map 8 SE58.
W Yorkshire, **Holme Moss** 1 m SW of Holme to East of A6024 Map 7 SK00.

WALES
Anglesey, **South Stack** in RSPB Reserve 3 m W of Holyhead Map 6 SH28. **Waun-y-Llyn** 5 m SE of Mold in country park Map 7 SJ25.
Dyfed, **Foel Eryr** 13 m NE of Haverfordwest ½ m W of B4329 Map 2 SN03.
Gwent, **Sugar Loaf** 3 m NW of Abergavenny Map 3 SO21.
Gwynedd, **Great Orme's Head** on top of Great Orme, Llandudno Map 6 SH78.
Powys, **Montgomery Town Hill** ½ m SW of Montgomery, off B4385 via unclassified road Map 7 SO29.

SCOTLAND
Borders, **Scott's View** 3 m E of Melrose Map 12 NT53.
Central, **David Marshall Lodge** 1 m N of Aberfoyle Map 11 NN50. **Queen's View, Auchineden** 6 m N of Bearsden Map 11 NS58.
Highland, **Bealach Na Ba'** *(Pass of the Cattle)* 5 m SE of Applecross Map 14 NG74. **Glen Garry** On A87 7¼ m from A82 at Invergarry Map 14 NH20. **Knockan Cliff** 8 m NE of Ullapool Map 14 NC20. **Struie Hill** 6 m SE of Bonar Bridge Map 14 NH68.
Lothian, **Blackford Hill** Edinburgh City Centre W of Royal Observatory Map 11 NT27. **Cockleroy** Beecraigs Country Park, 2 m S of Linlithgow Map 11 NS97.
Strathclyde, **Lyle Hill** 2 m E of Greenock, between A78 & A770 Map 10 NS27.
Tayside, **Queen's View** 6 m E of Tummel Bridge on B8019 Map 14 NN85.

INDEX

H

I

J

___ **T** _____

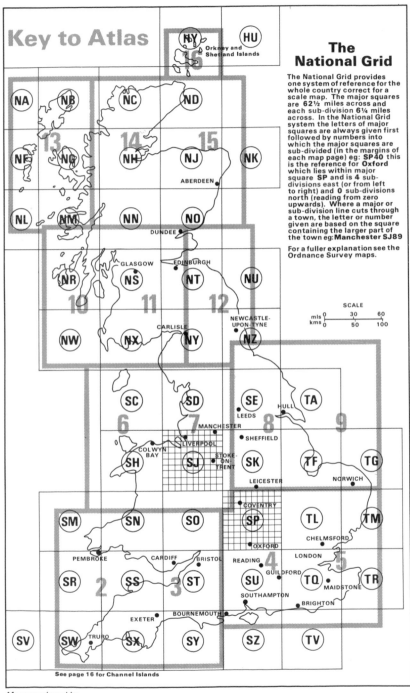

Key to Atlas

The National Grid

The National Grid provides one system of reference for the whole country correct for a scale map. The major squares are 62½ miles across and each sub-division 6¼ miles across. In the National Grid system the letters of major squares are always given first followed by numbers into which the major squares are sub-divided (in the margins of each map page) eg: **SP40** this is the reference for **Oxford** which lies within major square **SP** and is 4 sub-divisions east (or from left to right) and 0 sub-divisions north (reading from zero upwards). Where a major or sub-division line cuts through a town, the letter or number given are based on the square containing the larger part of the town eg: **Manchester SJ89**

For a fuller explanation see the Ordnance Survey maps.

SCALE

mls 0 30 60
kms 0 50 100

See page 16 for Channel Islands

Maps produced by

The AA Cartographic Department (Publications Division), Fanum House, Basingstoke, Hampshire RG21 2EA

This atlas is for location purposes only: see Members' Handbook for current road and AA road services information.

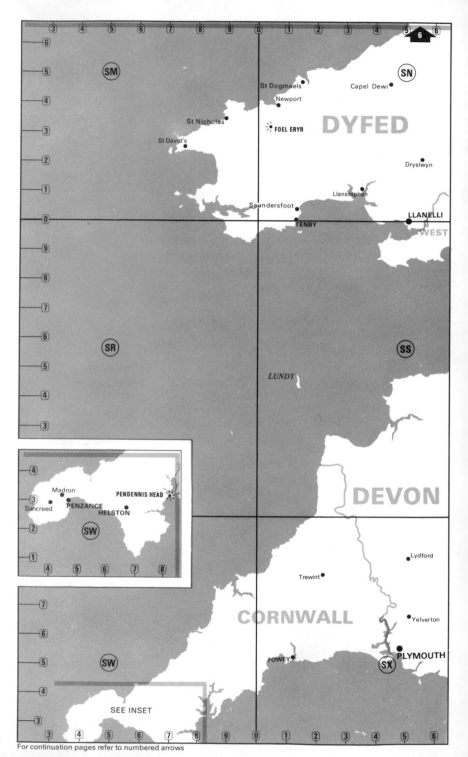

For continuation pages refer to numbered arrows

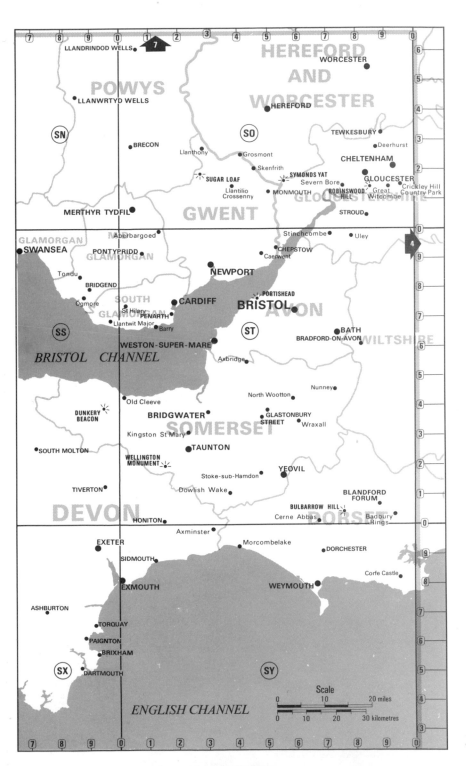

3

4

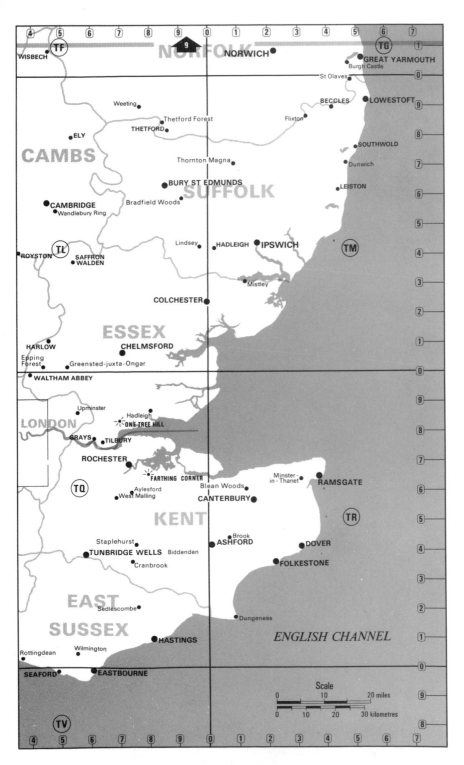

5

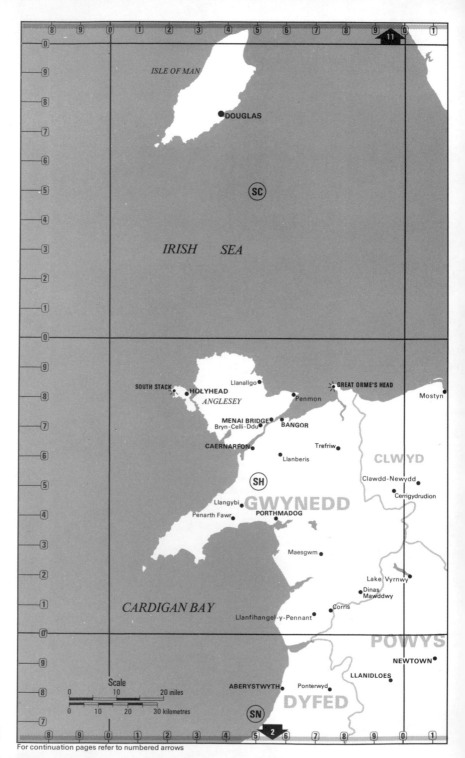

ISLE OF MAN

●DOUGLAS

(SC)

IRISH   SEA

SOUTH STACK● ●Llanallgo
HOLYHEAD●   ●GREAT ORME'S HEAD   ●Mostyn
ANGLESEY   ●Penmon
MENAI BRIDGE●   ●
Bryn-Celli-Ddu●   ●BANGOR
CAERNARFON●   ●Trefriw   CLWYD
                   ●Llanberis
        (SH)   Clawdd-Newydd●
Llangybi● GWYNEDD   ●Cerrigydrudion
Penarth Fawr● ●PORTHMADOG
        ●Maesgwm
                    Lake Vyrnwy●
                    Dinas●
                    Mawddwy
CARDIGAN BAY   Corris●   POWYS
Llanfihangel-y-Pennant●
                            NEWTOWN●
                    LLANIDLOES●
        Scale
0   10   20 miles   ABERYSTWYTH● ●Ponterwyd
0   10   20   30 kilometres   DYFED
                    (SN)

6

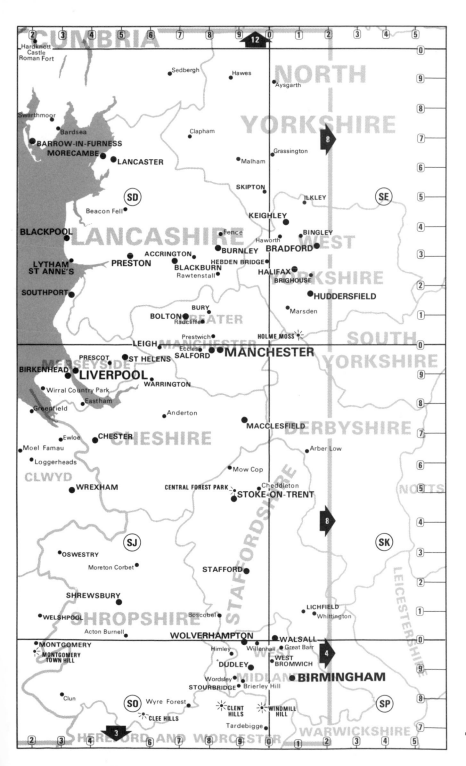

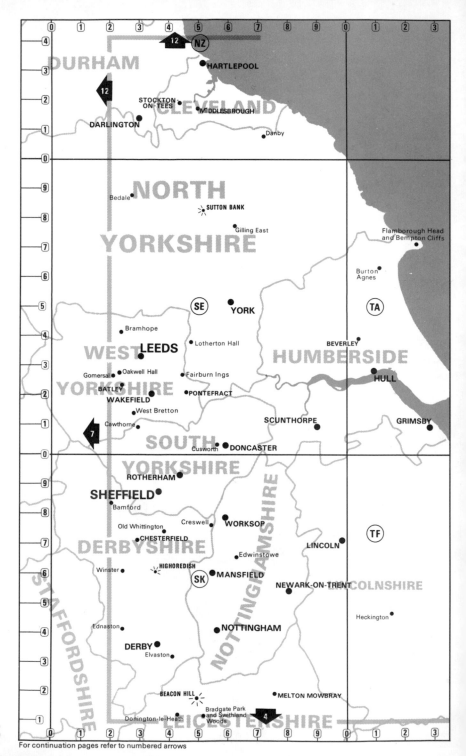

For continuation pages refer to numbered arrows